Wills of Rappahannock County, Virginia 1656-1692

Major George Morris's Survey of Estates Along the Rappahannock, 1680.

Wills of Rappahannock County, Virginia 1656-1692

By

WILLIAM MONTGOMERY SWEENY

CLEARFIELD

Originally published
Lynchburg, Virginia, 1947

Reprinted for
Clearfield Company, Inc. by
Genealogical Publishing Co., Inc.
Baltimore, Maryland
2002

International Standard Book Number: 0-8063-5174-8

Made in the United States of America

TO THE MEMORY OF MY

MOTHER

EUGENIA OCTAVIA REAGAN SWEENY

a descendant of Captain Thomas Graves
of "Doublin in the Realm of Ireland, Gent.,"
who came to Virginia, 1607, a Burgess in the
first Legislative Assembly in America held
at Jamestown, 1619; whose son Francis
patented land in Rappahannock
County, Virginia, in 1672.

CONTENTS

INTRODUCTION

The late William Montgomery Sweeny was well known for many years as a diligent, painstaking investigator in the local history of Virginia. His desire to review the descendants of Captain Thomas Graves of Jamestown, and Francis Graves, his son, who received a grant of land in Rappahannock County in 1672, led to a careful examination of the original wills and of the record books of that county. "Old Rappahannock" County as it is now referred to, was established in 1656; its original territory extended to the west and northwest of what was then Lancaster County, up both sides of the Rappahannock River, without any definite boundary limit on the west. The county was divided in 1692; that part on the northern side of the Rappahannock became Richmond County, and that on the southern side became Essex County. The wills of such a large region enlighten us not only on the territory of the present Richmond and Essex counties, but also on some of the early settlements of the upper Tidewater. Most unselfishly Mr. Sweeny made complete transcripts not only of the few wills which would be immediately useful to him in his own special project, but of all the wills for the benefit of other investigators of the social life of the region. This task, requiring many prolonged visits to the Court House at Tappahannock in the course of fifteen years, he accomplished with the utmost fidelity. To illustrate the difficulties he encountered in deciphering the early handwriting, there has been reproduced in this volume, in a full-page engraving from the original manuscript, the will of Isaac Hudson. Having studied these records for many years Mr. Sweeny was thoroughly familiar with the family names and topographical designations; this familiarity, together with his indefatigable industry, make his transcripts authoritative and dependable. The wills were not all conveniently copied and recorded by the county clerk in a set of books known as Will Books, but were scattered through the Deed Books and Order Books. In selecting the wills it was necessary for Mr. Sweeny to read over all the record books of Old Rappahannock, and all the early records of Essex and Richmond counties. In his search, he discovered a collection of twenty-four original wills, signed by testators, of which there is no copy in the records.

In these wills will be found details of the life of one of the earliest counties of Virginia, organized out of the scattered settlements in the middle region of the Rappahannock River basin only thirty-four years after the disastrous Indian massacre of the James River plantations in 1622, which almost destroyed Virginia; and twenty-four years after the establishment of the eight shires on the James and York rivers. What a wilderness, and how remote, when traveling was so difficult, from the center of social, business and political life at Jamestown. Rich and poor, educated and uneducated are represented in these wills. To those students who wish to construct a picture of the early life of Virginia, these wills will prove most acceptable and helpful. To mention only a few subjects, here will be found information on the extent and boundaries of early patents, the comfortable household equipment of a few of the inhabitants, the scanty equipment of others, the provision for widows and children, the maintenance of servants and slaves, the education of the children, the value of crops, the early deaths, the care of the sick, the family quarrels, the names of early estates, the names of merchants, the references to books, the importance of live stock, especially cows; truly a wide variety of subjects touching the early life of a newly settled community. Through it all there are glimpses of the arduous struggle to make a living; the standard of life, even among the more prosperous, was, necessarily, of unmistakable simplicity.

Some into whose hands this book may fall, will see only a few dates and names; others will find much more, just as much as they bring to it.

Fortunately Mrs. Sweeny was closely associated with her husband in his historical researches; to her for the faithful attention to his transcripts and notes, and for her careful supervision in seeing the work through the press, the students of Virginia Colonial life are deeply indebted. May this publication inspire others to undertake the compilation of similar volumes for all of the Tidewater counties.

E. G. SWEM

Williamsburg, Virginia.

FOREWORD

"Old" Rappahannock County is not to be confused with the present county of Rappahannock. "Old" Rappahannock was formed from Lancaster by act of the Virginia Assembly, December 11, 1656, and included territory on both sides of Rappahannock River, deriving its name, as did the river, from "the Indian tribe of the Powhatan Confederacy, . . . the people of the alternating (ebb and flow) stream." Lancaster had been formed in 1651 from Northumberland and York counties, which themselves had become entities only a half-dozen or more years prior to 1651. Northumberland was the name given the Indian district Chickacoan in February, 1645, and Charles River, one of the original shires, was changed to York county in 1642/3.

Thirty-six years—the period covered by this study—was the life-span of "Old" Rappahannock, for it became extinct in 1692, when its territory north of the Rappahannock River was erected into the county of Richmond and its territory south of the river was erected into the county of Essex.*

Coinciding in area with the political division of "Old" Rappahannock County was the church territory of Farnham parish, established in 1654. This parish was formed from a parish in Lancaster County, whose name, while not certainly known, is thought to have been Lancaster. In 1664 or earlier, Farnham parish was divided, and the new parish Sittingbourne included territory on both sides of the Rappahannock River. In or before 1683, Farnham was again divided, into North Farnham and South Farnham, the Rappahannock River being the dividing line.

RULES USEFUL IN INTERPRETATION OF THE WILLS

Rules to be followed deal chiefly with (1) relationship of one individual to another and (2) chronology.

RELATIONSHIP

Relationship as denoted in the seventeenth century proves puzzling today. For example, apparently the custom was to apply the term "cousin" to nieces and nephews as well as to actual cousins. "Father" referred to "father-in-law" as used today, when followed by the name of the person mentioned. Otherwise, "father" meant the parent himself. Of special note is that "father-in-law," "mother-in-law," etc., most frequently referred to step-father, step-mother, etc. "Junior" might refer to a nephew as well as a son as long as the older relative of the

---

*See Robinson's "Virginia Counties: Those Resulting from Virginia Legislation."

ix

same name, or the "Senior" in the family, was living. There is a noteworthy instance of this latter usage, incidentally, in the fact that John Washington, son of Capt. Lawrence Washington, was called John Washington, Jr., during the life of his uncle, Col. John Washington.

CHRONOLOGY

As to chronology, an excellent explanation appears in the "Note concerning Old Style English Calendar" in *The Virginia Magazine of History and Biography,* October, 1943, pages 392-3, the "Note" having been written by Mr. James P. C. Southall and having appeared in his article "Links in a Chain," as follows:

"A source of much confusion in English chronology is that until 1 January 1752 the English year began in March, for before then New Year's Day in England was the 25th of March. Accordingly, in all English documents, written records and letters, official and unofficial, an event that took place between 1 January and 25 March prior to 1752 was dated one year earlier than it would now be dated according to the new style.

"The same usage prevailed in the English colonies in America. For instance, 'The Muster of m' William Ferrar and m's Jordan,' as given in Hotten's *Original lists,* is dated '21th of January 1624,' old style, which is 31 January 1625, new style. Thus in order to convert old style into new style, the rule is to add ten (or eleven) to the day-number of the month; and in case the old style date comes between 1 January and 25 March, to increase the year-number by one."

Thomas Page made his will 10 March 1676, old style, or 20 March 1677, new style. John Newman's will dated 2 April 1676, old style, or 12 April 1676, new style, antedated Thomas Page's will nearly a year.

Only one other general rule should be borne in mind—that the stated ages of the witnesses to the wills represent their ages at the time of proving the wills.

ARRANGEMENT

1. The wills are subdivided with reference to the original books from which they were transcribed, and the page number of the will book is reproduced beneath each will.

2. Peculiar spelling, abbreviations, etc., appear as in the original— y^e (the), y^t (that), y^n (then), s^d (said), y^r (your), ff (Capital F), and so on. Omission of letters in the wills is incorporated herein.

"The Plott of New Plymouth Towne," 1680. By Act of the Virginia Assembly of 1705, Changed to the Indian Name of Tappahannock. Rappahannock County Record, No. 7, 1681-1688.

Wills of Rappahannock County Virginia, 1656-1692.

At Tappahannock, the County seat of Essex, formerly Rappahannock County, are preserved some of the oldest and most interesting records of Colonial Virginia, which fortunately have survived the "drums and tramplings" of three wars and "Time's destroying hand." Unfortunately, the original documents of Rappahannock County handed to the clerk for copying in the record books have been preserved only from the year 1677; all such papers prior to that date having been destroyed, it is said, at the time of Bacon's Rebellion.

The record books of (old) Rappahannock County appear to run apparently nearly in an unbroken series from the year 1656, when Rappahannock County was formed from Lancaster County, until the year 1692, when the county was divided, the part on the south side of the Rappahannock River becoming Essex County, and that on the north side, Richmond County; however, one or more books that contained wills evidently are missing, as we find mention of wills that were recorded in books which can not be found. These wills are as follows:—

WILLS OF WHICH ONLY A MENTION EXISTS

Will of Edward Berry. Order Book No. 1, at page 171, contains the following:

Court held 5 March, 1684/5: Edward Berry died seized of land on the south side of Rappahannock River, and by his last Will & Testament did devise the said land to the children of Catherine his then wife, and his own, to be equally divided amongst them. Edward George married Margaret, one of the daughters of the said Catherine. He asked the Court to divide the land according to the intent of the said Berry's will. The Court ordered it to be divided into three parts: John Berry, son of Edward Berry, to have the first choice and the other two parts to go to Margaret and Susanna, daughters of the said Catherine.

At a Court held for Rappahannock 6 January, 1686/7: "Charles Browne who married Susanna Daughter of Edward Berry, decd. & sister to John Berry did in Right of his sd wife Represent to the Court that the sd John Berry, hath been unheard of & in Remote parts for many years now past." *Order Book 1686-1692,* page 16.

Court held 11 June, 1696: "The Deposition of Margaret Pitman aged forty three years or thereabouts being sworne and Examined Saith That your Deponent's father Edward Berry gave to his daughter Mary Berry a Heifer by Will bearing date 1664 that same Heifer haveing produc't six Cowes, and further yor. Deponent Saith not.

"The Deposition of Sam^ll. Johnson aged twenty three years or thereabouts being Sworn & Examined Saith that about twelve years agoe he heard his Grandmother Blackbourne say that a Cow was given by her husband to yor. Deponents aunt Susana Berry and that Six Cowes came of that Cow, and further yor. Deponent Saith not.

"The Deposition of Francis Swinny aged fifty years or thereabouts Saith yor. Deponent about twelve years agoe askt M^rs. Blackbourne whether her husband gave two marks to ye Cattle, she pointing to one of the markes s^d. y^t that marke was Susan Berrys Cattle, and further yor. Deponent Saith not." *Essex County Deed Book 9,* page 51.

Will of Thomas Button, (who married by 18 March, 1662, the widow of John Gillett.) Will dated 1 March, 1669, names wife Jane as executrix. To brother, Robert Button, he devised the greater part of "Button's Range," in Rappahannock County. To Thomas Pettus he bequeathed 100 acres of land in Rappahannock County. To godson Henry Creighton, son of Henry Creighton, Sr., he bequeathed 100 acres, part of "Button's Range." *Orders &c., 1692,* pages 97, 347; *Deeds No. 8,* page 215. He died prior to 9 August, 1670. Jane, the widow of Thomas Button, married before 24 January, 1671, ――――― Watts. *Deeds No. 4, 1668-1672,* page 526. Shortly after his death, true to the tradition of Virginia widows, we find that in 1674 Mrs. Jane Watts had been wed to her fourth husband, Thomas Gordon. *Book No. 5, 1672-1676,* page 364.

Will of Colonel John Catlett. The first party to explore and reach the summit of the Blue Ridge Mountains was led by Colonel John Catlett, of Rappahannock County, as gleaned from "An Account of Virginia," communicated to the Royal Society in 1676, by Mr. Thomas Glover, "an ingenious Chirurgion that hath lived some years in that Country." (Blackwell's reprint, Oxford, 1904):

"There was a Colonel *Catlet,* that was a good Mathematician, who with some other Gentlemen took a Journey to make some further discoveries of the Country to the Westward, and arriving at the foot of the Mountains early in the morning, they left their horses and endeavoured to gain the tops of the Mountains, which they accomplished about four of the clock in the afternoon, and then looking further forward they discovered other Mountains, whereof they took the altitude and judged them inaccessible; which discouraged them from any further attempts, their design being chiefly to discover whether there were any Rivers that ran into the South-ocean."

Colonel Catlett married prior to 5 January, 1663/4, Elizabeth, the widow of Captain Francis Slaughter. *Deeds &c., 1656-1664,* page 326.

According to Dr. and Mrs. William Carter Stubbs in "A History of Two Virginia Families Transplanted from County Kent, England," Colonel Catlett was killed by the Indians while defending a fort at Port Royal, 1670. By his will he left his daughters, Elizabeth and

Sarah Catlett, 600 acres of land in Rappahannock County which he had purchased of Henry Corbin, Esq., and Alice, his wife, in 1667. This land had been patented by John Gillett, 28 September, 1657, and passed to Thomas Button on his marriage to Jane, widow of John Gillett. They sold the land to Henry Corbin, Esq., 12 May, 1664. *Deeds &c., No. 3, 1663-1668,* pages 58, 395, 396. Elizabeth and Sarah Catlett married brothers, Francis and Robert Taliaferro. On the 5 September, 1687, Francis Taliaferro, Gent., and Elizabeth his wife, conveyed to John Battaile, of Rappahannock County, 300 acres being one half of the tract of land left by Colonel John Catlett in his will to his daughters, Elizabeth and Sarah. *Deeds, &c., No. 7,* page 508; *Order Book 1686-1692,* page 25. Colonel Catlett's widow, Elizabeth married in 1672, to Rev. Amory Butler. *Book No. 5, 1672-1676,* page 40. Mrs. Elizabeth Butler, in her will, names her children, Francis Slaughter; Sarah, John, Elizabeth and William Catlett.

Will of Captain Alexander Fleming. He married, as his third wife Joyce Hoskins, a daughter of Captain William Jones and the rich and attractive widow of Anthony Hoskins, of Accomac County, who came to Virginia in the "George," 1635, aged 22 years, and, therefore was born *circa* 1613. Captain Fleming died testate about the latter part of the year 1668. In his will he names wife Joyce Fleming, Executrix, and Robert Payne, Gent., Executor. His estate "Westfalia" he left to his wife and other real estate to his daughters, Alexia and Elizabeth Fleming. Joyce with this large estate did not long remain a widow. She married, as her *third* husband, Captain Lawrence Washington, who emigrated from England to Virginia with his brother, John Washington, *circa* 1657. Later, Lawrence Washington returned to England, where he married first Mary, daughter of Edward Jones, of Luton, Gent. After her death, leaving his daughter Mary, to the care of her grandparents he returned to Virginia before 23 March, 1664/5. *Americana, Vol. XXXIII, No. 3,* pages 19, 23; *Deeds No. 4, 1668-1672,* page 163; Nugent: "Cavaliers and Pioneers," page 446.

Captain Lawrence Washington died in 1677. Between 25 March, 1677, when Joyce Washington appeared in Rappahannock Court and placed on record the mark of the cattle of her son John Washington, and 7 April, 1677, Joyce Washington married, as her fourth husband, James Yates, as indicated below:

"Know all men by these pʳsents that I James Yates of the County of Rappᵃᶜ planter doe acknowledge my Selfe Justly to be indebted unto John Washington Junʳ of the Same County his heires or assignes in the Just Sume of one hundred pounds Sterling money of England, to be paid unto the said Washington his heires or assignes upon all demands. In Witness whereof I have hereunto Sett my hand & Seale this 7ᵗʰ day of Aprill 1677.

The Condition of this obligation is such that if the above s^d James Yates shall relinquish att his decease the right that he hath of one third part of the lands formerly belonging to Capt. Alexander ffleming dec^d. & after to Ma^jr Lawrence Washington dec^d. & by them both given to Joyce Washington their wife to be by her disposed as she thinks fitt, the right he hath being now by marrying of her, & in case the above s^d James Yates shall relinquish his rights to his wife to be disposed of by her as she shall think fitt then this pr^snt obligation to be Void or otherwise to Stand in full power force & Virtue. In testimony whereof I have hereunto sett my hand & Seal the day & yeare above written.

Sealed and delivered in the
pr^sence of us

Christopher Blackbourne   James Yates   seal
Robert Pley
William Dacres
                            Recordat^r 18° die July An° 1677
                            Test Edm° Craske, Cl. Cur.
Rappahannock County Book of Deeds &c., No. 6, page 7.

Apparently Joyce Yates predeceased her husband, as his will, dated 9 January, 1685, makes no mention of a wife.

Will of John Gillett. Will dated 2 May, 1659. He was living 18 December, 1662, when he petitioned to the Governor & asked for "letters of Admr. on the Estate of Robt. Sharp late of Rapp^a County decd who went last year for England & shipped some goods in Capt. Plover his Ship intending himself to have come over in the said Ship —Sharpe died before he came aboard the sd Ship and the said Ship being now arrived in Rapp^a. river with the said Sharps goods in her and your petitioner being Left here as guardian to the said Sharp his son & sole attorney of the said Dec^d. Sharpe his son and only heir hereby ———— a let^r. of Administration on the said Decd. Robert Sharpe his goods that are aboard the Ship of Capt. Plover." John Gillett died before 18 March, 1662, leaving his estate "Nimcock" to his wife, Jane, whom he made Executrix of his will. *Deeds &c., 1656-1664,* page 269; *Deeds &c., No. 3, 1663-1668,* page 58.

Will of Francis (Gowre) Gower. The following reference to his will is of record in Order Book 1686-1692, page 349, 2 March, 1691: "Whereas a Nuncupative will of ffrancis Gowre of this County late decd. was duly proved in this Court whereby Stanley Gowre his brother is appointed Exor. ordered by the Court to take into his possession the Estate as also that he take under his care & tuition the children of the Said Francis."

Will of Bryan Hudson. The following reference to his will is of record in Order Book 1686-1692, page 75, 23 March, 1687/8: "Administration with the Will annexed is granted to Mrs. Mary Hudson on the Estate of her decd husband M^r. Bryan Hudson, his will Nuncupative being lawfully proved in this Court."

Will of Humphrey Perkins. The following reference to his will is of record in Order Book 1686-1692, page 41, 3 August, 1687: "Probate by oaths of Thomas Evett and Richard Taylor is granted upon the Nuncupative Will of Humphrey Perkins of this County decd. to W^m. ffreeman Exor. named of the s^d. Will."

Will of Stephen Thomson. The following references to his will are of record in Order Book 1686-1692, pages 18, 78, 2 March, 1686/7: "This day a Nuncupative Will of Stephen Thomson was proved by the Oaths of Two witnesses."

4 April, 1688: "Judgment is granted to M^r. Anth^o. Smyth as Exor. of Stephen Thomson against Roderick Jones for six hundred pounds of Tobacco."

Will of Colonel William Underwood. Deed Book No. 5, at pages 131, 201, 288, 297, 485, contains the following:

11 November, 1672: "William Ball, Jr.* who intermarried with Margaret Williamson & John Rosier who intermarried with Mary Williamson by virtue of the Will of Colonel William Underwood late of Rapp^a County deceased who did give and bequeath unto the said Margaret and Mary Williamson 882 acres of land and also confirmed by patent unto Margaret and Mary Williamson bearing date 11 March, 1662, may more fully appear and for as much as the said land is in joint tenant as by intermarrying as aforesaid and they are not willing the bounds thereof be laid out at present do agree &c."

---

*Son of Col. William Ball, great-grandfather of George Washington. Apparently the tradition that Col. Ball immigrated to Virginia with his family in 1650 is erroneous. He was designated as "William Ball of the province of Maryland planter," 15 February, 1659, when he was granted 420 acres of land, "Balleston, Lying on the West Side of Chesapeak Bay, and on the West side of a river in the said bay, called North West river beginning at a marked Locust Tree by the riverside running South West by the riverside for breadth Two hundred and five perches, to a Creek called Balls Creek, &c." *Liber No. 4* Folio 342, *Land Commissioner's Office, Annapolis, Maryland.*

10 June, 1671: "William Ball of the Collony of Virginia planter," having delivered the above grant to the Secretary's office to be made void upon record, the said William Ball was granted that parcel of "Land now Resurveyed called (Ballistone) Lying in the County of Baltimore on the west Side of Chesapeake bay &c." *Liber No. 16* Folio 268, *Land Commissioner's Office, Annapolis, Maryland.*

By the latter part of the year 1663 he had sailed down the Chesapeake Bay and settled at the mouth of Corotoman River, Lancaster County, Virginia. Nugent: "Cavaliers and Pioneers," page 491. It was here Col. William Ball erected the beautiful Georgian mansion, "Millenbeck."

26 February, 1673/4: William Ball, Jr. and Margaret his wife, of Lancaster County and John Rosier, and Mary his wife, of Westmoreland County, transferred to Thomas Kirton, Gent., of Rappahannock County, a plantation commonly called "Jackmans Folly," situated on the north side of Rappahannock River. The said land was granted Margaret and Mary Williamson, coheirs of James Williamson, of Rappahannock County, Gent., decd., by patent 1 May, 1665.

12 March, 1673: "Captain William Ball, Jr. Gent., and Margaret his wife, of Lancaster County, one of the Coheirs of James Williamson, Gent., late of the County of Rappahannock, decd., and Anthony Bridges, of Westmoreland County, Gent., Atty. for John Rosier, Gent., and Mary, his wife, of Westmoreland County, sold to Charles Dacres, Clerke, of Westmoreland County, 450 acres in Rappahannock County, whereof the said James Williamson died seized. Margaret and Mary Williamson had a brother, William Williamson, who died in his minority and they were the only heirs of the said James Williamson."

2 November, 1675: "Archidale Combes and Elizabeth his wife, formerly Elizabeth Underwood, widow of Major William Underwood, of Rappahannock County, decd. conveyed to Captain William Ball, of Lancaster County, her thirds in a tract of land given by Major William Underwood in his will unto the daughters of Mr. James Williamson, decd., Margaret and Mary Williamson."

The residence of Mr. James Williamson of Rappahannock County, one of the principal land owners and a wealthy merchant, contained a chamber, hall, parlor and buttery as is gleaned from an inventory and appraisement of his estate according to an order "of the Court 23 day of January 1656 by Tho: Goodrich, Andrew Gilson, Will Johnson, Hum: Booth." Among other items in the inventory was "A small parcell of old books" and "Certificate for rights 26 persons." Pages 57-79 are in fragments on which the inventory and appraisement were recorded in Rappahannock Records, 1656-1664.

Will of Colonel John Walker. His will dated 22 February, 1665, was proved 3rd and recorded 10th February, 1668, in Rappahannock County. A copy of his will was recorded in Richmond County, Virginia, 10 February, 1706. He was dead by 28 January, 1668/9, when his widow Sarah Walker, made her will. She was a widow before she married Colonel Walker and in her will she mentions her only son merely as "my Sonne Henry." She remarried, to Colonel John Stone. *Rappahannock County Deeds No. 5, 1672-76,* page 97, contains the following: "TO ALL CHRISTIAN PEOPLE to whom these presents shall come &C KNOW yee that I Sarah Stone Alias Walker of the County of Rappᵃ did in the time of my widowhood but before I had proved the will of Colonel John Walker my Late Husband deceased did set apart certaine young Negroes Certaine Cattle Some Plate and Household Stuff which I did intend to give to the children of Collᵒ

John Walker deceased as also to some of my owne had by him and to that Intent Richard Fox did make a writing of the Particulars soe Intended upon Consideration that I might oblige them the more to Love and Respect me and stir up filial affection in them unto me but finding contrary to Expectation I am for my good will and Affection to them Contemned & despised and Rewarded with Contumelious words and approbious actions and my loving husband John Stone molested by Litigious Lawsuits and daily threatened by more suits of Law doe by these presents of Wrighting Annulling Revoaking and making void all and Every the said Premises Part Parcell or Gifts therein Contained in the said Wrighting as if there Never was or had been such Gifts by writing made interesting and giving them fully to the disposing of my own loving husband and do further declare that I the said Sarah Stone alias Walker did never subscribe the said Writing but what is there subscribed is the act and subscription of Richard Fox and doe moreover with the consent of my loving husband John Stone make ordaine Constitute and appoint M^r. Henry Clerk my true and lawful attorney to acknowledge this as my act and deed in Court. IN WITNESS whereof I have sett my hand and Seale this 2nd day of November Anno 1672. Signum: Sarah (X) Stone (Seale). Signed Sealed and Delivered in the presence of Thomas Blissed and Henry Creighton. I acknowledge my Consent to this as Witness my hand and Seale the day and year above written: John Stone."

Will of Major John Weire. Will dated 7 May, 1671. He gave unto his wife, Honoria, all his real and personal estate to distribute between herself and their two children, John and Elizabeth Weire. George Jones, by intermarriage *circa* 1672, with Mrs. Honoria Weire, widow and sole Executrix of Major John Weire, decd., became possessed of the property, and at her request was to manage it for the benefit of herself and her two children, John and Elizabeth Weire. On the 30th December, 1672, George Jones conveyed the property back to his wife to dispose of as she saw fit. *Deed Book 5,* page 100. George Jones was dead by May Court, 1684, when administration on his estate was granted to his widow, Mrs. Honoria Jones.

Richard Gardner, of the Province of Maryland married Elizabeth Weire. Her brother John Weire died intestate prior to September, 1684 when administration on his estate was granted to his mother, Mrs. Honoria Jones. She failed to give proper security and when Court was held 1 July, 1685, administration on the estate was granted to Mr. Richard Gardner. "And forasmuch as Mr. George Jones late dec'd by intermarrying with the Relict and Sole Exct. of Major John Weire father of the aforesaid John Weire dec'd became possessed with all & Singular the Estate of the said John. It is therefore Ordered that the Estate of the sd John Weire be forthwith paid out of the Estate of the sd George Jones unto Mr. Richard Gardner Qualified as aforesd or his Order according as it shall appeare due by the Last Will & Testament of his dec'd father." *Order Book 1683-86,* page 139.

At a Court held for Rappahannock County, 6 June, 1688: "Mr. Luke Gardner Exhibited to the Court a copy of the last Will and Testament of Mr. Richard Gardner his brother of the province of Maryland late decd. and prayed that thereby Probate be granted of the s^d will which s^d copy the Court finds to be of credit and that it was a true copy of the s^d Rich^d. Gardner's original will by affidavit from the Province of Maryland thereunto annexed Have granted probate of the will in this Colony unto Clem^t. Hill, Esq., & s^d Luke Gardner Exors. therein named." *Order Book 1683-1692,* page 97.

Richard Gardner's will is not of record in Rappahannock County. His will was dated 19 April, 1687, probated 3 December, 1687, and recorded in St. Mary's County, Maryland. Among other Legatees were sons Luke and John Gardner. "To wife Eliza: and hrs., plantation in Va., and certain personalty during minority of son *Luke."* Cotton: "The Maryland Calendar of Wills," Vol. 2, page 19.

Wills of which the originals are in the Court House files, but the book of books in which they were recorded are missing:

Will of	Francis Brown,	proved	3	February, 1691.
" "	David Burk,	"	6	April, 1687.
" "	William Dunbar,	"	4	May, 1687.
" "	Isaac Hudson,	"	6	April, 1687.
" "	Edward Keeling,	"	1	June, 1687.
" "	Lewis Loyd,	"	5	November, 1690.
" "	Daniel Malle,	"	19	May, 1686.
" "	Josiah Mason,	"	4	May, 1687.
" "	Robert Moss,	"	3	April, 1689.
" "	Patrick Norton,	"	7	November, 1688.
" "	John Overton,	"	1	July, 1691.
" "	John Parsons,	"	6	November, 1689.
" "	Henry Reeves,	"	6	April, 1687.
" "	Edmond Riley,	"	4	September, 1689.
" "	James Simons,	"	4	May, 1687.
" "	David Sterne,	"	2	March, 1691/2.
" "	John Suggitt,	"	2	April, 1690.
" "	Robert Tomlin,	"	3	October, 1688.
" "	Walter Welch,	"	6	November, 1689.
" "	Richard Welsh,	"	16	December, 1691.
" "	Richard Wilcocks,	"	2	January, 1688.
" "	George Williams,	"	4	July, 1688.
" "	Henry Wilson,	"	10	March, 1688.
" "	Paul Woodbridge,	"	2	September, 1691.

None of the above twenty-four wills is given in Torrence's *Virginia Wills and Administrations.*

The following wills given in Torrence's *Virginia Wills and Administrations* have not been found of record in Rappahannock County:

1.	George Boyess,	1686.
2.	William Constantine,	1687.
3.	Peter Hopegood,	1677.
4.	John Maffitt,	1684.
5.	Patrick Norton,	1677.
6.	Thomas Roberts,	1683.
7.	John White,	1679.

Comments on these seven are as follows:

1. A Will of George Boycss (or Boyce) was proved 3 February, 1685/6. See page 120.

"The Estate of George Boyce was appraised by an order of the Court dated 3 February 1685/6 by Anth⁰ North Jn⁰ Wells Tho: Parker & Ralph Rowsey who met at the house of Mʳ John Daingerfield—under the heading "Bills due to the Testator is:　　lbs. Tobb

John Gatewood 0316
Rowland Thornton .... 0490"

Deeds, &c., No. 6, 1682-1686, page 74.

2. This will is dated and proved in *1697* and recorded in *Essex County Deeds No. 9, 1695-1699,* page 121.

3. The will of Peter Hopegood proved 7 May, 1679, is the only one of record. He married Sarah Godson, widow, in July, 1670. On 21 June, 1670, Sarah Godson, widow makes Deed of Gift to her four daughters, Sarah, Mary, Frances and Elizabeth Godson. 6 July, 1670, Peter Hopegood testified that he married Sarah Godson and authorized and confirmed the Deed of Gift. *Deed Book 4,* pages 310-311.

4. Should read John *Wassitt.* See page 111.

5. This is a deed not a will. Patrick Norton's will was proved 1688. See page 138.

6. Inventory and appraisement, 25 April, 1683, and recorded in *Deeds &c., No. 6,* page 6.

Wills in the Record Book entitled Deeds, &c., 1656-1664.

TEMPLE, JOHN,

Recorded in Northumberland County, 1658;
Recorded in Rappahannock County, *ca.* 1658.

The last will & Testament of Mr John Temple deced was proved in Northumberland County Court Mrs Ann Temple the wife of the said Mr John Temple being therein ordained to be Ex^rx

Test RI: FLYNT CL CUR

KNOW ALL MEN by these presents that I Ann Temple of the County of Northumberland widow & Ex^rx of the late deced John Temple her deced husband do im——————rge Dee my true and lawful Attorney to demand Sue imprisin release & discharge all ————— whatsoever Standing indebted to me by bill or account as if I myself were in ————— y as any law in Virginia shall confirme witness my hand this 27th—————————.

—————————   ANN TEMPLE   Page 51.

THRESH, CLEMENT,

16 ffebruary, 1656;
Proved or Recorded 1659.

The last will and Testament of Clement Thresh being in full sense and memory Imprimis I give my body to the earth and my soul to God almighty who I hope is my redeemer Secondly I give unto my daughter-in-law Ann Harris three years Schooling out of my Estate ————— to go ————— Mrs. Peacock to school and if it please God that Mrs. Peacock do dye ————— th Tho: Goodrichs Children where they do go and that the said Ann Harris is to remaine with Thomas Goodrich and when she comes to thirteen years of age to have half of the male cattle and if likewise any Lam ————— doth happen unto her I do Desire it may be paid out of my Estate Thirdly I give unto my daughter ffrances Thresh all my estate my debts being paid in the first place and ffraight being made good being 30 hogsheads my desire is that my servants may remaine upon the plantacon and a carefull man may be upon the ground I give unto my Godchild Benj^a. Goodrich one black heifer being two Years old and I give unto my Godchild Ralph Warren [Warriner] one heifer I give unto Thomas Goodrich five hundred pounds of Tobacco and also to Ann Goodrich one ————— of Tob————————— my horse to remain with Mr Gilson till the sa —————————Mr Andrew Gilson and Thomas Goodrich and John Gillet—————————————desire is that Mr Gilson and Thomas Goodrich and John Gill—————————

delivering three again when the said ffrances Thresh com————
—————————————————child doth die before she comes of age then
I do give the————————————————— unto I set my hand
C<small>LEME</small> ————————————

T<small>HOMAS</small> L<small>IDD</small>———— (Liddell?)
T<small>HOMAS</small> T Pow——— (Powell)
    his marke

What goods I ha——————————————————————bred since my
making my will ——————————————————————
daughter may h —————————————————————— between
them which is——————————————————————
ffrances Thresh —————————————————— and my daughter
-in-L ——————————————————————
broadcloth to —————————————————— ans to be
made——————————————————————
back to be gi——————————————————————and as for
————————————————— to be kept in my chest—————————ghter
ffrances Thresh and my pewter and the other things in th————
————————————————————e delivered unto the overseers
when my child Come of in————————bind again—————————give my
servant Robert Bennett one cow Calfe weanable when he have————
ved two years as witness my hand this 16th ffebruary 1656

Test   C<small>LEMENT</small> U T<small>HRESH</small>
    T<small>HO</small>^s T P<small>OWELL</small>   his marke
      his marke

    G<small>EORGE</small> X ———— (P<small>EARCE</small>?)
      his marke   Page 74.

SLAUGHTER, FRANCIS,   dated and proved *circa* 1656-7.
  Sick in body.

    To my mother-in-law Mrs. Margaret Upton ten shillings to buy
her a pair of gloves. To my brother-in-law Coll. Moore Fauntleroy
my book entitled Hooker's Eccleiastical Polity To Andrew Dew my
overseer as much broadcloth as will make him a suit. To my dear
wife Mrs. Elizabeth Slaughter all the rest of my estate and appoint
her executrix reserving and excepting my rapier and belt and young
mare that runs either about Lyons or Lower Chipoake Creek ————
river. I appoint my good friend and brother Humphrey Booth assistant to my wife and give him the said rapier and mare.

Witness P<small>HILIP</small> S<small>ANDERS</small>   Page 83.

29 December, 1657;
SMITH, TOBY,

No date of probate; inventory dated 15 Apl. 1658.

In the Name of God Amen the nine & twentieth day of December 1657. I Toby Smith being weak of body. My dividend of land called Rockingham on which I now live I give to my son——————— . heirs after the decease of his mother. The one moity of my divident ——————— acres of land in the freshes I give to my son Henry and his heirs the ——————— unto my son William and his heirs division to be indifferently made ———————take his choice. If either dies without heirs the land to belong to——————— ———unto my Honoured friend Henry Soane my dividend of three hundred ——————— of land which I purchased of Robt. Eyres to be to the———————est. that is to say to be sold to the best advantage and the produce to be delivered unto my executrix to the satisfying of my debts or relief of her and her children. Item——I give to my said loving friend Henry Soane ten pounds. I give to my honoured friend Coll. Francis Morrison ten pounds. I give unto Thomas Lane so much land as he can occupy for seven years where my executrix shall appoint him ———————. My stock of cattle I give between my Executrix ——————— youngest children. ——————— Executrix the liberty of taking ——————— eldest son & daughter ———————. The rest of my estate I give——————— ——————— do here nominate my wife ——————— to be sole executrix ——————— friend Mr. William ——————— as assistant to my ———————.

NEALE X PETERSON   TOBY SMITH   Seale
JOHN X LACEY   Witnesses
JOHN X WARNER   Page 84.

LAWSON, RICHARD,   (Nuncupative Will),   ———, 1658.

Delivered by word of mouth to Mr. John Catlett and Mr. John Paine; being the day before he departed out of this life which was ———ber, 1658. That his wife* enjoy his plantation that he ——————— during her life and afterwards Elizabeth Lawson the daughter of Epaphroditus Lawson ——————— case said Elizabeth die before his wife then his wife to dispose of the plantation. His wife to have and enjoy all his goods excepting that James Gaines

*Henry Corbin generall Attorney of Capt. John Whitty do hereby assigne over to Mrs Elizabeth Lawson als Page all the right Title & interest that the said Capt John Whitty Ever hath or hereafter shall have to an extent upon a parcel of Land of Richard Lawson decd her late husband & for a debt due to the said Capt. John Whitty as wit: my hand and seale this 2nd day of November 1659.

                    Henry Corbin   Page 98.

have another heifer; that John Taylor, his servant, have a heifer. If said John Taylor survive his m ——————— time with Elizabeth his daughter and if the said Elizabeth survive ————————— then she to have ————————— aforesaid heifer. ————————land upon the so ————————————— Occupation Creek ——————————— John Whitty according to mutuall agreement ———————————— deliver unto the said Lawson two men servants the age of sixteen and twenty years, having sufficient bedding and clothing. Note that the land was excepted in case the full tract were included within the bounds of the patent, and not entrenching upon any mans land.

JOHN CATLETT
JOHN PAINE

Postcript. In case the said Captain Whitty would not accept the said land in payment of his debt, it was to be sold to pay said debt.

Page 86.

WHITLOCK, THOMAS,   9 October, 1659;
20th November, 1659.

In the Name of God Amen I Thomas Whitlock being very Sick & weak in body but in perfect & sound knowledge & memory & calling to mind the uncertainty of this Life make this my last will & Testament revoking all former wills by me formerly made & by these presents rattify this to be my true will whatsoever shall appear to the contrary by m—————————ly under my hand or seale. Imprimis I Commit my soul to almighty God maker of Heaven & Earth who breathed in me the breath of Life humbly prostrating my self ——— footstoole of his throne of Grace for mercy believing that in and through the merits of Jesus Christ my only Lord & Saviour to obtain Everlasting Life & my body to the earth whence it came to be buried in such Christian buriall as shall ——————— by my Loving wife Mary Whitlock my sole Exe[x] & my overseer A ——————— Thomas Writte [Wright] & my worldly Goods in manner & form as foll. Item. I give unto my son Thomas Whitlock my Land Jno ————— lives on being in all Six hundred acres to come into his hand & be delivered unto him when he attains unto the age of one & twenty years but in case of his mortality in his minority the reversion thereof to ffall to my Loving wife Mary Whitlock my sole Ex[ex]. & further in case of my wifes mortality before my Son come to his perfect age then my said Son to be left with the use of my Land & such other money & goods as I shall leave him as hereafter shall be Specified & by the order of my overseers likewise my further desire is that the Land be not further made use on by planting or seating then the first deep branch that is commonly rid over that my son may have some ffresh Land to make use of when he attains to age. Item my desire is that all goods chattels & moveables whatsoever I dye possessed with & ——————— due by bill be praised to the Equall vallue in money or Tob°. the—————

————————————————————— sole use of my wife & the other halfe
part to be for the use of my son T ————————— security to be given
for it to pay him to the true vallue thereof when he —————————
age of one & twenty years & use thereof, till then to go to the maintenance of ————————————————— but in case my sd son should
dye before he attains to the age of one & ————————— to my
wife Mary Whitlock & further I desire my said wife to be good to my
————————————— in the fear of God & to let him be put to
School according as in her mature care will be thought Good & that
he be of age ————————————————— by my said Loving wife &
my overseers. Item my desire ————————— the two heiffers that
————————— my sons already being given him one by his God———
————————— Thacher & another ————————— given as by myself remain ————————— Sole increase mal————————— &
that they be kept upon the ————————— for the better—
————————————— male cattle to be sold to ————————— shall
be found ————————— by my wife or ————————— Death in
his ————————— my Wife as Joint ————————— better
improvement of my Land that an orchard be made upon my Land &
that my wife with the advice of my overseers see to the improvement
thereof and that it may be made with the Stock of trees due to me by
condition from my mate Samuell Nicholls fur——— with in hast was
forgotten my desire is that my Debts due unto any man by bill———
————————————— any other way lawfully due may be truly paid by my
Loving wife Mary Whitlock my Executrix & in case of her death or
debility by ov—————————r of my overseers ————————— or
the true ratification of this my writting Will I subscribe it with my
hand ————————— this 9th day of October 1659.

Signed & sealed in the presence of us   THOMAS WHITLOCK   Seale

ALLEX FFLEMING
JOHN RICHARDSON
JAMES YATES

Recorded the 20th day of
November anno 1659
P me
ANT STEPHENS Cl Cur Rapp[a].
Page 90.

—————————————1659 ;

WITHEY, AUGUSTINE,*   *circa* 1660.

    In the name of God Amen I Augustine Withey being visited with
Sickness under ————————— Almighty God but in perfect Memory

—————

*John Withy Citizen and painter stayner of the City of London———
    In September in the year 1659 he sent in the good ship Anthony of Lon-
don, Thomas James, Master, a servant named Henry Martin to his son Augustine Withy who died in Virginia before the arrival of the ship, & Captain
James sold the said servant. When Captain James returned to London he
paid John Withy full satisfaction and he (John Withy) renounces all his
claim, right, title and Interest which he or Coll. ffauntleroy in Virginia **may**
have to the said servant.
(Date missing but apparently *circa* 1662).

                                        Deeds, No. 2, page 144.

the Lords holy name be ever praised and magnified for his imence
mercy and if it be the pleasure of the Almighty ——————— ow to
call me out of this transitory Life I make & ordaine this to be my last
will & Testament Viz^t. P^o. (?) with a penitent & contrite heart
of ——————————— offences Rebellion against my God in whose
————————————————— bly through my self down at the footstool
of ——————————— nd of mercy yielding & committing my soule unto
him my maker through the merrits & righteousness of Christ Jesus
my beloved redeemer. I bequeath my body to the earth whence it came
to be decently buried at the will & pleasure of my Loving friend More
ffauntleroy the which being done my debts being paid which are unto
Henry Nicholls 270 lbs. tob^o. to Clement Herbert half a hhd & unto
Thomas Griffin 2 hh^ds. in equality & hard measures I make and appoint my ffriend More ffauntleroy gent my sole Executor of this my
last will & Testament bequeathing unto him all my ———————hold &
utensils whatsoever appertaining unto me In witness w ——————— re
underneath subscribed my name & affixed my seal this————————————
Anno 1659

———————————————SON

—————————————————N   AUG. WITHEY   Seale

Wills in the Record Book entitled Wills, Deeds, &c., No. 1, 1665-1677.

"Memorandum

That what is contained in this book from ye page 114 is truly transcribed out of part of ye book N°. F and faithfully Examined by me this VIth MDCCXXXj

WBEVERLEY Cl Cur"

WRIGHT, THOMAS,

23 October, 1661;
10 May, 1666.

Weak in body but perfect in memory.

I do make my Loving Wife Jane Wright my Sole Ex^r [Executrix] of all my whole Estate after my debts be paid onlye Desire that my female Cattle be Equally divided the one half to run for the use of my daughter Eliz^a. Wright and the other half to my Loving Wife likewise I do appoint M^r. John Washington Overseer of this my last will & Testam^t.

Wit. ROGER X RICHARDSON, ROB^T. SISSON.   Page 107.

13 November, 1671;
23 May, 1672.

BILLINGTON, LUKE, of ffarnham parish in Rappa County.

Of sound and perfect memory.

To my beloved wife Barbary Billington the house wherein I now dwell with all moveables and immoveables and Lands belonging thereunto belonging to the s^d Plantation with all the Cattle belonging to me as mares and horses sheepes and all the graine and corne and wheat servants and all my household goods within doors and without during the term of hir natural life and after her decease to fall to my son Luke Billington and his heirs forever and I doe oblige my s^d wife to provide and give unto my s^d daughter Elizabeth at hir day of marriage either a man servant or a maid servant of times as servants come into this country to serve. I give unto my son Luke Billington the mountain field wherein now Richard Peacock liveth to him and his heirs for ever and in case he dieth without issue then the s^d land to be divided between his fower sisters here nominated being Elitia and Elizabeth and Jane and Barbary my daughters and in case that any or either of my s^d daughters shall die without issue that the s^d land belong to their survivor or survivors. I doe oblige my sonne Luke to give and deliver at the day of marriage of my daughters Jane and Barbary to each of them a man servant or a maid servant for the full time or terme of years as servants serve their lawful apprenticeship in this Country. I give and bequeath unto my daughter Elitia three hundred and fifty acres of land belonging to the mountain fields as by pattent purchased appeareth and if my said daughter dieth without issue that then the s^d land fall and be divided between my three daughters Elizabeth Jane and Barbary and in case any of them die without issue to fall to the survivor or survivors. I give unto my daughter Mary apeece of plate to the value of thirty shillings and to her sonne my grandchild William Daniell a yew with a yew lamb by her side. I do further appoint and oblige my wife to pay and satisfy all or any just debts wch shall be made appeare that I owe either by obligation or accounts. I make my wife Barbary my whole and sole Executrix of this my last will and Testam^t. And further I desire my trusty and well beloved friends Mr William Travers and Mr Gyles Cale to be trustees of this my last will and Testam^t. that to their power as much as in them lyeth it be performed. Further D^r. John Russell to be a trustee to this my last will with Mr William Travers and Mr Gyles Cale.

Wit. HENRY SHEARES, aged 35 years or thereabouts,
JOHN RUSSELL, aged 26 years or thereabouts.

Page 114.

28 October, 1671;
MARTIN, SOLOMON,   No date of probate.

Sick and weak in body but of perfect sence and memory.

I doe wholly give and bequeath all my estate both reall and personall unto my well beloved friend George Mott and to his three children Elizabeth, Margaret and Anne all the living Creatures as well Cattle as horses & mares to be divided between them at the discretion of their father. Appoints George Mott Executor.

No witnesses.   Not signed.   Page 117.

27 August, 1670;
THOMAS, DAVID,   3 January, 1672.

Bequeaths all his estate to his well beloved friend Edward Lewis whom he makes his Executor.

Wit. WILLIAM X DAVIS, DAVID HUDNALL.   Page 118.

8 May, 1672;
WILLIAMS, WALTER,   3 July, 1672.

To Elizabeth Thatcher a cow. To John Cammock a young heifer. To Warwick Cammock and his heirs forever the land I bought of John Meader and Henry Peters wch Samuel Johnson hath a half in it he the said Cammock paying the remainder of the Tobacco that is due for it and I make and Constitute the s^d Cammock Executor of this my last will and desire that all my just debts be paid. To Silvester Thatcher a steere and to Mathew Thatcher a young heifer.

Wit. PETER DUNNIVAN, SAMUELL JOHNSON.   Page 119.

28th day of May in the 24th year of the reign of Charles II;

4 September, 1672.

WRIGHT, THOMAS,

of Moraticon Creek, Rappahannock County, Planter.

To wife Mary all and every the goods Chattles Cattle and whatsoever that she had when I married her, to her only use. To William Baldwyn's daughter living with one Isack Stannop on the South Side of Rapp^a. River the sume of Six hundred pounds of Tobacco to be laid out upon a Cow for hir use and my will is that my sonne in Law Edward Poole shall have the laying out of the Tobacco and that he see the Cow recorded with the increase to hir and hir heirs forever. To Edward Rylyes wives daughter the like Sum of Six hundred pounds of Tob° to bee laid out for a Cow for hir my will being that Thomas Madison have the laying out of the Tobacco and that he see the Cow recorded with the encrease unto hir and hir heirs forever. To my cozen Edward Carter my young mare and her increase and three hundred Acres of land joyning upon Mr Halls land and lying by Colonel Lees path and sold me by Mr Thomas Chetwood in part of satisfaction of 1000 acres which doth appear upon the records of Lancaster County. To sons in law Thomas and Robert Bryant my old mare and 1000 pounds of tobacco apeece. To my sonne-in-law Robert Briant 115 acres of land wch lyes by Moraticon mill being part of 230 acres of land between John Chine and myselfe. To my daughter-in-law's child Elizabeth Pool my old mare's foale which fell this p^rsent yeare and hir increase but in case the s^d Elizabeth Pooll doe decease without issue of hir body then the sd legacy shall return to Thomas and Robert Briant and their heirs for ever. To Brian Stott's children my stone colt which is at p^rsent above one year old and my will is that Brian Stott their father have the ordering of it as he thinks fitt. My will is that all my legacies which I have given away bee paid the next Cropp after my decease. My wife Mary Wright to be Executrix giving unto her my servants with all the remainder of my goods chattles cattle and household stuff whatsoever and all my debts which are due unto me she paying my legacies aforesaid and my debts I owe. Wit. BRIAN STOTT, aged 45 years or thereabouts,

ROBERT X BRIAN, aged 22 years or thereabouts.

Page 120.

24 July, 1672;

MANSELL, CAPTAIN DAVID,   4 September, 1672.

In perfect memory and sence yet sick and weake in body.

I make and depute my well beloved friend and nearest neighbour William Wheeler my full and whole Executor putting my whole trust in him my said Executor to take on himself the same charge and Care to bring up and educate my godchild David and to take to himself all the said David ffristo his Estate which I now possess or might possess and retaine until the said ffristo be come of age if lived. His Executor to pay all his lawful debts. To daughter Mary my sealed ring. To my grandchild Mansell Blagrave and his heirs and successors for ever one tract of land adjoining the land of Mr Robert Bayly on which land standeth a house called the block house there being neere 200 acres. To my said Executor William Wheeler the ½ part of my Estate that shall appeare to remaine after these debts and legacies be deducted out of the whole. To my said grandchild Mansell Blagrave the other ½ part of my Estate that shall remain after my debts and legacies be deducted as above said out of the whole. The remainder of my Estate to William Wheeler and Mansell Blagrave or their heirs or assigns either to be divided or sold by my aforesaid Executor or by him my said Executor to be retained putting in security for the ½ part to be delivered when my said grandchild cometh to be of age or whensoever my said Executor shall see best for both him and my grandchilds advantage.

Wit. JONAS X PAGE, aged 47 years or thereabouts,
MARTHA X LEWIS, aged 30 years or thereabouts.

Page 125.

| | 13 March, 1672; |
| HUTSON, EDWARD, | 6 November, 1672. |

Sick and weake but in perfect sence & memory.

To son John Barton two cows and their increase also three bills containing fower thousand pounds of tobacco and cask. Makes wife Dorothy Hutson his Executrix to whom he gives all moveables and immoveables during her lifetime. To Elizabeth Holt one cow calf.
Wit. ARTHUR HODGES, aged 33 years or thereabouts, PETER HOPEGOOD.

Page 127.

| | 5 March, 1671/2; |
| DEYOUNG, JOHN, | 6 November, 1672. |

IN THE NAME OF GOD AMEN I John Deyoung of the County of Rapp[a]. and parish of ffarnham being very weake in body but of Sound and perfect memory doe heere make my last will and Testament as followeth—Imp I bequeath my Soule to God that gaue it in hopes of a sure and certaine resurrection in and through Jesus Christ my lord and Saviour and my body to be buried in such decent manner as my friends hereafter named shall think Meet and my worldly goods in manner and form following—Item I giue unto my daughter Elizabeth Deyoung two Cowes & all my whole Stock of hogges which shall happen to bee after my decease and also one Steer of fower yeares old—Item It is my will that the rest of my whole Stock of Cattle both male and feemale bee equally deuided between my fower Children viz[t]. Elizabeth, Ann, Honour and John Deyoung—Item I giue unto

John Deyoung my Long gunn. Item I do moreover give unto my daughter Elizabeth, my best feather bed with the rugg and blanketts belonging thereunto— Item I doe giue the remainder of my goods & moueables to be equally devided betweene my aboues[d]. Children Elizabeth, Anne, John, & Honour Deyoung Item I giue my land unto my Sonne John Deyoung Item It is my will that my stock nor other estate bee noe waies remoued of the land if possibly it may be preuented— Item it is my will that my daughter Elizabeth together with my Bro[r]. in Law George Knott and my friend Thomas ffreshwater doe after my decease take care to see this my last will and testam[t]. in all particulars as neare as may bee performed And first before my legacies bee paid as afores[d] that my debts bee paid and Satisfied and in Confirmation of the p[r]misses I haue hereunto Sett my hand and Seale this 5[th]. of March 1671/2.

Signum

JOHN X DEYOUNG   Seal

Signed, Sealed, and
published in p[r]sence
of us——
      Signum
    ZACHERY X EFFORD
    WILLIAM DAUIS

        Wee the Subscribers doe declare that wee did see John Deyoung sign Seale and publish this as his last Will and testam[t]. and that he was then in perfect mind and Memory to the best of our Judgments

WILLIAM DAUIS
Signum
ZACHARY EFFORD

Jurautur in Cur Com Rapp[a]. Sexto die Nouemb 1672 et probat[r].

Test EDM[o]. CRASK Cl Cur p[r]d Ex[a].   Page 129.

13 June, 1672 ;
5 March, 1672/3.

TUFFLEY, WILLIAM,

To my Loving wife Elizabeth Tuffley all my land and housing I now enjoy with all my goods and cattle and hoggs which I am possessed of and in case of her mortality then I give and bequeath my land with all my goods and Cattle and hoggs unto my son in Law Griffin Carter and if it should please God to take him out of this life before he cometh to the age of one and Twenty years then I give and bequeath my lands goods and Cattle unto my loving friend Capt. John Hull whom I make my Executor of this my will.

Wit. FFRANCIS STONE, ROGER HULL, WILLIAM X WEBB.

Page 131.

8 February, 1672;
HARDESTY, JOHN,   5 March, 1672/3.

To wife Mary all my personal estate and likewise my seate of land
I bought of Mr George Pley in case my said wife be with child now
with eith^r boy or maide that then my wife shall have only her thirds
and my said child shall have the other two thirds both of goods and
lands but in case she is not with child then my said wife shall have as
aforesaid my debts and funerall expenses first paid. Wife Mary to be
my Executrix. Wit. ROBERT PLEY, EDWARD ROWZIE.

Page 133.

22 March, 1671/2;
HODGKIN, WILLIAM,   7 May, 1673.
of Rapp^a in Virginia being bound for England.

To my kinsman Samuel Peachy Sr. 2000 pounds of Tob. in cask
to bee paid by my Executors the next Crop, after administration. To
his eldest son Samuel Peachy my Godchild one Ewe and Lamb. To
his youngest son William Peachy one three year old heifer and one
ewe & lamb. To my Brother-in-law Henry Smith my bay mare. To
my servant John Booler one cow and calf out of my stock. To Mr.
Thomas Peenie the colt of my bay mare. To a minister of my Executrix her appointment 500 pounds of Tobacco to preach a sermon
in remembrance of me. To my loving wife Phoebe Hodgkin all the
remainder of my whole Estate in Virginia both personall and reall
my debts being first paid. Appoints his wife to be his Executrix.

Wit. RICHARD BRAY, RALPH GREAYDON.   Page 134.

Not dated;
7 May, 1673.

BUTLER, ELIZABETH, of the parish of Sittingbourne in the
     County of Rappahannock.

To son Francis Slaughter all the furniture of my chamber except
a chest of drawers which I give to my daughter Sarah to be delivered
to her at the age of seventeen years or day of marriage which shall
first happen and a close stool to my son John Catlett to be delivered
to him when he goes to housekeeping. To son Francis Slaughter all
the goods money plate rings and tobacco mentioned in an account
now in the hands of M^r. Daniel Gaines and one negro boy and an
equal share of the sheep pewter brasse and iron and also a great Chair
and Small Couch and one Chest and such things in my house as my
mother gave me by will the same to be delivered into his possession
when he comes to the age of nineteen years and that he shall not dispose or sell the same without leave and consent of my executor and
overseers hereafter named till he come to the age of one & twenty
years. To my daughter Elizabeth the bed and furniture as it now is

standing in the dining roome and the presse and cushion thereon and the great looking glasse and the drawing table and Turkey carpet and my child bed linen blanketts and fine baskett and my wedding ring and my biggest diamond ring my gilded bodkin and my necklace with the biggest pearle and one small Bible a silver sucking bottle and my small cabinett. To daughter Sarah two of my biggest stone rings a small pearle necklace and a silver bodkin and my new trunck and the napking Presse one small Bible and small Testament and a dram cup my wedding ring and oval table. To son John one small diamond ring the mapp in the dining room one rapier one great cutlash one pair of silver buttons and one paire of silver buckles and the Antimonial Cupp. To son William one small cutlash and a ring with a stone in it enamelled with blew and a silver seale. To my two daughters all my wearing cloathes and wearing linnen. To sons John and William all the books mentioned in the Inventory equally between them according to their fathers will. To my two sons John and William Catlett and my two daughters all my plate except three spoons with their names on them to whom they belong to be equally divided between them. I give and bequeath all my pewter linnen & other household stuffe unto my two sons John and William and my two daughters (except what is before bequeathed to my son Francis) with a bed furnished to each of my two sons and my daughter Sarah (except two suits of damask which I give to my two daughters) to be equally divided between my two sons and my two daughters aforesaid. To each of my three sons a carbine. I give and bequeath my gray mare with her increase unto the aforesaid fower children of my deceased husband John Catlett. My will is that my two daughters aforesaid shall have delivered to them their former legacies at their day of marriage or at the yeares of seventeen and likewise my two sons John and William have theirs delivered when they come of age. To my Couzen William Underwood the elder one stone Colt which came of the sorrel mare. To my Couzen Humphrey Booth the chest with the goods in it which were my mothers. To my Couzen Catherine Booth one silver Caudle cupp which was her grandmothers and in case she dyes to her Bro^r. Humphrey. If my son ffrancis dye before he comes of age then my surviving children to enjoy the whole estate both formerly and now bequeathed unto him. My will is that if my Executor hereafter mentioned shall brake up housekeeping that then all my household stuff aforesaid bequeathed to my Children shall be well packed and locked up and kept from use and that the linnen and other things that are in the Cask and trunck be forthwith locked up till the time of their delivery and that all my son ffrancis his household stuff be likewise reserved and kept by it self. To my sister Peirce a mourning ring of 20 shillings price in England. If my Executor hereafter mentioned shall voluntarily surrender up the estate that then Mr Daniel Gaines if he hath the children shall have the estate provided that he give good security to keep the said estate entire and deliver the same in kind according to my will and that my will bee by him in all respects performed as my Executor is bound to do. My will is that my Executor supply what Tobacco shall be required for the Childrens education now in England according to my husbands will and likewise that he make sufficient provision when they shall come from schoole for their accomodation and their bringing of them home to Virginia. My will is that all my wearing Cloathes which last yeare I sent for at the profit of my Tobaccoes be upon the arrival of the same locked up in my Cask kept for and divided between my two daughters and the rest my Executor to have for his household use. And likewise what moneys shall remain in Mr Geffries and Mr Manfords hands in London be disbursed by them for a bed and furniture for my son ffrancis in lieu of one his father-in-law did owe him and two small silver tankards (if it so holds out) to be added to the rest of the plate for the children of my deceased husband. My will is that the childrens estate be kept entire and not parted before their legacies given by me become due unto them and if the Court shall take my childrens estate out of my Executors hands that then my Children shall altogether bee maintained well educated and provided for by and with the profitt of their own estates and that my thirds and the profitts thereof shall remain in my Executors hands till they come of age. I do constitute and appoint my beloved husband Amory Butler sole executor of this my last will and Testament and Guardian to my Children and my Cousen Captain Thomas Hawkins my Bro^r. Edward Rowsee and Mr Daniel Gaines Overseers of this my last will and Testament Provided that if my said Executor do not educate and keep them well that then Mr Daniel Gaines shall have the Guardianship of my Children my s^d Executor allowing him a sufficient maintenance for their well being and education as my Overseers and Executor shall agree and if they do not what the Court shall determine for the same and if Mr Gaines shall dye my desire is that my Cousen Hawkins do take the children upon the same terms and if my Executor shall imbezell the estate or forsake the country then my will is that my Overseers shall call him to account and finding him delinquint my Executor shall be either bound to make good the same out of his own estate or else yield it up to Mr Daniel Gaines he the s^d Gaines doing as before for the security of the estate. Item that my s^d Executor do purchase as soon as he can a negro man for my sonn ffrancis by or with the profitt of the estate in lieu of one his father-in-law deceased did owe him. I give and bequeath of the cattle that were my mothers and now in the keeping of Thomas Kirk two of the females to my sister Peirce hir Children with their increase forever and also the other two of the female kind with their increase and eight steers to my Bro^r Booths children the said steers and increase of the female to be disposed of by my Executor to purchase for them a negro woman to be delivered to them with her increase when they come of age mortality excepted. My will is that if the estate of my children bee taken out of my Ex-

ecutors hands within halfe a year after my decease and if my executor
be compelled to make good of the sd estate what shall be falling short
my executor shall make good the same out of the increase of the
negroes that have bin since the same have bin committed to him the
sd increase to be delivered to my Children in Kind when they come
of age and if it shall not suffice then the same to be made good out of
my thirds or the profitts thereof as my executors shall think best for
my children. I give and bequeath to my well beloved husband Amory
Butler a bed and furniture with a mourning ring of 22 shillings price
in England. When my executors shall have paid all my Legacies that
then if there be remaining any of my thirds in his hands he shall
surrender up the same unto my Children the profitts thereof excepted.

Wit. THOMAS LUCAS, Senr., JOHN DAWSON.   Page 136.

                                        20 July, 1673;
GRAY, WILLIAM,   3 September, 1673.
    Sick and weak but of perfect memory.
    To sons John and Warwick Gray equally to be divided between
them the tract of land I now live on containing 728 acres with houses
edifaces thereunto belonging. To sons William and Abner Gray 461
acres of land adjoining to Occupancy Run equally to be divided between them and if either of my sons die before they reach the age of
twenty one that then that moyity or half of land to return to the
Survivor which did belong to him. My will is that my Executor and
my Executrix or either of them shall buy a young mare for my sons-
in-law Toby and Thomas Ingram between this and the last of
April 1675 with the increase of the said mare. To son Abner a black
mare and all her increase which was purchased with a gift from Mr.
Abernethy. To daughter Mary Gray the first mare colt that my mare
brings. To my grandchild Elizabeth Bowler a cow called Mad Buck.
To wife Maudlin and son-in-law James Bowler Executrix and Executor.

Wit. WARWICK CAMMOCK, aged about 37 years,
        Signum
    FRANCIS F STERNE, aged about 35 years.

                                        Page 143.

                                        — December, 1672;
SWELLIVANT, CORNELIUS,   19 November, 1673.
    To John Burridge all my land during his life and one feather bed
and one chest one trunck and all my working tools and all my household goods and my boate. To Thomas Norton sonne of Patrick Norton
three hundred and fifty acres of land of the upper side of the divident
and after the decease of Thomas Norton and John Burridge the land
to fall to Patrick Norton. To John Kelly sonne of Mathew Kelly I
give one hundred and seventy five acres joyning upon the land that

the s^d Mathew Kelly now liveth on in the meantime may put it to what use he please and after the decease of John Kelly the land to fall to Mathew Kelly his father. What cattle the s^d John Burridge shall receive of Cornelius Sullivant he to leave so many in kind to Thomas Norton. To John Dowty I give one Dowlas shirt one pair of Kersey breeches and one Coate and three pewter dishes. To Patrick Norton I give my hanger.

signum

Wit. WILLIAM MAJOR, JOHN F O ORGILL.   Page 148.

30 January, 1673/4;

PETERS, HENRY,   4 March, ———.

Sick and weak but of sound and perfect memory.

To wife the two girls Elizabeth Walker and Mary Peters as their mother deceased desired that John Smith should not meddle with them so likewise it is my will and desire. To James Allen my wife's son 300 acres of land lying near Pewmondsend to be laid out together to him and his heirs forever. To my daughter Elizabeth Walker two cows and a mare a year or two old to be paid hir the day of hir marriage. All the rest of my estate reall and personall to my wife Jane Peters and my daughter Mary Peters to be divided equally between them by my loving friends Mr Lawrence Washington John Meader Francis Sterne and Warwick Cammock within three weeks or thereabouts after my decease and my request to them is that they would divide it equally as they can to the best of their judgments because my will is that there be no appraisement made of any part of my estate. Wife Jane to be sole Executrix.

Wit. PETER DUNNIVAN, JOHN GIBSON, WARWICK CAMMOCK.

An addenda to the will.

If wife dies before his daughters Elizabeth Walker and Mary Peters come to be of age then Daniel Gaines and Warwick Cammock to take charge of them and their estate and if said Gaines and Cammock die in the meantime the survivor is hereby impowered to choose another.

Wit. PETER DUNNIVAN, JOHN GIBSON.   Page 149.

14 Oct. 1669;
27 May, 1674.

LUCAS, THOMAS, the Elder, of Sittingbourn Parish.

In good health & sound memory but aged.

To son-in-law John Catlett ten shillings. To son-in-law Captain Thomas Hawkins ten shillings. To my grandchild Mary Hawkins one young heifer with a cow calf and all their female increase to be delivered by my executors hereafter named unto my sonne Hawkins aforesaid to keep for hir within one year after my decease and the male increase for his charge and care in keeping them and he the said cattle and female increase to deliver to hir at her age of one and twenty years or day of marriage which shall happen first. To son Thomas Lucas all my lands and tenements and hereditaments with the appurtenances to him and his heirs forever. All the residue of my goods and chattels my debts and legacies being paid I give and bequeath to my son Thomas Lucas aforesaid whom I make my sole Executor.

Wit. EDMUND DOBSON, RICHARD R WEST.

signum

An addition made March 24, 1673/4.

My Executor to pay all my debts in due and convenient time after my decease and in particular my will is that my loving sister-in-law Mrs. Margaret Plammer be paid as soon as may be after my decease £5 Sterling or the just value thereof in sweet scented tobacco. To my loving son-in-law Thomas Hawkins one thousand pounds of tobacco to be paid in two years after my decease. To my loving friend Daniel Gaines ten shillings Sterling. Requests that his son-in-law Thomas Hawkins be aiding and assisting to my son and my Executor Thomas Lucas in what he shall reasonably require of him either for advice or otherwise.

Wit. THOMAS HAWKINS, DANIEL DS SHIPLEY.   Page 152.

sign

| | 7 March, 1673; |
| WARRINER, RALPH, | 27 May, 1674. |

My body I desire to be buryed home with or near my father and mother at the discretion of Thomas Gouldman. To ffrances Keys my Cow Squirrel as useth Coll Vassells old plantation that was. To William Dyer my horse. I give all the Tobacco that belongeth to me out of the crop or is otherwise properly due to me unto my guardian Thomas Gouldman he laying out of the same for my sisters particular use five hundred weight of the same in such necessarys as he shall think fitting. To my sister three young black cows and one steer three years old or thereabouts and one bull of two years old and one yearling heifer and also two sowes that I have on the plantation.

Wit. ROBERT X PARKER, WILLIAM X DYER.   Page 155.

| | 18 April, 1673; |
| PACKSTON, (PAXTON), JOHN, | 27 May, 1674. |

. This is my will and desire that my three hundred acres of land shall be at my landlady's Sarah Bowyer's disposal to doo what she thinks fitt to sell or otherwise and if the said Sarah Bowyer die without any will then the said three hundred acres of land to be divided between Samuel Flood and Bridget Essex the daughter of John Essex and she to have one heifer about 2½ years old and also I give one steer about the same age to Samuel Flood and further my will is that my Landlady Sarah Bowyers shall have the rest of my cattle and hogs to do what she please either to sell or otherways what she shall think fitt.

Wit. JOSHUA LAWSON, THOMAS X WARRING.   Page 156.

31 March, 1674;
27 May, 1674.

MOTT, GEORGE, of the Parish of Sittingbourne, in the County of Rappa., Planter.

Sick & weak of body but of perfect sence & memory.

And for my part of the divident of land on the north side of Rapp[a] River granted to my Brother John Mott and I by Pattent dated at James City the seventeenth day of October 1670 my will is that my well beloved wife Elizabeth Mott shall enjoy one-third part thereof during hir natural life and that the land be equally divided among my Children Viz[t] Elizabeth Margaret Anne and Ellen and if it shall happen that my wife be with Child at my death and the child live that it shall have an equal part with the rest but if it be a son my will is that if any one of my daughters afores[d] depart this life before she comes to age or marries then the son shall enjoy hir part of the land and in case more of my children dye my will is that the Survivors bee joynt heirs Then as for my personal estate my will is that my well beloved wife have and enjoy one third part thereof forever to be at her disposall and the other two-thirds to be equally divided among the Children to be delivered in kind as in respect of age and quality either when they marry or come to the age of seventeen years And whereas my Bro[r] and I have joyntly given to the Children some certain Sheep and Cattle my desire is that they may be distinguished by a marke and that they with their increase bee by my wife improved to the Childrens best advantage And I doo make and appoint my well beloved wife to bee my sole Executrix of this my last Will and Testament and I doe desire that my well beloved Bro[r] John Mott would be Assistant to hir in management of the estate and for the pformance thereof my desire is that an Inventorie may bee taken of all the psonall estate appertaining to my bro[r] and I and that noe division be made thereof but that they would live together upon the Plantation with the estate joyntly as my bro[r] and I formerly have done onely dividing the Cropp yearly & each to have the disposall of their part at their own discretion but if it should happen that any inconvenience should arise that they shall see cause to devide the estate and live apart that then my brother shall have half of the profitts of the Orchard during his life and I do further give liberty to my Execut[x] and my Bro[r] to sell 1000 acres of the divident of land aboves[d] the division thereof betwixt them and to divide the produce thereof betwixt them equally and the remainder of the land to be equally divided betwixt my Bro[r] and my Children and whereas there was an Instrument of writing made betwixt my Bro[r] and I under our hands & Seals on purpose to destroy joynt tenancie betwixt us bearing date the 10th of October 1671 wherein mention is also made of certain parcells of land conveyed and to bee conveyed to severall persons as allso 2000 acres of land sould & acknowledged in Court to Mr. William Thornton therefore it is my will that if my Execut[x] or any of my Children shall act or do anything contrary to the true intent & meaning of our severall agreements with these parties that then the damages arising thereby shall bee made good out of their or any of their part of my estate and I do likewise constitute and appoint my well beloved wife Elizabeth Mott to be my Executrix of the last will and testament of Mr Solomon Martin and do desire that my said wife having the consent of my Bro[r] John Mott (if living) to dispose of the increase of the estate given to my Children by the sd Solomon Martin as also of the estate aboves[d] already in their possession to the use and benefit of my Children and to no other purpose.

Wit. JAMES HARRISON, JOHN BOWSIER, HENRY X HACKERY.

Page 157.

NOTE. He revokes all other wills and testaments made by him heretofore.

28 April, 1674;
ELDER, PETER,   5 August, 1674.

I do bequeath my son Peter Elder unto Mr Richard Peacock he being my soul Godfather whom I have made choice of above all others and as for what stock of Cattle I have I give to my son Peter and the heifer of three years old due by bill from John Arnold due to be paid according to bill And as for what stock of Cattle I have I give to my son Peter M[r] Peacock to have the benefitt of them until my son come to be one and twenty years of age M[r] Peacock to have the male & my son the female And as for my Plantacon and all moveable goods else M[r] Peacock is to take into his custody until the boy comes to bee one and twenty. My loving friend M[r] Richard Peacock to be my Executor.

Wit. GEORGE HOWELL, RICHARD X APPLEBEE.   Page 161.

28 July, 1674;
DRUIT, (or DREWITT), JOHN,   5 August, 1674.

To Elizabeth Saxon one yearling heifer called by the name of Browning and to Anne Saxon daughter of the sd John Saxon I give one Cow Calfe not yet marked the remaining part of my estate I do give to Richard Glover making him the sd Richard Glover full and sole Executor of this my last Will & Testament.

Wit. THO: FRESHWATER, JOHN X JONES, JOHN SAXON.

Page 163.

	7 August, 1674;
BILLINGTON, BARBARY,	21 October, 1674.

Sicke & weake in body but of perfect mind & memory.

I give to my daughter Jane one pair of large andirons. I give to my daughter Barbary one large Copper kettle. All the rest of my estate moveables and immoveables Chattels Servants debts and all worldly estate belonging unto me my just debts being first Satisfied I give and bequeath to bee equally divided amongst my Children Elisha Russell Luke Billington Elizabeth Billington Jane and Barbary and in case of the mortality of any of them before they attain to their lawfull ages my desire is that their part be equally divided amongst my Surviving Children and doe ordaine and appoint my daughter Alisha Russell Luke Billington my Sone my full and Sole Executors of this my last will & testament desiring my friends Mr Robert Bayly Mr Henry Clark and Mr Samuel Peachy to be Overseers of my sd Children and their estate until they attaine to their respective ages and in case any difference should happen among my sd Children in the division of their legacies or the explanation of this my intent in my will and to avoid lawsuits and expences that may happen thereby I refer and leave it totally and fully to the determination of my aforesaid Overseers.

Wit. JNᵒ STONE, HENRY WILSON, aged 46 years or thereabouts, NATHANIELL RICHARDSON, aged 28 years or thereabouts.

Page 164.

Proved 21 October, 1674;
Recorded 10 day of 9bris, 1674.

STOAKES, WILLIAM, (Nuncupative Will),

The deposition of John Stringer aged 30 years or thereabouts sworn & Examined Saith—

That William Stoakes lying sick at yʳ deponts house he your deponent being to go from home asked the sᵈ Stoakes if it pleased God to take him out of this world before my return how will you dispose of your bills the sᵈ Stoakes replyed unto my Cozen Samuel Parry & further Saith not.

signum

Jurator Coram   JOHN X STRINGER

nobis ROBERT ABRAHALL

    ROGER MALLARY

Commission of Administration is granted to Samuel Parry junior on the estate of William Stoakes deceased upon the testimony of John

Stringer the 21st of October 1674 nine months being now expired
since the death of the sd Stoakes no other heirs appearing & no other
person to crave Administration.   Page 166.

                                        19 October, 1674;
MADDISON, THOMAS,   4 November, 1674.

Sick & weake but of perfect sence & memory.

To Wife Catherine Maddison all my Moveable goods within dores
and without that are mine or that belongeth or appertaineth to me
the sd Thomas Maddison I do also give and bequeath unto the said
Katherine Maddison my wife all Cattle in General both Young and
old and hoggs likewise both young & old that are running within my
plantation or without or wheresoever else that belongeth or appertaineth properly unto me the sd Thomas Maddison furthermore I the
sd Thomas Maddison doe leave my plantation and all my land to
cleere and discharge all my debts which I owe onely 300 acres which
I sould to Richard White and a parcel of land which I sould to Richard
Simms and all the rest of my land I doe leave to discharge my debts
which belong to my patent or patents and if there bee anything left
over and above more than shall pay my debts then it shall return to
Katherine Maddison my wife furthermore I doe leave my loving
friends and neighbors Richard White and Thomas Bryant Executors
of this my will and Testament to be assistant to Katherine Maddison
my wife and I doe allso give my long gun to Thomas Bryant and my
short gun to Richard White I do also give to my Godchild Rebecka
Pettie the daughter of Robert Pettie one heifer of two years old and
furthermore I do give and leave unto Katherine Maddison my wife
my money which I have in England with my Bro^r Leonard Maddison
which is the sume of seaventy pounds Sterling.

Wit. PETER CALVIN, JOHN BIFOREST.

A probate hereon is granted to Coll Willm Travers in behalfe of
Anne Maddison by order of the Court.   Page 167.

                                        11 June, 1674;
BLAKE, ELIAS,   6 January, 1674:

By the name of God I Elias Blake being sick in body but of perfect
mind and memory make this my last will & Testament I give my
Soul to God and my body to the Earth to be buried at the discretion
of Henry Mouncaster and for my worldly goods I bequeath as followeth Item I give unto my Brother Walter Blake my mare ffinally I
give and bequeath all the residue of my estate to Henry Mouncaster
who I make my sole Executor of my last will and Testament and for

By the name of God I Elias Blake
being Sick in body but of perfect mind and
memory make this my last will & Testament
I give my Soul to God and my body to the
Earth to be buried at the discretion of Henry
Mouncaster and for my worldly goods
I bequeath as followeth Item I give unto
my Brother Walter Blake my mare finally
I give and bequeath all the residue of my
estate to Henry Mouncaster who I make
my Sole Executor of this my last will and
Testament and for confirmation hereof I
hereunto Set my hand & Seale this Eleventh
day of June 1674 ———   Elias Blake (Seale)

Signed Sealed & published
and declared as his last
will and Testament in
presence of us ———⟩ Wee the Subscribers do declare
Test John D Goudg ⟩ upon o.r oaths that this within
                   ⟩ written was the last will and
Elizabeth O Castlett ⟩ Testament of Elias Blake and
                   that he was in perfect Sence
                   and memory at the Signing thereof
                   to the best of our Judgment

Jurant.r in Cur Com̃ Rapp.a 6.o die   John Goudg
January 1674 ———   Elizabeth Castlet
Test Edm.o Crask Cl. Cur
& Probat.r & recordat. ———

Will of Elias Blake Recorded 6 January, 1674, by Edmond Crask, Clerk
of Rappahannock County.

confirmation hereof I hereunto set my hand & seale this Eleventh
day of June 1674—

Signed Sealed & published	ELIAS BLAKE seale
and declared as his last	
will and Testament in	
presence of us	Wee the subscribers do declare upon o^r.
signum	oaths that this within written was the
Test JOHN D GOUDG	Last will and Testament of Elias Blake
signum	and that he was in perfect sence and
ELIZABETH O CATLETT	memory at the signing thereof to the
	best of our Judgment

JOHN GOUDG

ELIZABETH CATLETT

Jurant^r in Cur Com Rapp^a 6° die Januarij 1674—

Test Edm°. Crask Cl. Cur.

Ex^a. Probat^r. et recordat^r.   Page 170.

27 January, 1674;

BOLLIN, (or BULLIN), JOHN   5 May, 1675.

I doe give and bequeath all my land unto *Mathew Harwood* and
her heirs after the death of my mother to *Martha Harrod* and her
heirs forever. I do give unto Peter *Harod* one yearling heifer for
ever I doe give and bequeath all my Cattle to my deare mother making
her my lawful Extrx.

Wit. RICHARD X KING, aged about 40 years,

THOMAS X HINES, aged about 22 years.   Page 171.

18 April, 1675;

5 May, 1675.

SPEEDE, JOHN, of the parish of Sittingbourne in the
Countie of Rapp^a.

After my debts are truely & honestly paid a decent funerall to be
made for the accomodation of my neighbors & friends I doe give unto
Sarah Allen two Cows in the first place this p^rsent year and to enjoy
them for ever it is my will that a Cow Calfe should be given from
one of the aboves^d. Cows this next year unto William Thorpe and
then my real and personall estate to be divided between John Evans
and Sarah Allen equally.

JOHN X SPEEDE   seal

Witness

PETER CORNWELL, aged 41 years or thereabouts,

FFRANCIS X JENKINS,* aged 27 years or thereabouts.

A probate hereon is granted to Martin Johnson in behalf of
Jno. Evans.   Page 172.

*He signed Francis FE *Jennings*. Signum.

22 April, 1675;
LOES, RICHARD,   7 July, 1675.

Sick in body but of sound & perfect memory.

To my son-in-law James Tacket all the estate I have in Maryland both Tob° good debts & otherwise and whereas I did ship home for Lime (Lyme) 50 hhds of tobo out of Maryland and Consigned them unto Walter Tucker Merchant in Lime (Lyme) I also give and bequeath unto my sd son James Tacket the full produce of the sd 50 hogsheads unto him & his heirs forever. I give and bequeath unto my son-in-law James Tacket the ½ part of all the stock of Cattle horses & mares that I am now possessed with & two Christian servants for the full time they have to serve at their coming into this country to be delivered him the next Shipping one fowling gun one pot two pewter dishes & two basons & all the pewter which was his mothers decd. I also ordaine that my sd son James Tacket & Servants have ground to work on & house room to cure their crops & for their accomodation on the plantacon whereon I now live for and during the space or time of four yeares next ensuing after my death & to have free privilege to grind his Corne at my mill toll free during his life or the time of his abode in this river. I give and bequeath unto my son-in-law Mr Henry Williamson all my Lands lying in Nimcock in Rappa River which I formerly purchased of Richard Bennett & Henry Corbin Esqr unto him the sd Williamson and his heirs forever I give & bequeath unto my sd son-in-law Mr Henry Williamson all the rest of my personall estate both Negroes, Indians, Mullatoes horses Mares Cattle Moneys & all other estate of wt. nature or Kind soever here in this Country or elsewhere unto him the sd Williamson and his heirs for ever And I do hereby ordain and appoint my sd son-in-law Mr Henry Williamson my Sole & absolute Executor of this my last will and testament willing to pay all my debts & legacies above menconed.

Wit. MARY X HODGES, RICHARD GRIMSTED, aged 28 years or thereabouts, EDWARD THOMAS, aged 32 years or thereabouts.

Page 174.

RUSSELL, JOHN, (Nuncupative Will),

Thomas Erwin aged 46 years or thereabouts sworn Saith That on or about the beginning of March last past this deponent being at the house & plantacon called Irland where John Russell then lived And the said Russell being at that present deprived of his speech but according to my Judgment in perfect sence and memory did first according to this deponts understanding make signes to William Serjent to follow him the sd Russell they went into a little shed and the sd Russell took two pewter dishes in his hand & made Signes to his Sonne to give him one of of the sd. dishes And according to this deponents understanding the sd. Russell made signes to give the other dish to his daughter & coming out of the sd. shed went & opened a small box & took out two silver spoones & delivered the one of the s^d. spoones to his afores^d son & the other spoone according to this deponents understanding the s^d. Russell made signes to give to his afores^d daughter And afterwards the s^d. Russell took out a small box out of which he took one Gold ring & one Silver seale & delivered the Same to William Serjeant the s^d. Serjeant saying to the s^d Russell what to me the s^d Russell made signes to the contrary then the s^d. Serjeant said to the s^d Russell what to my wife the s^d Russell then made signes according to this deponents understanding that he did give the same to the s^d Serjeants wife after all which signes the s^d Russell put up the severall things above mentioned in the respective places where they were And there they Continued till the s^d Russells decease to the best of this deponents Judgment & further saith not May the 17th 1675. Probated 7 July, 1675.   Page 177.

SHERMAN, QUINTILLIAN,
15 May, 1675;
1 September, 1675.

Sick and weak in body but of good and perfect memory.

To son Quintillian Sherman 100 acres of land wch land make all the clear ground orchard & all thereabout it & 100 acres of woodland ground I do give unto my son Martin Sherman the same so equally to be divided *as it may not p^r.vidus on the other Senr.** To daughter Anne Sherman two Cowes by name Starr & Cherry with their increase forever. To son Quintillian one cow by name Lilley with her increase for ever & further it is my will and desire three years hence that my son Quintillian & my daughter Anne give my son Martin each of them a heifer apiece out of the increase of the Cows aboves^d & further I give my son Quintillian my gun. All the rest of my Estate that I have I doo freely give to my beloved wife Jane Sherman the same to be at her own disposing.

Wit. RICHARD DUDLEY, HENRY TILLERY.   Page 178.

COOPER, THOMAS,
29 July, 1675;
1 September, 1675.

Sick in body but sound in mine & of perfect memory.

First my Will is that my body be decently buried by my wife in Piscataway Churchyard. To John Jones the eldest son of Richard Jones deceased all the devident of land upon which my dwelling house now standeth on soe far as the branch which leads to Thomas Harper for ever. To Richard Jones another son of Richard Jones aforesaid all that devident of land beyond the s^d branch. To Dorothy Petty one red cow known by the name of Browning. To Dennis Conniers my stuffe Coat & my large drawers. All the rest of my wearing Cloaths to my servant Thomas. To John Soper my gun which is now in my dwelling house. To Jane Jones daughter of Richard Jones decd aforesd

*So in record book.

one mare foale which now runneth by the old mares side wth the sd Coalts increase for ever. All his just debts to be paid. Executrix Avis Jones widow to whom he bequeaths "all my household goods & stock of what nature or kind soever & all debts due to me & my servants she to enjoy the aforesaid devident of land during her natural life and after her decease to return as afores^{d}."
Wit. JOHN BAGWELL, FRANCIS X WEBB.   Page 180.

1 December, 1673;
1 September, 1675.

SWELLIVANT, DENNIS, of the County of Rapp. and Parish of ffarnham in Virg^{a}., Planter.

Weak in body but of perfect minde and memory.

To son Dennis Swellivant the land I now live on from the lower pte thereof as farr as the place called by the name of Dennits Cove wth the land purchased of Thomas ffreshwater if when he comes to the age of sixteen years he will accept thereof or else to have the upper part of my devident (Viz^{t}) from the s^{d}. Dennits Cove to the upper end of my devident soe my s^{d} son Dennis to have his Choice either pte when he attain the age of sixteen years. I give unto my son Daniel the upper pte of my devident vizt from the s^{d} Dennis Cove to the upper end and provided my son Dennis doe not make Choice thereof and if he should then my s^{d} son Daniel to have the other pte that I now live upon and to enjoy the same at the years of sixteen but it is my will that neither of my s^{d}. sons shall dispose sell or convey away any parts thereof until they attain the age of one and twenty years and if either of my s^{d}. sonnes dye before they attaine the s^{d}. age of one and twenty years without issue then it is my will that the Survivour should enjoy the whole Item I give and bequeath unto my wife Joane my whole personall estate during the time she shall remaine aWid^{w}. and if she shall happen to Marry then my personall estate to be divided into three equall pts Viz^{t}. my s^{d}. wife one third and my s^{d} sones each of them athird and if she shall die in time of her widowhood then to be equally divided between my two sonns Dennis and Daniel Item I give unto my daughter Sarah the wife of Henry Lenton three Cowes and one steer of five or six years of age and I give unto my grandson Anthony Lenton one Cow Item I do make constitute and appoint my s^{d} wife Joane Swellivant my sole executrix of this my Last will and testament Item I do hereby intrust my well beloved friends M^{r}. Robert Baylie, M^{r}. James Samford, Henry Lenton and Thos. ffreshwater as overseers of this my last will and in confirmacon thereof have hereunto set my hand and Seale this first of December 1673

Signed Sealed & publish^{d}.   DENNIS X SULLIVANT   Seal
in p^{r}sence of
    WILLIAM MAJOR
        sign
    JOHN X HORYESLY   Page 183.

1 March, 1674/5;

JAMES, EDWARD,   4 November, 1675.

In perfect sence and memory.

To the children of Robert Welch taylor living in back street in Bristoll all my estate both personall and reall onely I desire that Robert Peck should have my estate in his possession till the above said Children do come or send for it and likewise I desire that Robert Peck as soon as he doe hear of my decease that he doe immediately send the aboves^d Children word of it and y^t the s^d. Robert Peck do give a Just account to the Children of my s^d. estate.

Wit. JOHN PHILLIPS, ELIAS YATES.   Page 185.

24 March, 1671;

PAYNE, ROBERT, Gent.,   4 November, 1675.

IN THE NAME OF GOD AMEN I Robert Payne of the County of Rapp^a. in Virginia Gent—considering the frailty of all flesh & the uncertain estate of this transitory life & knowing that I was born to die when it shall please God do make constitute ordain & declare this my last will & testam^t. in manner & form following revoaking and annulling by these p^rsents all and every testament and testaments will and wills heretofore by mee made & declared either by word or writing & this is to be taken only for my last will & testament & none other— And first being penitent and sorry from the bottom of my heart for my sins past most humbly desiring forgiveness for the same I give and commit my soule unto Almighty God my saviour & redeemer in whom by the meritts of Jesus Christ I trust and believe assuredly to be saved & to have full remission & forgiveness of all my sins and that my Soule with my body at the generall day of resurrection shall rise again with joy & through the meritts of Christs death & passion possess & inherit the Kingdom of heaven p^rpared for his elect & chosen my body I commit to the Earth to be buried in such place where it shall please my executrix hereafter named to appoint, and now for the setling of my temporall estate & such goods Chattels, and debts as it hath pleased God farr above my deserts to bestow upon me I do order give & dispose the same in manner & form following That is to say ffirst I will that all those debts & duties which I owe in right or conscience to any manner of person or persons whatsoever shall be well & truely contented & paid or ordained to be paid within Convenient time after my decease by my Executrix hereafter named Imp^rs. I give & bequeath unto my son Robert Payne all and singular my estate as well lands as other my estate of what quality kind or Condicon soever it be of within this Colony of Virginia reserving to my wife her accustomed third thereof onely Item my will is that both my lands and other estate before & above bequeathed to my son Robert be enjoyed by him & his heirs for ever Item my will is that if my son Robert depart this life before he attaine to one and twenty years of age or have issue lawfully begotten that then I do give all and singular my s^d. lands & all and Singular my other s^d. estate (excepting four thousand pounds of to bacco & casque, which I will that my son Robert have delivered him at the age of Sixteen years to improve his genius with by my Executrix hereafter named out of my s^d. estate) unto my s^d. loving wife and her heirs for ever Item my will is that if my s^d. son Robert shall depart this life before he attaine to one and twenty years of age or before he hath issue lawfully begotten and that my s^d. wife allso shall die without more issue of her body lawfully begotten that then my will is that William Clapham, Alexia fflemming, & Mary Clapham enjoy all and singular my s^d. lands equally to be devided between them and to their heirs for ever Item my will is that after my debts are paid that adivision be made of my said personall estate and what servants especially and Cattle belong to my said son be put on some one of my best plantatons and there managed for his interest & education & according to their cropps encreased in number of Servants and that the remainder of my other personall estate appertaining to my s^d. Son be disposed of by my said Excutrix for the interest of him & no otherwise and that my s^d. Son have education allowed him suitable to his estate not impoverishing the Same & that if he desire to enter thereon that he be Suffered so to do when he shall by gods grace attaine to the age of Seventeen years. Item my will is that if it shall please God that my wife happen to be with Child during my life and that the Same live to full age or being afemale to Sixteen years of age or day of marriage which shall happen first & have issue lawfully begotten that it have & enjoy fifteen hundred acres of the land taking it together whereon I now live to it and its heirs for ever & one third pte of my psonall estate Excepting one Servant more to my s^d. Son Robert, Item I give the first mare foale that falls of my Sorrel mare to Mary Meedor my Goddaughter with all its increase to her & her heirs for ever Item I give the second mare foale that comes of my s^d. mare to Mary Clapham & her increase to her & her heirs for ever Item I give the fourth mare foale that shall come of my s^d. mare to Elizabeth Madestard with her increase to her & her heirs for ever Item I do hereby nominate appoint and ordain my well beloved wife Elizabeth Payne sole Executrix of this my last will & testament desiring M^r. Warwick Camock to see that this my will be performed in all respects as neare & as fully as Can be & that whatsoever person shall intermarry with my wife be Compelled to give bond with good Securitie for performance hereof before he be invested with any part of my son Roberts estate & that if M^r. Camock die before that the Court of Rapp^a. see the same effected which is also my will so to be done. Item my will is that my son Robert have from the time of my departure of this life as well the male as female increase of his mare Rose & to him & his heirs for ever IN WITNESS of all & singular the p^rmises I the s^d Robert Payne have hereunto put my hand & Seale this 24th day of March 1671.

Signed, Sealed, & publish: ROBERT PAYNE   Seale
ed in p^rsence of us
    RICHARD BARBER
    JOHN MEADOR

John Meador aged 38 years & Richard Barber aged 30 years or thereabouts depose & say that this within written is the last will & testament of M^r. Robert Payne formerly Clerk of this County and that he was in p^r.fect Sence and memory to the best of their knowledge when he signed, Sealed & published the same—

                JOHN MEADOR
                RICHARD BARBER

Probat^r. P Sacramentum Johis Meador, & Richardi Barber 4° die Novembr 1675—

        Test Edm°. Craske Cl Cur et Recordat^r Test Edm°.

Craske Cl Cur. Ex^a   Page 187.

                          22 February, 1674/5;
COX, HENRY,   2 November, 1675.

Very sick and weake in body but of good and perfect memory.

I will and my meaning is that whereas Edmund Craske Clerk of Rapp^a County standeth engaged with me that I shall make a good assurance of the half or moiety of my land I now live upon to Mr John Hasslewood for and in consideration of his delivering up a certain bond of mine of five hundred pounds Sterling bearing date the 8th day of July 1673 as allso for the passing of bills of exchange for the payment of forty five pounds Sterling money to me or my Order now my will is that my Executors hereafter named make good the sale of the moyitie or halfe part my land according to obligation and save the said Edmund Craske harmless and indemnified from the s^d Mr Hasslewood his heirs or assigns or otherwise take care for the satisfying of the s^d. Haslewood his just debt and take in the bond aforesaid & for non performance then I will and my meaning is that the s^d Edmund Craske shall be possessed with so much of my estate both reall and personall as shall discharge and satisfie the oblegacon wherein he stands engaged with me to the sd Haslewood untill such time as the sd debt be satisfyed and the sd Craske saved harmless from all such charges or damages he shall be at by being become bound with me as aforesaid. I give and bequeath to Mr James Miller now living with me my sword and belt to be delivered to him immediately after my death. To my brother-in-law Richard Cawthorn my best Cloath Suite my best hatt a pair of french falls and a pair of stockings both new to be delivered to him immediately after my death.

I give unto Richard Cawthorn jr my nephew and to Amelia Cawthorn my neece each of them a Cow and Calfe to be delivered them about the beginning of June next after my death. To Mr Thomas Gordon of Rapp^a County and M^rs. Jane Gordon his wife each of them tenn shillings to buy them two mourning rings to be paid them by my Executors within two months after my decease. To my friend Edmund Craske twenty shillings to buy him a Mourning ring to be paid him by my Executors within two months after my decease. All the rest of my estate as lands goods chattels cattle and all implements of household stuffe or husbandry bills bonds ready money and debts owing me I freely and willingly give and bequeath them all to my Executors hereafter named for and during their natural lives and after their decease unto William Cox my son hereby willing and requiring my said son William within one year after he shall be possessed of my estate as aforesaid to give unto the child my wife now goeth with a good assurance of the moitie of the land he shall be possessed withall by this my will or the value thereof (as two men indifferently chosen shall adjudge it worth) at the discretion of my s^d son but if the s^d child should happen to die before my s^d son William shall be possessed with my estate as aforesaid then the whole estate to be and remain with my son William and his heirs forever. Appoints as Executor and Executrix "my father-in-law Mr William Strachey of Glocester County and Arabella Cox my now wife hereby willing and requiring them to pay all debts as I shall Justly happen to owe at the time of my death to take care of and provide for my children during their minorities and to bring my body decently to the ground and it is my earnest desire that my father-in-law would come and live with my wife and assist her in the management of her estate.

Wit. CORNELIUS MELAGHLEN, WILLIAM HARDING, aged 28 years or thereabouts, THOMAS HART, aged 25 years or thereabouts.

Page 191.

PAGE, THOMAS,

10 March, 1676;
3 May, 1676.

Very sick in body but of proper memory.

To Elizabeth West eldest daughter of Richard West one cow with her increase called Starr. To Mary Noell eldest daughter of Cornelius Noell one cow and her increase called Violett. To my grandchild Samuel Allen my plantation and land belonging to it wch I formerly lived upon to him and his heirs forever. To my son Valentine Allen 200 acres of land where he now lives to him and his heirs forever. To William Hodges children 300 acres of land being part of a devident where my sonn Allen now lives to be equally divided between them and their heirs forever. All the rest of my estate my debts being paid

I give to my daughter Mary Allen and her heirs forever. Executrix my daughter Mary Allen.

Wit. WILLIAM FFOGGE, ROBERT X RUDERFORD.

A probate hereon is granted to Capt. Tho: Hawkins upon Mary Allen's Consent.   Page 195.

	20 March, 1675/6;
BERRIDGE, JOHN,	3 May, 1676.

Sick and weak of body.

To loving friend Francis Suttle all that debt of tobacco that is due to me from Henry Durrant. To my loving friend Jane Barrett all that she hath in her possession of mine. To loving friend Richard Mathews two bills one of William Talbutt that 1100 pounds of tobacco and one of Robert Moss that 1200 pounds of tobacco and one gunn at Robert Mosses. All the rest of my estate to my loving friend Francis Suttle. Executor Francis Suttle.

Wit. JOHN STONE, WALTER TURNER.   Page 196.

7 January, 1674;
3 May, 1676.

SHERLOCK, JOHN, of the County of Rapp{a}. and Parish of Farnham.

I John Sherlock being very sick and Weak but in true and perfect memory Praised be God for it and Knowing the frailty of this life do here make my last will and testament in Manner and form as followeth Imprimis I give and bequeath My Soul to the Almighty God my Maker in hopes of a resurrection in and through my Lord and Saviour Jesus Christ My worldly goods I dispose of as followeth I give and bequeath Unto my Son Andrew Sherlock three hundred and sixty acres of land and do appoint that my wife shall have her being and livelihood upon the sd Land during her life without Molestation and after her decease do order Andrew Sherlock to be full and Wholly Executor and Administr{r} thereof I give and bequeath to my Sonn John Sherlock fifty acres of Land Joyning upon William Davies land to him and his heirs forever I give and bequeath all my Cattle and hoggs to my wife and my son Andrew Sherlock and do appoint that they Shall be equally devided When Andrew is of age I give and bequeath to my Son Johns Children Hanna and John One Cow Calfe belonging to Cherry this Calfe to run till the girl is married or marriageable and to be equally devided between the boy and the girle my Son John having the male increase for looking after them. I give and bequeath to my son Bartholomew Leaburs Children John and Bartholomew One Cow Calfe and do appoint that the female increase shall be equally devided between them When they are of age and their father to have the Male for looking after them I give and bequeath one Cow and Calfe that is at John Jones towards building of a house for my Wife and Andrew to live in and all my Moveables to be equally devided between my son Andrew and my wife and for my debts I leave bills to pay them with my wife of Thomas Freshwater and Hezekiah Turner and this I do declare to be my last will and testament as Witness my hand the 7th of January 1674—

Signum

JOHN X SHURLOCK   Seal

Signed Sealed in the presence of

Signum

EDWARD JONES, WILLIAM XX BRAY

I Edward Jones do testifie that I did see the within mentioned John Shurlock Senr. Sign and Seale and Publish this his last will and testament and that he was then in perfect mind and memory to the best of this deponents Judgment

EDWARD JONES

Juratus est Jones in Cur Com Rappa 3º die May 1676

Test EDMº. CRASKE Cl Cur

Probatr. et recordatr. xxº die Ejusdem Mens Anº. Suprd.

Test EDMº. CRASKE Cl Cur

Page 198.

19 January, 1675;

ERWIN, THOMAS,   3 May, 1676.

IN THE NAME OF GOD AMEN I Thomas Erwin of the parish of Sittingburn in the County of Rappa: being sick in body but of sound & perfect memory do hereby make and ordain this my last Will & Testament hereby revoaking and making void any testament heretofore by me made either by word or writing & this only to be taken for my last Will & Testament (My wife to be my onely Executrix hereafter) Imprs. I give and bequeath my Soul into the hands of Almighty God hoping and trusting through the mercies of Jesus Christ to obtaine full and perfect remission of all my sins and my body to the earth from whence it was taken to be buried in comely and decent manner according to the discretion of my wife & relations and as for my worldly goods I thus bequeath them Item—I give and bequeath to my wife one bay mare & if in case she bring forth a mare foal it is to run for the good of all my children and likewise there be three mares more & a horse which I do order & Constitute to be given to my children in generall & a young gelding in the same manner for the use of my children Item—I give and bequeath to my children eight cows & their increase & them to be kept upon my said plantation for the use of all my children & no exception to be made but equally to be devided Item—I give and bequeath to my two eldest Sonns all my land consisting of two hundred & thirty acres & the said land equally to be devided when they come to age that is to say sixteen yeares & then to be free to enjoy accordingly to live together upon one plantation that then my eldest son provide proportionally so much land in some other place convenient as my Second Sonn thinks fitt otherwise to concurr to live unanimously together according to my will & desire Item—it is my will and command that my wife have the third part of the land & half the orchard for the use of her and likewise her children forever without any molestation whatsoever Item—I give and bequeath to my two youngest Sonns two hundred acres of land lying in the ready way to Coll: Washingtons & if it please God they should depart before they come to age to enjoy it then the said land to fall to my two eldest Sonns & if in case they should die then it to go to the use of my daughters Item—it is my will that my wife shall have all my personal estate that is to say all cattle hogs & all immoveables whatsoever as tobaccoes debts dues & whatsoever belongs to me in order to the education & bringing up of the children Item—I do hereby make ordain and appoint my loving wife Ann Erwin the whole Executrix of this my last will & testament to see it performed & further I do ordain & appoint my loving friends John Matlin William Serjeant & Henry Creighton Overseers & assistants to my wife & in case of the death of my wife to take care of my childrens estate & education IN WITNESS whereof I have hereunto set my hand & Seal this 19th day of January 1675.

Signum

Signed Sealed & Delivered to   THOMAS X ERWIN   Seale
be his last Will & Testament
in the presence of us
    JOHN PAYNE
    THOMAS BARKER

I underwritten do depose and say that I did see the within named testator Signe Seale & publish the within mentioned to be his last will & testament & that he was in perfect Sence & memory at the Signing Sealing & publishing thereof to the best of my judgment

JOHN PAYNE

Juratus est Payne in Cur Com Rappa: 3 die May 1676.

Test EDM. CRASKE Cl Cur

Probat. et recordat XX die ejusd Mensis Ano Supd

Test EDM. CRASKE Cl Cur
Page 200.

26 June, 1675;
HULL, JOHN,   2 May, 1677.

Well in body & of good and proper memory.
His debts to be paid by his executors Hereafter named.
My son-in-law John Carter to be paid his five hundred pounds
due him for his wives dower according to speciality but if it should
so fall out that what monies and debts and merchantable goods will
not pay it without disposing of my wife's plate and Jewells then part
of my land to be sold to pay it, To my son John Carter and his wife
each of them a ring of forty shillings price. To wife Elizabeth Hull
all the plate and jewells I die possessed of. To son Roger Hull and his
heirs forever all my land I die possessed of. To wife Elizabeth and son
Roger all my monies goods and chattles I die possessed of equally to be
divided between them. My will is that my loving wife Elizabeth Hull
may have any of my plantations with the lands and houses belonging
to the same that she will make choice of during her life and then
return to my son Roger Hull or his heirs. Wife Elizabeth to be
Executrix.

Wit. THOMAS COLLINS, aged 22 years or thereabouts, THO: SMITH,
aged 22 years or thereabouts.

NOTE: The witnesses called the testator "Lieut. Col. John Hull."

Page 202.

22 January, 1672/3;
SIMMS, RICHARD,   2 May, 1677.

To John Penn should I die without wife or issue all my reall and
personall estate that is lands goods and chattels as well moveables as
unmoveables to his heirs and assigns forever. Executor John Penn.
Wit. THOMAS HARWARE, aged 34 years or thereabouts,

HENRY WILLIAMSON, aged 34 years or thereabouts.

Page 205.

13 January, 1676/7;
PENN, JOHN,   2 May, 1677.

Sick & weak in body but in proper memory.
To Anne Sharp daughter of John Sharp the plantation I now live
on and £50 Sterling money in England. To Judith Sharp daughter
of John Sharp deceased £50 Sterling money in England. To Elizabeth
Harware daughter of Thomas Harware £50 Sterling in England.
The above £50 and the plantation to be delivered the day of their
marriage by my Executors hereafter named. To Edward Dracas
Thomas Cocker and Mary Peyton each one cow to be delivered on
demand and likewise she the said Mary Peyton to be free at my decease
for all other moveable stock cattle and horses and mares and servants
and what other estate in Virginia Maryland, England or elsewhere

I give and bequeath to my Executor Thomas Harware and his heirs forever only paying my debts. To Thomas Talbutt son of William Talbutt a young Mare about three years old and likewise two cows to be delivered on demand. Should Anne Sharp die without issue then the land I give her to my friend Thomas Harware otherwise to her and her heirs forever.

Wit. PETER HOPEGOOD, aged 30 years or thereabouts, JOSEPH PRICE, aged 26 years or thereabouts.   Page 206.

21 April, 1676;
6 June, 1677.

BISHOP, ROBERT, of the County of Rappahannock & Parish of Farnham.

To John Grigory Jr., the land I bought of Mr Henry Awbrey to him and his heirs forever likewise all my personal estate. Executor John Grigory, Jr.

Wit. THO: WHEELER, aged 30 years or thereabouts, JOHN GARNER, aged 25 years of thereabouts, JOHN X BURNETT.

Later 24th of May 1676 he gave his Executor power and command to demand and receive two hundred and thirty five pounds of good tobacco of John Jones my brother-in-law which is to be paid by October 10, 1676 and the sd John Grigory is to produce an heifer with the sd tobo for the use of John Jones, Jr. with the increase of the sd. heifer untill the sd. John Jones comes of age and likewise I give John Grigory, Jr order to receive one heifer which is at Capt. John Grigory's pen marked with a cropp and a slitt in the left eare one year old of a red colour with her increase male and female when the said John Jones shall come of age and likewise one sow when the sd John Jones shall come of age and the sd John Grigory to keep the sd two heifers with their increase until the sd John Jones shall come of age and then deliver them with their increase.

Wit. THO: WHEELER, RICHARD GRIGORY.   Page 209.

2 February, 1676;
MILLS, PETER,   2 May, 1677.

Very sick in body & weak but of perfect memory.

To my sister Elizabeth Mills all my whole estate both reall and personall only I give and bequeath to Mary Borkett daughter of my brother John Borkett the youngest mare filly that now is and likewise one black yearling to Jane Wall wife of Samuel Wall. To Mary Raw the cow calfe that comes of the cow called Stone. To John Boginton a sow shoate. To Richard Middleton a sow shoate. To my brother Borkett my old sow. To my father two young barrows. To John Mills a young red sow. To Joseph Shipp a young sow. To Samuel Ward the yearling which my sister Margaret gave to me. My sister Elizabeth

Mills to have possession of all my estate soe soone as I am dead to live where she pleases. I desire that my Executrix Elizabeth Mills pay the Doctor and other necessary charges for my funerall.

Wit. SAM WARD, JOHN MILLS.   Page 211.

BAXTER, NATHANIEL,   22 May, 1676;
                                    2 May, 1677.

In the Name of God Amen.

I Nathaniel Baxter of the parish of ffarnham in the County of Rapp^ac Planter, being by God's grace intended forth for the warrs do make and ordain this my last will & Testament in manner & form following Imp^rs. I bequeath my Soule unto Almighty God who gave it in full & certaine hope in and through the meritts of Jesus to inherit Eternal life and my body to return to the earth and likewise it is my will & I do hereby give & bequeath unto my naturall Sonn Nathaniel Baxter and his heirs forever all the bounds of my land from Piscataway Creek unto M^r. Parrys little Creek and the remainder of my divident of land which lyeth on the other side of M^r. Parrys Creek towards Thomas Dayes formerly Huttsons by virtue hereof I will unto my daughter Ann Baxter and to her lawful heirs forever Provided allways that if it please God to take to his Mercy either my son Nathaniel or my daughter Anne before they be of the age of one and twenty years or be married the first of them so dyeing his or her part of the land abovesd shall fall and descend to the Survivor for ever. To wife one young gray stone horse with a small slit in the right eare and a black pied heifer comonly called by the name of Fitt with all her increase to be wholly at her disposing. To my daughter Elethias Baxter one cow commonly known by the name of Cherry with all her increase male and female to her and her heirs for ever and in case the said cow should die without any increase then the sd Elethias to have a heifer out of the stock with her increase male & female for ever Provided allways and it is my desire that in case the said Elethias shall die without issue then the said cow or heifer to returne with their increase to my abovesd Children. To wife in lieu of her thirds and to my abovenamed son and daughter Nathaniel and Anne equally to be divided after my debts satisfied all my personall estate moveable and unmoveable for ever. Executrix and Executors my wife and my son Nathaniel and my daughter Anne and likewise my beloved friends Mr William Young senior & Thomas Roberts to see this my will executed.

Wit. THOMAS X JENKINS, JOHN JOLLY, BARBARY X ANDREWS.

Thomas Roberts, aged 28 years or thereabouts, testified that he the deponent did write and see Nathaniel Baxter sign said will in the presence of Thomas Jenkins, John Jolly & Barbary Andrews.

                                                        Page 213.

Not dated;
JACKSON, GEORGE,   2 May, 1677.

Sick in body but in perfect sence & memory.

To Robert Eaid son-in-law of Edward Freeman one hundred acres of land betwixt the said Robert Eaid and Edward Freeman lawful son of the said Edward Freeman. Executor Robert Freeman.

Wit. THOMAS X HARPER, aged 50 years or thereabouts,
SYMON X BUTLER.   Page 216.

Proved 2 May, 1677;
Recorded 21 June, 1677.

JENKINS, THOMAS, (Nuncupative Will),

The deposition of Elethias Perkins aged 49 years or thereabouts That your depon^t being in the house where Thomas Jenkins did make his will in writing and did heare him give his whole estate to his son-in-law William Price after the decease of his mother or day of marriage onely two Cows and a Calfe to William Price his sisters Children and further depon^t Saith not

ELETHIAS X PERKINS

The deposition of Thomas Roberts aged 28 or thereab^{ts} Sworn and examined Saith that y^{or}. depon^t. did write and witness a will of Tho. Jenkins wherein he did give all his estate to his son in Law W^m. Price after the death of his wife onely excepted two Cows or heifers which were given to W^m. Price his sisters Children and further y^{or}. depon^t. Saith not

THO: ROBERTS   Page 217.

23 February, 1675;
2 May, 1677.

ELLWERD, (ELLVERD, ELLWENE), THOMAS,

Lying very sick & weak.

To daughter Betty one hundred acres of my land beginning at the further side of the devidend of the sd land and one brown heifer of three years old and her increase and all the rest that I have besides to be divided between my wife and my son my wife to have the disposing of it till my son comes to age.

Wit. THOMAS NAYLOR, aged 35 years or thereabouts,
SUSANNA WHITE, aged 29 years or thereabouts.

Page 219.

27 September, 1675;
WASHINGTON, LAWRENCE,   6 June, 1677.

In the Name of God Amen I Lawrence Washington of the County of Rapp^{ac}. being sick & weak in body but of sound and perfect memory do make and ordaine this my last will & testament hereby revoaking

annulling & making void all former wills and Codicills heretofore by
me made either by word or writing & this only to be taken for my last
will & testament Imp^rs. I give and bequeath my soul into the hands
of Almighty God hoping and trusting through the mercy of Jesus
Christ my Savio^r. and redeemer to receive full pardon and forgiveness for all my sinnes and my body to the earth to be buried in a
comely & decent manner by my Executrix hereafter named & for my
worldly goods I thus dispose them Item I give and bequeath unto my
loving daughter Mary Washington my whole estate in England both
reall & personall to her & the heirs of her body lawfully begotten for
ever to be delivered into her possession immediately after my decease
by my Executrix hereafter named. I give and bequeath unto my
afores^d. daughter Mary Washington my smallest stone ring and one
Silver cup now in my possession to her and her heirs for ever to be
delivered to her immediately after my decease. I give and bequeath
unto my loving son John Washington all my bookes to him and his
heirs for ever to be delivered to him when he shall come to the age of
Twenty one years. I give and bequeath unto my son John and Daughter
Ann Washington all the rest of my plate but what is before exprest
to be equally divided between them and delivered into their possession
when they come of age. Item my will is that all my debts which of
right and Justice I owe to any man be Justly and truely paid as also
my funeral expences after which my will is that all my whole estate
both reall and personall be equally divided between my loving wife
Jone *(Joyce)* Washington and the two children God hath given me
by her Viz^t. John and Ann Washington. I give and bequeath it all
to them and the heires of their bodies lawfully begotten for ever, my
sonnes part to be delivered to him when he comes of age, and my
daughters part when she Comes of age or day of marriage which shall
first happen. Item my will is that and which became due to me in
right of my wife lying on the south side of the river formerly belonging to Capt Alexander ffleming comonly known by the name of West
ffalco be sold by my Executrix hereafter named for the payment of
my debts immediately after my decease. Item my will is that the land
I have formerly entered with Capt W^m. Mosely be forthwith after my
decease surveyed and pattented by my Exec^x. hereafter named and if
it shall amount to the quantity of one thousand acres then I give and
bequeath unto Alexander Barrow two hundred acres of the sd land
to him and his heirs for ever the remainder I give and bequeath unto
my loving wife afores^d and two Children to them and their heires for
ever to be equally divided between them. Item my will is that if it
shall please God to take my daughter Mary out of this world before
she comes of age or have heir of hir body lawfully begotten then I
give and bequeath my land in England which by my will I have given
unto her unto my son John Washington and his heires and the psonall
estate which I have given hir I give and bequeath the same unto my
daughter Ann Washington and her heires for ever. Item I do hereby

make and ordain my loving wife Jone (*Joyce*) Washington Executrix of this my last will and testament to see it performed and I do hereby make and appoint my dear and loveing brother Coll[l] John Washington and my loveing friend Thomas Hawkins (in case of the death or neglect of my Executrix) to be the overseers and guardians of my Children untill they come of age to the truth whereof I have hereunto Sett my hand and Seale this 27[th] of September 1675.

LAWRENCE WASHINGTON   seale

Signed sealed and declared to
be his last will & testam[t].
in the p[r]sence of us

CORNELIUS WOOD
sign
JOHN B BARROW
HENRY TANDY jun[R]

A Codicill of the last will & testament of Lawrence Washington annext to his will and made Septemb[r]. 27[th] 1675 Item my will is that my part of the land I now live upon which became due to me by marriage of my wife, I leave it wholy & solely to her disposall after my decease Witness my hand the day and year above written

Signed, Sealed, and declared
to be a Codicill of my last will &
testam[t] in the p[r]sence of us

LAWRENCE WASHINGTON   seale

CORNELIUS WOOD
HENRY TANDY jun[R]

The above named Henry Tandy jun[r]. aged 17 years or thereabouts sworn examined saith that he did see the abovenamed Lawrence Washington Sign, Seale, and publish the above mentioned to be his last will & testament and that he was in perfect sence and memory at the Signing Sealing & publishing thereof to the best of your deponents Judgment

HENRY TANDY

Juratis est Henricus Tandy in Cur Com Rapp[ac] Sexto die Junij An°. 1677 p Sacram p[s].d et recordat

Test EDM CRASKE Cl. Cur.   Page 219.

Wills in the Record Book entitled Deed Book No. 5.

A Copy of a Will. IN THE NAME OF GOD AMEN the 30th day of March 1666 according to the Computation of the Church of England I James Gowner son of Francis Gowner of the County of Rappa being of perfect memory and Remembrance praised be God doe make and ordaine this my Last will and Testament in manner and forme following Vizt First I give and Bequeath my soule into the hands of Almighty God my maker hoping that through the meritorious death and Passion of Jesus Christ my only Saviour and Redeemer to Receive free Pardon and Forgiveness of all my sins and as for my Body to be buried in Christian Buriall Item I give to my Brother Francis Gowner Two hundred and fifty acres of Land lying in Hoskins Creek & one Cow & her increase forever Revoaking all other will & testament In Witness whereof I have hereunto Set my hand and seal the day and year first above written

                                                    Signum
Test DENIS CONNIERS   JAMES X GOWNER
          Signum
     MATHEW M HUMPHREY

                    Recordatr. Xo. die Maij 1676
                    Test EDMo CRASK Cl Cur   Page 511.

Note. January 18, 1675, Francis Gowner transferred the above 250 acres to his brother Stanley *Gore.*

                              Deed Book 5, page 512.

Wills in the Record Book entitled Deeds No. 4, 1668-1672.

---

2 February, 1669/70;
WARRENER, RALPH,   3 February, 1669.

IN THE NAME OF GOD AMEN I Ralph Warraner Being Sick in Body But Perfect in Mind and Memory make this my Last Will & Testament in manner and Forme as Foll my body to ye Earth and my Soul to God who gave me it As for my worldly Estate I give and Bequeath it As Followeth Item I give unto my son Ralph Warraner my whole Estate as Land Chattles Hoggs household Stuff he paying unto his *ytes* (sister) Mary Warrener three thousand pounds of Good Tobbacco or else six young Cowes w^ch: he Pleaseth to be delivered when she shall attaine seaventene Yeares of age and if she shall Chance to Depart this Life Before then the s^d: Legacy to Fall to Ralph Warraner before Expressed. ITEM my will and desire is that Thomas Gouldman have the manageing of the said Estate during the Childrens Minority and alsoe my desire is that the said Gouldman have the keeping of the said Children alway provided that he give them Education as to teach the boy to write and the Girle to sew. KNOW ALL MEN by these p^rsents that I Ralph Warrener of the age of Sixteene yeares but under the age of one and twenty son of Ralph Warraner of the County of Rapp^a: deceased do hereby Elect & Chuse Thomas Gouldman of y^e: Aforesaid County now Resident uppon my Fathers Plantation my curator or Guardian to take administration of the Goods & Cattell of my said Father and to employ the same for my Benefitt during my minority and all other effects of Law w^t:soever pvided he the said Gouldman put in security according as is Usuall in such Cases and for Confirmation hereof I hereunto Sett my hand this 2^d. day of February anno 1669/70.

RALPH WARRENER
Test
Ro PAYNE
Recognit^r: 3 of Feb: 1669
Test Ro PAYNE Cl Cur   Page 238.

Wills in the Record Book entitled Wills No. 2, 1677-1682.

NICHOLLS, GEORGE,

Not dated;
Proved 2 May & 6 June, 1677.

Mr George Nicholls his last Will & Testam^t being sick and weak in body but of sound and perfect mind Impr^s doe give and grant to my Grandchild George Glascock foure hundred acres of land to him and his heirs for Ever it being part of the Devident of my own land & the foure hundred acres to adjoyn wth the five hundred acres wch I have already Confirmed to my Daughter Anne Glascock. To son Zacharias two hundred Acres of land Joyning to the Plantation now in the possession of Mathew Wilcocks to him and his heires for Ever. To my grandchild Anne Downing three hundred Acres of Land to her and her heires for Ever it being all of one Devident. To my Grand Child George Glascock my whole & sole Estate with the goods here mentioned 2 Chests & one Court Cupboards two Tables one six foote & one foure foot & one form one Great looking Glass & one Couch & one great Joyned Chaire & one paire of Andirons fire Shovells & Tongs one Great Iron pestle 3 Wedges one Gun one Iron pott of nine Gallons one Iron Kettle of Six one Iron Skillit one feather bed & furniture two high beadsteads two pair of Course Sheets & pillow beeres twelve napkins & one large table Cloath Sixteen pieces of Pewter & one Pr of Pottracks one plow Chaine one Sett of Coopers Tooles & two Cows & one Calfe & two heifers of two Years & if it should please God that the said George Glascock should depart this Life before he Comes at age then the mentioned Legacy to Stand good to his Father and Mother Thomas & Anne Glascock & their disposall Son in Law & own Daughter to the above mentioned Mr. George Nicholls and alsoe I give to Jane Glascock my Grand Child one piece of Plate being about five pounds value And the said Thomas Glascock to be the Sole Executor & Administrator of the Estate.

Wit. THOMAS X DEWSIN, aged 29 years or thereabouts,
PAULE WOODBRIDGE, aged 46 years or thereabouts.

Page 1.

26 December, 1676;
6 June, 1677.

BUTLER, JOHN, of Westmoreland County, Planter.

To son Thomas my Plantation I now live upon lying & being in the forrest in Quantity of Acres one hundred and fifty to him and his heirs for ever also one Mare filley about Eight Months old my daughter Grace to have the first Mare foale that the said Mare filley shall bring & her increase for ever; also to my son Thomas one brown

Heifer about 3 years old having a hole in Each eare Cropt in the Left her & her female increase for ever. My will is that the feather bed I now lie Upon with the furniture thereunto belonging (In Case I now die) Remaine in my Wifes possession Soe long as she keeps herselfe Single & Unmarried & afterwards to be delivered Unto my Sonn Thomas in Case she marry. All the rest of my Temporall Estate both Moveables & Immoveables Shall be sold to discharge & pay all my Debts as Shall appeare Lawfully due by me unto any person or persons. To daughter Grace the first Cow Calfe that falls from any of my Cattle to be Recorded for her & her heires for ever. To son Thomas one Small pott of about 3 or 4 gallons. Appoints as his Executors & Overseers of his will Mr Henry Berry of Rappac County & his eldest son Henry.

Wit. JAMES TAYLOR, aged 28 years or thereabouts,

JOHN X THOMAS, of Stafford County, aged 32 years or thereabouts.   Page 3.

KENNY, WILLIAM,
                                            17 January, 1676;
                                            Sexto die Junij 1677.

IN THE NAME OF GOD AMEN I William Kenny Sick in body but in good and perfect memory Blessed be God doe now make and Ordaine this my last Will & Testam^t: & for my body I committ it to buriall thereof to the disposing of my friends & my Soule into the hands of Almighty God Amen & as for my Worldly estate I dispose of it as followeth Imp^is: One halfe of my land I give to my Sonn in Law John Jackson when he come of Age the other halfe of my land I give to my wife, but if we die w^th:out heires the land I give to John Kennadys Children to be equally divided as for all my Goods moovable and Unmoovable I give to my wife & my sonn in Law to be equally divided IN WITNESS whereof I have hereunto sett my hand & Seale this Seventeenth of January 1676

                                            Sign
Witness   W^M: X KENNY   Seal
    JOHN SAMSON
       Sign   JAMES CHEED JUNIO^R:
    SARAH X CANNADY

The above named John Sampson aged 26 Yeares or thereabouts Sworne & Examined saith that he did see the above named W^m: Kenny Signe Seale & publish the Above mentioned to be his last Will & testament & that he was in perfect Sence & memory at the Signing Sealing & publishing thereof to the best of his Judgm^t:

                                            JOHN SAMPSON

Juratus Est Sampson in Cur Com Rapp^a: Sexto die Junij 1677 p^r. Sacram: praedic Probat^r: Et Recordat^r:

            Test EDM^o. CRASK Cl Cur   Page 5.

26 February, 1675;
WILLIAMS, ROGER,   6 June, 1677.

To my two sons Roger Williams and Shadrack Williams I doe give 225 acres of land apiece which is 450 acres between them. To wife Joane Williams I doe give the Plantation with 200 acres of land at the Plantation I say wherein she is at this present living. To eldest daughter Betty Williams one heifer marked in the right ear & a crop & two slitts on the left & a nick underneath. All the rest of my cattle to my wife with the before-mentioned plantation & lands.

Wit. GERRARD GREENWOOD, ROBERT SISSON,

Proved by Robert Sisson 2 May, 1677 and by Gerrard Greenwood, aged 34 years or thereabouts, 6 June, 1677.   Page 7.

29 August, 1676;
TOONE, JAMES,   6 June, 1677.

To my three sons James William & John Toone A Seat of Land Lying between the Land of Henry Austin & Robᵗ Bedwell It being 300 acres with 150 acres of Land by me formerly bought of Richard Powell and joining to one corner of the said devident to be equally divided between them but if either of them die without issue the land to fall to the survivor but if either be minded to sell, their brothers to have the Refussall of it. To my other two sons Haster and Mark Toone my other seat of land wch John Massy now liveth on to be equally divided between them but if either die without issue the Land to fall to the Survivour but if Either be minded to Sell his brother to have the first Refusall of itt. To my daughter Anne Toone my Mare Filley Called Betty with her Increase for Ever onely the Second Mare foale that shall Come Either by her or her Increase I give unto my two Sonnes in Law Andrew & Thomas Dew if she die in her minority the mare with her Increase to Returne to her brothers to be divided amongst them I give to my five sonnes above named my other three Mares with their Increase to be divided as they Come to Age To my Son James my Feather bed which was his Mothers & a gunn which was his Grandfathers To my daughter Anne One Young Cow called Blossome. To Sonn William One Cow called Bese, To son John one Cow Called Browners To my Sonnes James William and John one Yoake of Steeres. I appoint my well beloved wife Anne Toone to be my Sole Executrix and do give unto her all the Remaining part of my Estate to her disposall & my Children to her Guidance during the time of their Minority. He appoints as Overseer of his will his friends William Barber John Suggitt and Samuel Pechey [Peachey].

Wit. JOHN JACOB, aged 50 years or thereabouts, ROBERT X HUGHES, aged 26 years or thereabouts, WILLIAM BARBER.

Page 8.

26 December, 1674;
ROWZIE, EDWARD,   6 June, 1677.

To son Edward Rowzie 400 acres of land lying at the head of Occapacie when he comes of age. To sons Lodowick Rowzie and John Rowzie my Land I now Live Upon to be Equally divided among them as they Come of Age. To my daughters Sarah Rowzie and Elizabeth Rowzie 1000 acres of land that lyeth in the Freshes of Rapp^ac: River at the South side to be Equally divided between them when they Come of Age or When they are Married W^ch of them shall First Happen. To daughter Sarah Rowzie my Black Mare & all her Increase only the first Mare fole she brings I give unto my Daughter Elizabeth Rowzie & her increase. To wife Mary Rowzie a Horse the Choice of them wch She pleaseth & further it is my will that all my personall Estate be brought to an Appraisem^t w^thin foure Moneths after my decease the mare & Horse only excepted as aforesaid & my Estate to be prized in money Sterling my Debts & funerall expences first paid & then all my personall Estate to be equally divided between my Wife & Children according to Law. Wife to be Executrix.

Wit. ROBERT PLEY, aged 42 years or thereabouts, GEORGE BOYCE.

Page 15.

In Rapp^ac: in Virginia this 15th of X^ber 1676;
DEMPSTER, JAMES,   ~   6 June, 1677.

His body to be decently buried by his Loving Friend & Executo^r: John Fenner of the County of Rapp^ac:

To Godson John Brailhatt one heiffer that is now at M^r: W^m. Mosses aged about three Yeares w^th: a long Starr in her Forehead White bellied To Godson John Brailhatt all my Goods that is in my Chest & now at this present at the house of John Wood & Alsoe what debts are due to me from any person or Persons in this River. Also to his said Godson all Goods & Chattels that in any wise Or Right in Conscience belongs unto me in the County of Rapp^ac: from any person as is before Exprest. He leaves his Godson to the care and tuition of his Executor John Fenner & by him to be brought Up till he is of mans Estate & Able to provide for himselfe. Should my Godson die before he comes to Enjoy what I have Given him then I give and bequeath what belongs Unto me unto John Fenners three Children to be equally divided amongst them. Item It is my Will & desire that these persons indebted unto me doe after my decease make paym^t & Satisfaction unto my Executo^r for my Use & Alsoe that what debts I in right or Conscience doe owe to any Person desire that it may be Satisfied by my said Executo^r.

Wit. JOHN RYMAN, ALEXAND^R MARSH

Proved by the witnesses June 6, 1677.

An Account of debts due James Dempster	1 Tob
Mr Robt Thomlin for trayes	120
Mr George Taylor	200
John Motley	100
Patrick Norton	060
	480

M^r: Blackbourn one Barrell of Corne
John Wood one Barrell
John Wood Seaven Bushels of Corne
that I bought of Thomas Webb
It. a new Suite of Cloaths about 10 Ells of Dowlas & 3 Y^{ds} Kersey
Gent. these I desire may be Satisfied by you to my Executo^r: John
ffener Gent. for my Use
Wit. JOHN RYMAN, ALEXAND^R MARSH.   Page 17.

                                    19 January, 1676;
KILLMAN, JOHN,   6 June, 1677.

To daughter Anne one brass pott and a Whislett & Corall and the
first foale that my Mare brings and a Rug & a Cow & a yearling. To
daughter Sarah a Small Ring & a Cow & a yearling & a pott & the
second foale my Mare brings. To my daughter Mary the third foale
that my Mare brings & a Cow & a yearling & a pott & two Pott Racks
& all the Rest of my household goods to be Equally divided betwixt
my foure Children onely my Gunn & one pott I doe give unto my
Son George & my Mare & the Rest of my Cattle. Appoints son George
his Executor. John Dike and Thomas Greene to be Overseers. Thomas
Greene is to see that the estate be not removed of the plantation and
that William West shall live on the Plantation rent free till my son
George be 16 years of age. All my land to my son George and his
heirs forever.

Wit. THOMAS X COCKIN, aged 50 years or thereabouts,
     BENJAMIN X RANDALL (or RANDLE) aged 40 years or there-
     abouts.   Page 20.

                                    30 March, 1672;
BERRY, HENRY,   No date of probate.

Executor my Loving friend Robert Peck he to act in any Case as
if I my Selfe were present. To William Kerton 100 acres of Land.
All the rest of his estate to be divided amongst his children "except
my wives thirds and to him that shall have the Girle named Jane

Stowe to have two Cows more than the Rest. To John Rolt one heifer two years old. I will that all my children have a great Care of the keeping the said Jane Stowe soe long as she lives & that my sonne Richard may have learning as well as the Rest."

Wit. JOHN ROLT, aged 50 years or thereabouts,
HANNA X MADDING.   Page 21.

28 August, 1673 ;
30 June, 1677.

PROSSER, JOHN, of Golden Valle in the Parish of Sittingbourne in the Freshes of Rapp^ac County.

To be buried by my first wife Martha. To my wife that now is I mean my Loving wife Margarett 500 acres of land and ½ of my moveable Estate my debts and funeral charges being paid and if my moveable Estate will not pay my debts then soe much of my Land back upon Pewmansin to be sold by her as will fully satisfy all. Wife to be Executrix. To eldest son John Prosser his Plantation called the Nutgrove and the land thereunto belonging. If he dies without issue the surviving Bretheren to have it divided amongst them equally. To second son Samuel Prosser 400 acres of land adjoining his brother John and if he dies without issue the land to be divided among the surviving Bretheren. To wife Margaret my plantation of the Golden Valle and the land in the Neck during her naturall life and then to fall to my eldest son John Prosser and his heirs forever. To his two sons Roger and Anthony Prosser jointly a dividend of land containing 1100 acres lying upon Mattapony Swamp to be divided by lott when the Eldest of them come of age and if they die without issue to be equally divided between the surviving Bretheren yet this shall be no barr to any of them to hinder any one of them from selling his own proper inheritance if occasion require. To sons-in-law Robert Goffe and Thomas Goffe 200 acres of land jointly joining upon my back line of my dividend of the Golden Vall. What land I have over and above what I have disposed of aforesaid to be equally divided among my four sons by name John Prosser Samuel Prosser Roger Prosser and Anthony Prosser. Leaves his sons under the protection of his wife until they come one after another to the age of Eighteene and to whome she shall think fitt to put them too and I doe hereby desire Mr James Kay to assist my said Executrix in performing all my will & Testament & whereas I have sold some Land that as yet hath no conveyance do hereby impower my said Executor Mr James Kay or his or her certaine attorney to give conveyance for the same & to acknowledge it to be recorded.

Wit. JOHN WAIGHT, HUGH X PALLMER.   Page 23.

24 May, 1676;
EALLES, (EILLS), WILLIAM,   2 May, 1677.

To my loving friend John Michell my worldly goods and Lands as followeth I give and bequeath my house and lands and all my worldly goods and chattels with all that doth belong to me.

Wit. PETER HOPEGOOD, aged 30 years or thereabouts, JOHN X FISHER.

Page 26.

2 April, 1676;
Proved 2 May & 4 July, 1677.
NEWMAN, JOHN, of the County of Rappa. in Virginia.

To eldest son Alexander Newman 600 acres of land that lie at Morattico Indian Towne it being the halfe of 1200 acres of land taken Up betweene Paule Woodbridge and myself onely my sonne Alexander shall give & grant unto his brother John what Timber he shall have occasion to use upon the Plantation which his Father have given him as long as they two shall live. To son John Newman the Plantation where I now live. To son Samuell Newman 20,000 pounds of Tob. and a breeding mare. To sons Alexander & John all the rest of my Estate moveables & unmoveables. Son Alexander shall take possession of my whole Estate after my decease till my other sons Samuell and John comes to age, provided these friends below mentioned doth see that he doth not Embezill nor waste the Estate. Further my desire is that my Friends should look into the Estate Every Yeare & if they should see that ye Estate should be wronged my desire is they should take it into their Custody till my Children come of age & if in case my son Alexander should Embezill any thing of ye Estate whilst he may have it in his custody then I doe Order he shall pay to his brother Samuell 20,000 pounds of Tob. & in case he should increase the Estate then he shall pay to his brother Samuell five Thousand the first yeare he comes to age & 5000 the second year. Likewise I order that my sonne John shall pay to his brother Samuell 5000 the first yeare that he comes to age and 5000 the second yeare. Further I would desire Capt Leroy Griffin Mr Paule Woodbridge Mr Thomas Glascock as this my Will doth Specifie Likewise I would desire them to Act according to it further I would desire my friend Paule Woodbridge once a Week Come & give my sonne advice & for the consideration thereof I give him 500 pounds Tob. p^r Yeare.

Wit. RICHARD X BOWLER, W^M WOODWARD, aged 20 years or thereabouts, THOMAS BARBER, aged 34 years or thereabouts.

Proved by W^m. Woodward 2 May, 1677 and by Thomas Barber,* 4 July, 1677.   Page 27.

*He signed as Thomas *Bankes.*

12 March, 1676;
BROWNE, WILLIAM,   4 July, 1677.

To my three sons William John and Maxfield all my land I am now possessed of not only that I live on but any where else to be equally divided between them. I doe Ordaine the Rest of my Children what my Executor & Executrix hereafter mentioned shall think fitt to Ord^r. them out of my Estate not having respect to one More than the other. Wife Elizabeth Executrix and friend Evan Morgan Executor. His horse to be sold for the better payment of his debts. And that the Mares & Cattle I have Run for the good of All my Children if my aforesaid Executor think fitt.

Wit. MALLACHY PEALE, aged 28 years or thereabouts,
    PETER X BUTLER.   Page 31.

3 January, 1676/77;
FRITH, NATHANIEL,   4 July, 1677.

To sons Nathaniel & William Frith my Plantation wch I now live on and the Land belonging to it wch is in all 150 acres to be equally divided betwixt them and if one dies the other to have it all. To wife Elizabeth all my moveables & Cattle saving only one cow calf to be delivered to my God daughter Rebecca Williams daughter of Jone Williams. Wife Elizabeth Executrix and if she die Afore they come of age then my two sons Nathaniell & William to be possest wth their land at 17 years of age.

Wit. RUPERT BERKER HEAD,* aged 27 years or thereabouts,
    LEWIS X JONES, aged 40 years or thereabouts.   Page 32.

BLISSED, (BLISFED), THOMAS,

IN THE NAME OF GOD AMEN this I ordain my last Will & Testam^t: Revoaking all Others being in perfect health & memory First I bequeath my Soule to Almighty God & my Saviour Jesus Christ by Whom I hope to Receive Salvation, & my Body to the Earth from Whence it Came Imp^{rs}: I bequeath unto John Willson sonne of Elias Willson & Susanna his Wife to w^{ch}: Child I am God Father three thousand pounds of Tobacco to be Conveniently laid out for his Edification when he shall Attaine to the Age of Eight Yeares old in Learning the Word of God. Secundas. I bequeath to Phebe Willson Daughter to the sd Elias & Susanna thirty Shillings or the Value in Tobacco to buy her a Ring when she shall Arrive at the age of Seventeene Yeares. Tertius. I bequeath unto Elizabeth Jones Daughter in Law to M^r: George Taylor, Twenty Shillings to buy her a Ring At the Value in Tobacco. Quartus. I Bequeath to M^{rs}: Mary Harper & her Eldest Daughter Elizabeth Bowlware twenty Shillings a peice to buy them two Rings or the like Value in Tobacco. Quinq^e I be-

---

*He signed as *Berkenhead.*

queath unto Sarah Harper one thousand pounds of Tobacco & twenty Shillings to buy her a Ring or the Value in Tobacco. Sep I doe ordaine & Depute Edward Freeman & William Serjeant, to be my whole & Sole Executo[rs]: to See my Will performed after my debts paid to See all the Legacies paid According to my Will but if any of the Legatees Should die before the Probate of my Will, then to Redown to my Executo[rs] & all the Remaining Part of my Estate in What Sort or kind Soever to be Equally divided between them onely my Silver Tobacco Box to be given to Susanna Willson & my Signet to M[r]: James Miller of York, this being my last Will & Testament all others Renounced & Revoaked I doe here in perfect health & memory Put to my hand & Seale this 7[th]: day of February 1676/7

Sealed & Delivered in the   THOMAS BLISFED   Seale
     p[r]sence of

     JOHN SAVAGE
     DAVID ROMER

THE W[th]:IN Named John Savage aged 29 Yeares or thereabouts & David *Roomee* aged 32 yeares of thereabouts Sworne & Examined Saith that they did See the w[th]: [within] named Thomas *Blissed* Signe Seale & publish the w[th]:in mentioned to be his last Will & Testam[t]: & that he was in Perfect Sence & memory at the Signing Sealing & publishing thereof to the best of their Judgm[ts]: & further Saith not
                                                       JOHN SAVAGE
                                                       DAVID ROMER

Jurant[r] Savage Et Romer in Cur Com Rapp[ac]: 4⁰ Die Julij 1677
                              Test
                              EDM⁰: CRASK Cl Cur
          Probat[r] Et Recordat[r] Test
                              EDM⁰: CRASK Cl Cur
               Ex[d].   Page 35.

IN THE NAME OF GOD AMEN The last Will & Testament of Anne Evence widd being Sick but in perfect Sence & Memory. Item I give & bequeath to my Lord & Savio[r]: Jesus my Soule from whome I Received it, & I committ my Body to y[e] Ground there to be decently Buried, & my Worldly goods I bequeath as followeth Item I give & bequeath to my Daughter Sarah Cook one Feather bed & what belongeth to it, Item I give to Sarah Cook halfe y[e] pewter, Item more one Skillet. Item I give & bequeath to Anne Soaper 1 Hat Apron & handercheft Item more to Sarah Cook one Kettle Item more to Sarah Cook three Spoons Item more to Sarah one Chaire, Item I give & bequeath to Sarah Cook halfe my living, onely I give & bequeath to Dorathy Armstrong one hankercheife one *quoife* & *Andressen*, Item I give & bequeath to Mary Armstrong two *Quoifes* & two Neck Cloaths

Item I give to Sarah Cook one White winscote Box & one Gold Ring & one Skimmer & one Pewter Porringer more one Suite of Serge. Item I give unto my Sonn William Younge all ye Remainder of my Worldly Goods as Witness my hand this twentie first day of Aprill in ye Yeare of O^r Lord 1677

Sign

Test   ANNE m EVENCE

    JOHN SOAPER
    JOHN PATRICK

THE DEPOSITION of John Soaper aged 34 Yeares or there-abouts Sworne & Examined in Court this 1st: of August 1677 that he was p^rsent when ye deced Woman w^th :in Mentioned did declare ye w^th :in Will to be her Last Will & Testam^t & that all things w^th :in Specified were Ord^red to be disposed of according to ye Within forme but ye Suite of Cloaths for Sarah Cook & one laced apron & one laced hankercheife given to my Wife was put in after ye w^th :in Will was Signed & Deliv^red but whether by ye decds ord^r or not, I know not, & further Saith not

JOHN SOAPER

Juratus Est Soaper in Cur Com Rapp^a : 1°. die Augusti 1677. Probat^r p^r Sacram Johan Soaper Et Recordat^r

Test

Ex^a.   EDM^o : CRASK Cl Cur

Page 37.

IN THE NAME OF GOD AMEN I Thomas Pannell being Sick & Weak but thanks to God in Perfect Memory, do Make Constitute & Appoint this to be my last Will & Testam^t : Imprimis I bequeath my Soule to God & as for my Worldly Estate I doe give & bestow as followeth Imp^rs : I give my lands Goods & Chattles Equally to be divided between my Beloved wife Katherine Pannell & my three Children William & Mary & Isabella Pannell & alsoe the Child she now goes w^th : & all my Estate to them & their heires for Ever. Item I give to Anthony Prosser a Tract of Land lying at Matapony Branches w^ch : was taken up between his Father John Prosser & my Selfe in Copartnership, ye s^d Land I say to be divided between my own Children & him & to their Heires for Ever, and doe hereby make & appoint my beloved wife Sole Executrix, & my desire is that she Acknowledge all Deeds of Land from me due, And Alsoe I appoint my Loveing Friends Warwick Cammock & Daniell Gaines to assist my Wife, & in Case of her Mortality to take Care of my Children. In Witness whereof I have hereunto Sett my hand May 11th *1676* (these Words interlined) & alsoe y^e. Child she now goes with in y^e. 8th: line & to y^e. heirs for Ever in y^e. 12 line

sign

THOMAS X PANNELL

Witness:

JOHN POWELL, aged 33 years or thereabouts,
WILLIAM CLAPHAM, aged 23 years or thereabouts.

Proved 3 Sept. 1677.   Page 39.

26 January, 1676;
CREIGHTON, HENRY,   6 7^{bris} 1677.

To son Henry Creighton the Devident of Land where I now live with all ye housing and Orchards thereunto belonging and if he dies without issue I doe hereby give ye same to my sons William and Thomas Creighton to be equally divided between them & upon ye decease of ye said William or Thomas to the survivor & his heirs to Enjoy ye whole Estate for Ever but his wife Jane Creighton to enjoy it during her widowhood until my said son Henry shall attain ye age of 21 years and that my said son Henry shall enjoy y^e ½ profits thereof during her widowhood. To sons Henry William and Thomas and their heirs forever all my parcell of Land lying in the Freshes of Rapp^{ac} (as by pattent will appear) to be divided into three parts between ye said Henry Thomas & William ye said Henry first Choosing his part thereof and William next of his part thereof. To Charles Elizabeth and John Bredgar all my female Cattle belonging to the Lower Plantation the said Cattle to be appraised and ye Value thereof to be equally shared between them. All the rest of my personal estate to be sold at an out Cry for money or tobacco to pay my debts first and then equally to be divided between my said wife Jane Creighton and my sons Henry & William Creighton each of them one-third part thereof. Executors his loving friends Mr. Thomas Gouldman and Mr. Robert Tomlin.

Wit. PATRICK X NORTON, aged 35 years or thereabouts,
JOHN HUBBARD.   Page 41.

8 December, 1676;
PELLS, TIMOTHY,   5 day of 7^{bris} 1677.

To daughter Kezia my mares first Filly foale that will be produced by her & that this next spring it may be sett on foote unto the use of my said daughter also two cows (Viz^t) Colly & Gentle and the Female increase of them. To daughter Susanna the first Filly that Cometh of my said Mare alsoe two Cows Commonly known by ye name of Doll & Browny wth their Female Increase. To daughter Elizabeth two Cows (Viz^t) Cherry & Cramp also ye heiffer Yearlings that now are

on foot. To both my eldest daughters my seat of land to be equally
divided betwixt them Both as it shall be then equally divided each paying a like for yᵉ same. Executrix wife Alice Pells.

Wit. LAW. ROCHFORT, aged 31 years or thereabouts,
JOHN GRAVES, aged 28 years or thereabouts.   Page 44.

DART, THOMAS, (Nuncupative Will),

The deposition of Barnaby Wells aged 40 years or thereabouts Ex-
amined & Sworne Saith that yoʳ deponᵗ being in the Company wᵗʰ:
Thomas Dart at yᵉ House of Mʳ Donathan about yᵉ Month of March
last was twelve-month did ask yᵉ sd Dart if You should die in yᵉ
Condition You are in now who will you give yoʳ Estate to the sd Dart
Replied that he freely Gave all his Estate he had in yᵉ world to John
Bowen Excepting onely one Cow Calfe wᶜʰ: said he I give to my God
Son but yoʳ deponᵗ is ignorant who that Godson is & not long after
yᵗ sd Dart was Murthered by Indians these or yᵉ like words is yᵉ
whole Trueth to yᵉ best of yoʳ deponᵗˢ: Judgmᵗ & further Saith not

sign
BARNABY X WELLS

Sworn to in Court August 1, 1677.

The deposition of Richard Hollis, aged 40 years or thereabouts,
Examined & Sworne, Saith That yoʳ deponᵗ Living at yᵉ house of
John Bowin did heare one Thomas Dart (who put in at yᵉ House as
he was Going to Mʳ Donathans, Say that if he was Kild by yᵉ Indians
he freely gave all his Estate to yᵉ said John Bowen & soone after yᵉ
said Dart was Murthered by Indians these or like words is yᵉ Whole
Truth to yᵉ best of Yoʳ Deponts knowledge & further Saith not

sign
RICHARD X HOLLIS

Sworn to in Court August 1, 1677.

Probated 5 die 7ᵇʳⁱˢ Ano 1677.   Page 46.

GODFREY, JOHN, (Nuncupative Will),

The deposition of Henry Woodnutt, aged 39 years of thereabouts,
is Ready to depose that John Godfrey deced & John Blaxon being
Mates John Godfrey he went into yᵉ Freshes said that if he died John
Blaxon should possess all he had, being in discourse wᵗʰ yoʳ deponᵗ
Concerning their Mateship saying that by Reason John Blaxon did
help to work for it he should Enjoy it & further Saith not

sign
HENRY X WOODNUTT

The deposition of Thomas Grime aged 30 years or thereabouts, is
Ready to depose that upon a falling out between John Godfrey and
John Blaxon, John Godfrey said to Blaxon give me from undʳ yoʳ

hand that you will pay for halfe ye Land, & I will give you from und^r: my hand for halfe ye Land then, said John Godfrey there is no Need of such ceremonies, for I have no body to give but you neither shall Any have it but you & further Saith not
THOMAS *Grahame*

Sworn to by Thomas Grahame May 2, 1677. Probated September 11, 1677, by the oaths of Henry Woodnut and Thomas Grahame.

Page 47.

8 September, 1677;
22 November, 1677.

SCOTT, SAMUEL, of Headington in ye County of Hills, [Wilts.], Gent.

Sick & weak in body but of perfect memory and Sound Judgm^t: My body to the Ground to be buried in Goodman Constables Orchard. I give my servant William Glew unto Nicholas Constable during ye Remainder of ye time he hath to serve me & I give my Gelding Saddle & bridle unto ye sd Nicholas Constable. To Thomas Chilly ye Remainder of my Estate. Appoints Thomas Chilly his Executor.
Wit. ROBERT SCOTT, EDWARD FRYAR.   Page 49.

27 February, 1675;
9 May, 1677.

DOUGHTY, ENOCH,

Estate to his children (not named), "and as my desire is that they may goe out of this Country I doe impower my Overseers Francis Doughty and James Phillips to put on sale all my lands and goods and Chattels for money Good for my Children."
Wit. JOHN SIMPTON, JONATHAN BATES, HUGH X MANE.

MEMO. 16 hhds of Tob. that my brother carried to England is properly upon my account for him to make use being my own crop & 500 acc^t my Brother owes me a Bill of Thomas Becks to my Brother I have paid him for it & another of George Grime I have received many Bills in Stafford of my Brother in my name & have given him a list of them some Mares wch I have of his, three of his being about at my Plantation & ye other in Potomack Ward. Feb. ye 27, 1675.

Page 51.

8 October, 1675;
17 January, 1677/8.

MOTT, JOHN, of ye Parish of Sittingbourne in ye County of Rapp^ac, Planter.

All my land to my four nieces Elizabeth, Margarett, Anne & Ellen Mott & their heires to be equally divided to them. Desires to be buried by his beloved brother George Mott. To Ellen Pigg two cows & calves. To my niece Ellen Mott a young mare. And it is my Will that my nephew John Vickers shall hold & enjoy my Plantation wch I am now going to cleare wth soe much land as he shall have occasion to make use of (he making no wast of ye Timber but wch shall be for his necessary use about ye Plantation) Untill ye first of January wch shall be in ye yeare of O^r Lord one thousand Six hundred Eighty & five & then to Render it up to ye Uses of my nieces aforesaid wth all Houses & Fences wch shall then be upon it in good Repaire & for my personall Estate (after debts & Legacies paid) to be equally divided betwixt my nephew John Vickers & my 4 nieces Elizabeth Margaret Anne and Ellen Mott to be delivered to my Neeces at ye age of 16 yeares or day of marriage wch shall first happen & if any of them shall die before, ye survivor of them to be their heires. Executor my nephew John Vickers.

Wit. RICHARD X WALLICE, WM. WINN.

Sworn to by William Winn, aged 28 years or thereabouts, 20 November, 1677.   Page 53.

8 February, 1675;
20 January, 1677.

HAWKINS, THOMAS, of the County of Rapp^{ac}: & pish of Sittingbourne.

To my two sons Thomas & John Hawkins all my lands to be equally divided between them but in case my Loving wife Frances Hawkins be wth Child if a Sonne then I give & bequeath him an Equal part of All my lands & if any of them should happen to dye before they Come of age ye Land still to fall to ye Surviving Sonnes or Sonne & if they all dye then to my daughters wch I now have & wch other it shall please God to send Me by my Now wife to be equally divided among them and ye heires of their bodies lawfully begotten for ever. All ye Rest of my Estate I give & bequeath Equally to be divided between my Loving wife Frances Hawkins & ye Rest of my Children wch I shall have in Esse or posse at ye time of my death excepting one negroe Girle & one English Servant to my Loving Wife above her equall part & my former wifes Diamond Ring & pearl Necklace wch I give to my daughter Elizabeth Hawkins if she lives to ye age of sixteen years but if she die before I give ye same to her sister Hannah Hawkins above their equal parts. Appoints his wife Frances Hawkins Executrix and brother Samuel Blomfield Executor, provided they give good security for ye performance of my will & well bringing up of my children otherwise I leave it to ye Courts disposal. To brother Blomfield a mourning Ring my sword & belt & small pistolls.

Wit. JOHN GRAVES, aged 29 years or thereabouts,

ABRAHAM RAW, aged 33 years or thereabouts, WILLIAM X SAILE.

Page 55.

30 January, 1676;

CLARK, RICHARD,   2 January, 1677/78.

To my Loving Friend Theophilous Whale all my Woodland ground or to his heires and do make him Sole Executor of all w^ch : I am now posest wth both of Goods and Chattels giving to my Loving Friend Edmund Pagett my light Coloured Suite of Cloaths and my God Daughter Elizabeth Whale one Cow Calfe.

Wit. ANTHONY NORTH, aged 50 years or thereabouts,

EDMUND PAGETT, aged 30 years or thereabouts.   Page 58.

4 January, 1675;

NANGLE, GEORGE,   3 January, 1677.

IN THE NAME OF GOD AMEN I George Nangle of ye Citty of Doublin in Ireland merchant being very Sick in body but of Good & perfect memory thanks be to almighty God, therefore doe make & ordaine this to be my last Will & Testament : in manner & forme following first I committ my Soule to God & my body to the Earth to be decently buried at ye discretion of my Executor^s : hereafter mentioned And touching what worldly Estate God hath Blessed me, I dispose of as followeth I give & bequeath unto my very good friends William Smith & Robert Akins both Merchants of ye Cittie of Doublin & to Gerrard Nangle my Brother & Judah Nangle my Neece all of ye Citty of Doublin aforesaid my whole Estate both Reall & personall lying & being in ye Citty of Doublin ye Kingdome of Ireland in Virginia or Else where they paying ye Severall Legacies hereafter Menconed or Allowing ye same to my Executor^s : who I impower to make paym^t : of ye Said Legacies. Item it is my will & desire that all my Estate in this Collony be Converted into Tobacco w^th : what Convenient Speed may bee by my Executor^s hereafter Named, and that ye same Tobacco be by my Executor^s : transmitted to England by ye first opportunity If to ye port of London, then to be Consigned to Thomas Wise and Lombard of ye Citty of London and in Case of their Death or Absence, then to Thomas Hardis of ye same Citty Merchant, If to ye Port of Bristow in England, to be Converted to Peter Wadding of ye s^d Citty merchant, or if opportunity present to Leaverpoole then to be Consigned to M^r : ffarham of ye same Towne together w^th : Letters of advise according to ye purport of this my Will, alsoe I desire that a Coppie of this my Will be sent home to M^r : William Smith and Mr Robert Atkins, ye produce of all my Tobacco at what port Soever exposed to Sale whether by Thomas Wise and Lombard or Thomas Hardis of ye Citty of London, Peter Wadding of ye Citty of Bristow or M^r : Farham of ye Towne of Leaverpoole, to be delivered to ye above mentioned William Smith & Robert Akings Gerrard Nangle and Judah Nangle or their known Attorney, and that ye produce of all Tobacco's Sent home be Equally divided between them or

Soe many as shall be Liveing. I give unto Mary Evans thirty shillings. I give to Jugg five Shillings. I give to M^r: Benj^a: Goodrich my best periwigg. I give to Thomas Gouldman a peece Remnant of Cloath Serge and ye buttons and Silk belonging to itt. Y^e produce of all ye goods I brought into Virginia together wth: what tobacco I have in ye hands of Coll: W^m: Traverse (my debts first paid and funerall Charges Satisfied) be wth: all Expedition sent home for ye Uses aforementioned. My Executors shall not Exceed twenty pounds upon my funerall. Executors Co^{ll}: Thomas Goodrich and Mr Thomas Gouldman giving unto each of them one thousand pounds of Tobacco and Cask.

Wit. GEORGE MORRIS, JACOB LUMKIN.

Sworn to by George Morris 4 July, 1677, and by Jacob Lumkin Tertio die Januarij 1677.   Page 60.

25 December, 1677;
25 January, 1677.

TURNER, HEZEKIAH, of ye Parish of Farnham in ye County of Rapp^{ac}.

The plantation whereon I now live to be sold to pay my debts and in case that ye value does not extend to make full ye said payments then soe much of my Cattle or of my other plantacon in ye woods be sold to Compleat ye said payments. Executor ye Wor^{full} Court of this County to see that my Lands and Goods as aforesaid be sold to its Best Value and ye produce Justly employed to ye Use and Uses aforesaid according to the true Intent and Meaning of this my Will and Testament and that ye remainder of What shall be Left of ye said sale be carefully employed and delivered unto ye use and uses of Elizabeth my wife my Sonn Hezekiah and my Daughter Michell Jointly to be enjoyed by them for their better Maintenance in Living during my wifes life and after her decease equally to be divided between my said sonn and daughter. I do reserve unto my Friend and Neighbor James Samford that in case he thinks fitt to take this plantacon at ye price of 10000 lbs. of Tob. that then it be firmly sold and delivered unto him and his heirs forever. To my Grand Child Anne Chissell 150 acres of land lying in ye woods being ye place where her Mother now lives bounding on that side where Martin Hamman and Job Hamon now live and Running ye whole Breadth of my said Land at that End. I doe bequeath my son Hezekiah to ye tuition and Care of Mr Jno. Saffin for the Terme of nine years from ye date of these p^{r}sents.

Wit. JAMES SAMFORD, aged 53 years or thereabouts,

ROGER BAGWELL, aged 24 years or thereabouts.

Page 64.

5 March, 1661;
6 February, 1677.

STEPHENS, JOHN, now bound for England.

To John Fulcher Sonne in Law to Mr Richard Webley Gent 1000 acres of land lying in Rapp^{ac} Creek on ye same side ye Indians liveth on as P a pattent more at Large Appeareth & ye other 500 to Alexander Dudley Sonne unto Richard Dudley to them and their heirs forever. To Mr. Richard Webley 500 acres of land lying in Rapp^{ac} Creek and being part of 2000 acres deserted by————————Henry ——————————————— granted patent unto Walter———————— unto ye sd Mr. Richard Webley his heirs and assigns for ever; to Mr Richard Webley ½ or moyitie of my hoggs that I have in Rapp^{ac} Creek they being of the same Mark of John Wraskams wch is upon Record onely a Neeck on ye Right Eare and all ye increase to him and his heirs forever; to Mr Richard Webley and Richard Dudley all my Estate that shall be after my Debts be paid to be equally Divided betwixt them.

Wit. CLEMENT HERBERTS, THO^s LIDDLE.

Proved by comparing ye Witnesses hands (they being dead) in open Court this 6th day of February, 1677.   Page 66.

4 May, 1676;
7 February, 1677/8.

GIBSON, WILLIAM,

To daughter Elizabeth Gibson the 150 acres of land I bought of Nicholas Catlett and one young mare one year old. To James Bartlett 100 acres of land where I now live ye said James Bartlett to deliver unto ye said Elizabeth 200 apple trees and 100 quince trees when ye said Elizabeth is marriageable. To Thomas Bartlett 150 acres of land which I last took up provided if any of ye Children die without issue that his estate be equally divided between the rest. Executrix wife Mary Gibson to manage my said estate to ye best Advantage Untill my Children be of age and in case she Marries that her husband be bound to make good every Particular thing belonging unto ye sd Children & Every of their heirs to be Equally divided amongst ye sd Children.

Wit. LAW ROCHFORT, aged 30 years or thereabouts, JNO. PATTERSON.

Page 68.

23 November, 1676;
7 February, 1677/8.

JONES, RICE,

To son John Jones and ye heirs of his body forever all that plantation or Devident of land whereon I now live Called Nimcock point wch said land I formerly purchased of Richard Bennet Esqr and if my said son John should die without issue then I bequeath my said divident of land unto my son Rice Jones and the heirs of his body

and if both my sonnes die without issue then I bequeath my said
divident of land unto my daughter Anne Jones and ye heirs of her
body and if all three die without issue then to my daughter Mary
wife of John Broche and ye heirs of her body forever. To son John
Jones ten silver spoons one new Silver Sack Cup two Christian Servants by name John Powell and John Diett and three Negroes by name
Ockery Masea and Seniora. To son Rice Jones 800 acres of land it
being part of ye devident of land whereon my sonne John Jones now
Lives bounded on ye Dragon Swamp in ye County of Middlesex at
ye North West End of ye divident and if my sonne Rice Jones die
without issue then I bequeath my said devident of Land unto my
Sonne John Jones and ye heirs of his body and if both die without
issue then I bequeath my said devident of Land unto my daughter
Anne Jones and ye heirs of her body and if all three die without issue
then to my daughter Mary wife of John Broche and ye heirs of her
body forever. To son Rice Jones three Christian Servants by name
Robert Blackley Zachariah Mullen and Elizabeth Holland and two
Negroes by name James and Dido and my Silver Tankard and one
New Copper Kettle and one New bell Mettall pot. To daughter Anne
Jones and ye heires of her body forever 500 acres of Land it being y^e
remainder of that Devident of land whereon my sonne John Jones
doth now live on ye Dragon Swamp in ye County of Middlesex as
above Expressed at ye South East End of ye said Devident and if my
sd daughter die without issue then I give ye said 500 acres of Land
unto my sonne Rice Jones and ye heires of his body and if both die
without issue I give the sd 500 acres of Land to my sonne John Jones
and ye heires of his body and if all three die without issue then to my
daughter Mary wife of John Broche and ye heires of her body forever.
To daughter Anne Jones two Negro lads by name Peter and Tom
to be delivered for her use immediately after my death and four paire
of Shoes and two pair of fine Worsted Stockings three Ells of Holland
and Seven Ells of Dowlas and 100 pounds Sterling to be paid her y^e
next Shipping Ensuing ye Day of her Marriage and 8000 pounds of
Tob. the said tobacco to be paid her ye next Cropp after she is married
and ye other four thousand ye next year following and one Mare and
foale of aboute a year old to be Delivered for her use as Soone as
they can be gott in; they being now in New Kent County. To daughter
Anne Jones my Feather Bed and furniture wch is in ye little roome
and a new feather bed and boulster teeking and a new green wosted
Rugg wch is sent me from London this Shipping and one new Ver-
million Sett of Curtaines and Vallance wrought with Red Wosted
and my Trunk in ye little Room and New Chest and all her Mothers
and Sisters Wearing Cloathes both Linnen and Silk except one black
Taffety petticoate and wastcoate of her mothers wch I bequeath unto
my daughter Mary ye wife of John Broche. I bequeath that my
daughter Anne Jones shall have her Diett and accomodation wth her
Brother John Jones Upon this Plantation whereon I now Live and

ground for her two Negroes to work on and house room for their Corne and Tobacco Untill yᵉ day of her marriage or death wch Shall first Happen, I bequeath if it shall please God to take my Daughter Anne Jones before she be married Unto my two Grand Children Barbary and Margaret Broche the daughters of John and Mary Broche fifty pounds Sterling to be equally divided between them and yᵉ Remainder to my two Sonnes John and Rice Jones to be Equally Divided between them To my Son in Law John and daughter Mary Broche Each of them a gold Ring of Twenty Shillings price and to their Daughters Barbary and Margaret ten Ells of Dowlas and ten Yards of Serge To my Grandchild Margaret Broche yᵉ Daughter of John and Mary Broche one Negro Child Named Kate wch I desire may be nursed by her Mother Dido untill she be three Years Old and then to be delivered unto my said Grand Child mortality Excepted To my Friend Edward Thomas one hhd of Tobacco Conteyning 500 weight and three Ells of Holland To my Sonne and Daughter in Law Henry and Jane Creighton each a Gold Ring of 20 shillings price To my two Sonnes John and Rice Jones all other my estate English goods households moneys Debts Cattle Horses hoggs and all other my Estate of what nature or kind soever or in what place soever to be equally divided between them and doe appoint and earnestly request my loving friends Mr Humphrey Jones Mr Nicholas Cock Mr Henry Williamson and Mr. Richard Symms to make an equall division of all things between them. My loving friends Mr Nicholas Cock and Mr Henry Williamson to be overseers in trust and guardian to my daughter Anne Jones and her estate that she may not be wronged by her brothers or any other Either in person or Estate. Executors sons John and Rice Jones.

Wit. PETER HOPEGOOD, JOHN POWELL, EDWARD THOMAS.

Page 70.

1 March, 1677;
HOPKINS, ROBERT,   6 March, 1677.
March Cᵗ: 1677/8

IN THE NAME OF GOD AMEN I Robert Hopkins being Sick in body but of perfect Sence & memory, Doe make this my last [Will] & Testamᵗ: in Writing in manner & forme as followeth (Vizᵗ:) First I bequeath my Soule into yᵉ hands of God that gave it, & my body to be Decently buried at yᵉ discretion of my Executrix—And as for my Estate, I bequeath it as followeth, I give & bequeath unto my Deare wife Katherine Hopkins & her heires for Ever, in barr of her Dower all my Land lying from yᵉ Slashett to yᵉ Miles End, I give and bequeath unto my three Sonnes Thomas Hopkins Robert Hopkins & George Hopkins & their heires for Ever all my Land lying from yᵉ Slashett aforesaid, to yᵉ side of Rappᵃ: river to be devided in three Equall parts between them by my Loveing Friends Wᵐ: Moss & John Fennell, and as for my pˢonall Estate my Will is that it shall be Disposed of for ye paym^t: of my Debts, And I doe make my deare wife Katherine Hopkins my Sole Executrix of this my Last Will & Testam^t: dated ye 1st day of March 1677.

ROBERT HOPKINS   Seale

SIGNED SEALED & ACKNOWLEDGE to be ye last Will & Testam^t: of ye Robert Hopkins in ye P^rsence of

Jo^N HUBBARD

FRANCIS DOWNER

THE ABOVE NAMED Francis Downer aged 31 Yeares or thereabouts Sworne & Examined Saith that he did see ye abovementioned Testat^r. Signe Seale & publish this as his last Will & Testam^t: & that he was in perfect Sence & memory at ye Signing, Sealing & publishing thereof to ye best of his Judgm^t: & Further Saith not

FRANCIS DOWNER

Probat^r P Sacrament Francis Downer in Cur Com Rapp^ac: 6°. Die March 1677

Et Recordat^r xx6° Die ejusd Mens An° Sup^rd

Test

EDM° CRASK Cl Cur

Page 77.

| | 4 May, 1676; |
| BARBER, RICHARD, | 3 April, 1678. |

Of sound and perfect memory.

I Richard Barber being intended to goe in pursuite of ye Indians Doe make this my last will & Testam^t I bequeath all my Lands unto bothe of my Children Richard and John to be Equally divided betwixt them and their lawful heires for ever and in Case ye one should die before ye other and have no heire then the whole to descend to the other Like wise I bequeath my whole personal Estate to my said Children two mares onely Excepted to pay my Debts To sonne Richard my Negro Boy and in Case ye said Negro Should Die another to be delivered to him of ye same age when ye said Richard becomes of age Executrix my Loveing wife Mary Barber to manage my Estate to ye best use she can for my two Children And should ye said Children both die without heires then ye whole Estate both Reall and personall be Conferred unto my said wife and her heires for Ever and in Case she should die w^thout Issue that then my Estate both reall and personal to be disposed of as hereafter (Viz^t) my Land to be a Glebe two hundred Acres excepted wch I bequeath unto unseated persons to begin ye world wth all my personall Estate to be turned wholly in Cattle towards ye maintenance of ye poore upon ye said Land therefore I earnestly desire that ye Vestry may be Carefull from time to

time to See and ord[r]. that y[e] sd Estate may be Allwaies looked after
and putt to y[e] best use for y[e] poore that possibly it may be putt to.
Wit. LAW: ROCHFORTE, FRANCIS X HAWKINS.

Sworn to by Lawrence Rochforte, aged 30 years or thereabouts,
6 March, 1677 and Francis X Hawkins, aged 26 years or thereabouts.

Page 79.

Date of Will obliterated;
GODFREY, JOHN,   Recorded 3 April, 1678.

In perfect sence and memory, but God above doth know how soone
I may be visited with Sickness or Cut off with some other Untimely
end for wee have a faire Election to be destroyed by ye heathen and
no more then or desertes for it is Just with God to Cut us of for or
Sinnes and wickedness that is Daily enacted amongst us Yet I hope
ye Lord will have mercy upon Us and give us his Grace that wee may
Render him praise and thanks for all his benefits continually bestowed
upon us from ye beginning of ye world untill this day hoping ye
Lord will not Suffer us to Come to such an Untimely End as to be
Destroyed by ye heathen but wee cannot expect no other for wthout
Sound Repentence from ye botome of ye heart there is Small hopes
of Grace Therefore this is to Certifie all persons whom it may Con-
cerne that this is my last Will and Testament First I bequeath my
Soule to Almighty God that gave it to me unto ye meritorious death
and passion of my Blessed Savio[r] and Redeemer Jesus Christ that was
Crucified for my Sinnes next my body to the Ground to be buried
according to Christian Buriall to ye best disposing of my Friends as
they shall think fitt or Convenient Amen Therefore as God shall allot
it I give and bequeath unto my welbeloved Friend————————all
my personall Estate moveables or Unmoveables land Cattle Hoggs
household Goods or anything that is properly mine Given und[r] my
hand and Seale this————————————.

No witnesses

Page 82.

NOTE. The above will leaves a space for the name of the beneficiary, whose
name is given in the depositions made by Richard Hollis and Henry Woodnutt.
See Nuncupative Will of John Godfrey probated 11 September, 1677, page 47.

21 March, 1677/78;
2 May, 1678.

FULLERTON, JAMES, of Piscatacon, in ye County of Rapp[ac].

First my will and desire is that my two Daughters Mary and
Hannah having Sore heads have their Heads Cured and Satisfaction
made for ye same out of such Debts as are Due me after wch done
and performed ye Remainder of such Debts as are due me whether by

Speciality or otherwise be equally divided amongst my wife and children Secondly I will and bequeath that my whole Stock of Cattle be Equally divided amongst my wife and children wch pte of Cattle and Debts thus given unto my wife in lieu of her thirds and no otherwise. To my Sone James Fullerton one bay horse of two Yeares old and all my armes now in possession or otherwise Offensive and defensive and all my wearing Apparell. To my daughter Mary one Bay Mare. To my daughter Hannah one Young Mare. To my wife one black Mare And as touching my household Goods and furniture my will is that it be Equally divided amongst my wife and children my wifes pte thereof to be in lieu of her thirds as Abovesaid. To sonne James and his heires forever All my lands and tenem[ts] held by pattent or otherwise Excepting 400 acres of land wch I give to my two Daughters Mary and Hannah and their Heires forever to be Equally Devided betweene them when by Either of them or their heires required wch 400 acres of land is pte of a Devidend of 900 acres Scituate and being in ye Maine Swamp of Piscatacon Creek Provided allwaies that if any of my Children Sonne or Daughter die before they be at ye age of twenty one or be married that his or her pte of Land Stock Household goods or debts be Equally devided betweene ye Survivors. My friend Thomas Gaines to be my Executor till my Sonne James attaine ye age of Sixteene Yeares and then I appoint Thomas Gaines and my Sonne Joynt Executors till my Sonne James attaine ye Years of one and Twenty then I appoint my Sonne James Sole Executor My will and desire is that neither Court nor Justices of ye peace of ye abovesd County intermeddle wth my Children or any pte of my Estate but that all be at ye disposall of my Executors or Executor.

Wit. THO: EDMUNDSON, THO: WHEELER, JAMES BOUGHAN.

Page 83.

| | 4 March, 1677/78; |
| DRENN, EDWARD, | 2 May, 1678. |

I bequeath ye foure hundred acres of land that is my pte of ye land betwixt John Smith and me to be Equally divided betwixt Richard West and his three Children Elizabeth Mary and Ellen and should any of them die to be Equally divided betwixt ye Rest and ye said land is to be Leased unto Andrew Boughan and David Jamison Seaven Yeares after ye date hereof and I do obleidge my Self or my Executor to build Houses for their present Use (Viz[t]) twenty foot dwelling House and forty foot Tobacco house upon ye said Land Executor my friend Richard West All my other goods I bequeath unto ye said Richard West and his heirs forever.

Wit. LAW[E] ROCHFORTE, DAVID X JAMISON.   Page 87.

29 November, 1677;
CURTIS, JOHN,   5 June, 1678.

To my well beloved friends Doctor Peter Hopegood and Randoll Peters all my worldly goods they paying all my Debts and to bury me in a decent manner. Executors Dr. Peter Hopegood and Randoll Peters.
Wit. SIMON GRAY,
     THOMAS GRAHAME,
     JNO. WHITE

Proved by the oaths of Symon Gray, aged 30 years or thereabouts & Tho: Grahame, aged 30 years or thereabouts, 7 February, 1677.
Page 89.

23 November, 1677;
13 June, 1678.
WHITLOCK, THOMAS, of Sittingbourne Parish, in the
     County of Rapp^ac.

To my sisters Sarah, Elizabeth and Katherine Rowzie my Seate of Land which my Father Mr Thomas Whitlock left me on ye North side of Rapp^ac River equally to be divided amongst them when they come of ye age of Eighteene Yeares or day of Marriage which shall happen First to them and their heirs forever. To my loving brother Edward Rowzie my Cow. To my loving brother Lodowick Rowzie my Yearling All the rest of my personal Estate to my loving Brothers and Sisters Edward Lodowick John Sarah Elizabeth and Katherine Rowzie equally to be divided amongst them when they come of age. To loving Uncle Robert Gullock and loving Friend Robert Pley a mourning Ring apiece of the value of fifteen Shillings each. Executors my Uncle Robert Gullock and friend Robert Pley.
Wit. THO: ROBERTS, JONATHAN BATHO: Page 91.

26 February, 1677;
13 June, 1678.
WILLCOCKS, MATHEW, of Totaskey in ye County of Rapp^a:
     planter.

To wife Rebecca my white Mare Bonny with the bed and furniture wch is in my Roome and ye new Chest and 500 acres of Land lying next Mochotuck path My Godson Zachariah Nicholls I make my sole heire and give him all the Rest of my land and ye horse and Gunn and all my wearing Cloaths my old Chest ye bed and furniture with two paire of Sheets that is in ye Porch Chamber and ye Tables and Cupboards to stand as Heirdum for ye good of ye house Ye remaining part of ye Stock to be Equally divided betweene my wife and my Godson when they shall think fitt and if my said Godson die w^thout

Issue then his Estate to fall to my kinsman William Nutt and if he die to his Younger Brother And likewise I give to my Godson my Mill wth all ye Utensils belonging to her, and doe leave him to ye tuition and Guardianship of William Barber and John Alloway Executors William Barber and John Alloway.

Wit. Dan^{ll} X Hawkins, Thos. X Chittie, Jno. X Alloway, W^m: Barber.   Page 94.

31 March, 1678;
MOSS, THOMAS,   13 June, 1678.

To wife Elizabeth and two daughters Elizabeth and Frances all my goods Chattles Cattle horses mares household stuffe and Implements of household stuffe and all my personall Estate equally to be divided between them share and share alike my debts and funerall charges being first paid. To my two aforesaid daughters all my Lands to be Equally devided between them as they shall attaine to their respective ages Onely my Loving wife enjoying her thirds of ye Same During her life according to Law. Wife Elizabeth Executrix.

Wit. Abraham Stapp, Henry Moncaster.   Page 97.

6 March, 1676/7;
Proved by the witnesses 5 June & 7 Nov. 1678.

TALBUT, WILLIAM,

To son Thomas *Tabutt* ½ of my stock of Cattle male & female onely ye two biggest Steeres Excepted also 200 acres of Land w^{ch}: I had wth: my Wife by a Deed from her Father John Sharp dec^d. only my Wife Mary *Tabutt* to have a share in it her life according to law. To wife 50 acres of land purchased of Capt. George Morris also all my Chattels horses mares household goods and moveables she paying all my debts.

Wit. Henry Mawdsley, Thomas Harware.   Page 99.

23 November, 1672;
PETERSON, NEALE,   3 July, 1678.

To son John Peterson two cows Lye and Pye with their Increase. To daughter Mary one cow Tobey and two heifers Swan and Coale with their increase. To daughter Anne two Cows called Nobard and Toby with their Increase. If his children die then to be equally divided amongst the rest. All the rest of his estate to his wife onely my Spit and Tongs to my daughters Mary and Anne after my wifes decease.

Wit. William Johnson, Henry X Jordan.   Page 102.

14 April, 1678;
FULLERTON, JOANE,   3 July, 1678.

To Elizabeth Meades one cow called Pye. To John Topp, Jr. one cow called Muge. To Thomas Cunniers one black mare. All the rest of my worldly Estate to Robert Doewell. To Samuel Parry, Jr., one gold ring.

Wit. Sam^LL. Parry, Humphrey Perkins.   Page 104.

18 December, 1677;
GRIGORY, JOHN,   4 September, 1678.

IN THE NAME OF GOD AMEN I John Grigory being very Sick and Weak in body but in perfect mind and memory Doe make this my last Will & Testam^t: First I give my Soule to God that gave it me in a Sure and Certaine hope that after this life Ended, that at the last day my Soule & body shall be United together, & my body to the Earth to be buried in a Terestiall buriall as my Friends shall think Fitt & as for my worldly Goods I bestow as followeth Item I give unto my Sister Mary Grigory foure hundred and Eighty acres of Land being a Tract of land formerly bought by Robert Bishop of M^r: Henry Awbrey to her and her heires forever but if my Said Sister Die w^th:out Issue lawfully begotten of her, that then the said Land to Returne to the nearest of Bloud, Alsoe one pied Cow w^th: her Increase to her and her heires for-Ever, onely the first Cow Calfe, the said Cow shall bring to be delivered to Katherine Armstrong to her and her heires for Ever. Item I give to my Sister Elizabeth one Red Cow with all her Increase to her and her heires for Ever Alsoe I doe appoint my Brother Richard Grigory my whole and Sole Exec^r: of this my Will to See it performed As WITNESS my hand this 18th. of Decemb^r: 1677

Test   John Grigory
    Tho: Games
    James Fugett

THE W^TH:IN NAMED Thomas Games Doth depose that he did see the w^th:[in] mentioned John Grigory Signe Seale and publish the w^th:in mentioned to be his last Will and Testam^t: and that he was in perfect Sence and memory at ye Signing Sealing & publishing thereof to the best of his Judgment

                                        Thomas Games

Juratis Est Games in Cur Com Rapp^ac: 4°. Die 7^bris. 1678 Et Probat^r: P^r:

Sacrament Thom: Games Et Recordat^r: 5°. Die Octob^r. An^o. 1678

                        Test
                EDM^o: Crask Cl. Cur.   Page 106.

18 April, 1678;
CLARK, HENRY,   28 January, 1678/9.

To son John my bay mare with what increase she shall have after
my decease. To son-in-law Francis Gore one man servant which shall
then have his full time to serve in this country to be bought with part
of my estate by my Executrix and delivered to him. To daughter
Elizabeth wife of Argell Jacobus and the heirs of her body lawfully
to be begotten 200 acres of land next adjoining to the land of M^r
William Fauntleroy at the South West part of that devident of Land
where I now live and for want of such issue to my son John and his
heires and all my other Lands and hereditaments whatsoever provided
that Joane my wife shall enjoy the housing and plantation I now dwell
on during her natural life. All the rest of my Estate not before bequeathed I give to my said loving wife Joane whom I make Executrix
of this my will.

Wit. JOHN SAMPSON, JOHN TAVERNER,
STANLEY GOWER, aged 19 years.   Page 108.

24 March, 1677/78;
DIKE, JOHN, Sr.,   6 November, 1678.

To son John all my land and both plantations to him and his
heirs forever. Also to son John he paying my debts all my Cattle
Hogs household goods and all that appertains to me to him and his
heirs forever. Appoints son John Executor.

Wit. HENRY MAUDSLEY, DANIEL FAUTES.   Page 111.

21 August, 1678;
29 January, 1678/9.

BUTLER, AMORY, [Rev.], of the Parish of Sittingburne
and County of Rapp^ac., Clerk.

To my loving Brother Mr Wm Butler minister of Washington
Parish all my Books Sermon Noats and papers. To brother John
Butler all my wearing Cloths Linnen and Woolen and 2,000 pounds
of Tobacco and Cask. To Valentine Allen 60 pounds of Tob. in lieu
of a paire of Shooes I owe him. To my Godson Wm Pannell one Bible
and one Bible to my Godson Cawthorne. All my other Estate I
give and bequeath unto my Godson and nephew John Underwood
my debts first paid out of the same by my Executor Mr Daniel Gaines.
This my last Will and Testament Satisfying and fulfilling all therein
as shall appeare to be just and True and which he in his Conscience
knows and is perswaded soe to be Referring my sd Executor to the
assistance of my brother Wm Underwood who may give him knowledge
in my Concernes and ordering that Mr Sam^ll Bloomfield According

to his Demand be First Satisfied out of my Estate for mine and my Brother John Butler's accomodation at this house. I give unto my Executor before named his Choice of my three Bookes in my Studie. Wit. Sam^{LL} Blomfield, Law^E Rochefort.   Page 113.

23 March, 1678/9;

BUCKSOME, ANANIAS,   3 April, 1679.

Aprill Court 79 begins

IN THE NAME OF GOD AMEN The last Will and Testam^t: of Ananias ·Bucksome being Sick and weak in body, but of Perfect [mind] and memory—IMP^{is} I bequeath my Soule to God that gave it, wherein and Through the Merrits of my Savio^r: Christ Jesus I hope to Inherrit Eternall Salvation, my body to be Decently buried and my worldly goods I bequeath as Following It. I give to my Loveing wife all my worldly Estate, as Lands, Catle, Goods & whatsoever to me appertayneth, making and ordaining my said wife, *Jane Wilson* my Sole heire and Executrix as Witness my hand and Seale this 23th day of March 1678/9.

Ananias X Bucksome   Seale

SIGNED SEALED
AND ACKNOWLEDGED in the p^rsence of Us
        J^{no} Stone
            Sign
        Sarah X Bowyer

Co^{ll} John Stone aged 48 years or thereabouts being Sworne Saith that he did see the above Named Ananias Bucksome Signe Seale and Publish the above mentioned to be his last Will and Testam^t & that he was in perfect sence and memory at the Signing Sealing & publishing thereof, to the best of his Judgm^t.

John Stone

Juratus Est Stone in Cur Com

Rapp^{ac}: 3° Die April 1679
Et Probat^r: P Sacrament p^rd Stone
Et Recordat^r: X°. die Ejusd Menss. An°. Sup^rd
Test
Edm°: Crask Cl. Cur.

Ex^a.   Page 114.

15 March, 1678/9;

GOODRICH, THOMAS,   3 April, 1679.

To eldest son Benjamin 200 acres of land on the River Side which I bought of Clem^t Thresh and ½ the divident of land I now live upon with all the profits commodities and emoluments thereto belonging. Also to son Benjamin five negroes Wills, Jermine, Nan and her daughter Moll and her son Ben and one mulatto boy called Will Brandy. To son Joseph ½ the dividend of land called Matepony to him and his heires forever Devident Conteyning 1800 acres of which I will to be equally Devided into Two Moyeties and my Sonne Joseph to have his first Choice and if my Sonne Make Choice of that Moyitie which Contains the plantation and houses then my Will is that my Sonne Joseph shall build half soe much housing upon the Other Moyetie of the said land as is now upon that part he lives upon for those to whom hereafter I shall bequest it. Also to son Joseph one Negro called Saw one Negro Woman called Cutchenah and her Child that now Sucks with all the Stock that is now upon the Land wth all their increase forever. To son Charles one tract of land containing 400 acres adjoining to a Devident of Land called Buttons Range and to his Heires For Ever wth: all the profitts and commodities and three Negro Slaves Mary and her son George and one boy Manall. Also to son Charles all the profits of 600 acres of land Joining upon the Devident which I formerly Settled Upon Hoskins Pocoson. To daughter Anne 900 acres of land with the profits it being one Moyetie of a Devident of 1800 acres called Matapony as abovesaid and to the heires forever, Also to daughter Ane four Negroes Betty Watts Tho: Evans Fuller and her now Sucking child to be delivered to my said daughter upon her Marriage Day or at the age of one and twenty years which shall first come. To son Peter and to his heires forever 800 acres of land it being part of a devident of 4000 acres scituate and being upon Hoskins Pocoson and likewise six head of cattle the ½ male and the other female with all their increase. Also to son Peter two mulleto boys Isaac and Toby when my son reaches the age of twenty one. To daughter Katherine and to her heires forever 800 acres of Land it likewise being part of that Devident of 4000 acres as abovesaid and two Negro boys Kyeto and James at her marriage or at the age of twenty one which shall first happen. To eldest sons Benjamin Joseph and Charles each a feather bed and furniture and likewise the same to my eldest daughter Anne. All the rest of my estate to my wife whom I appoint Executrix and my eldest son Benjamin whom I appoint Executor. And lastly it is my will and mind and desire that no Court or Justices Whatsoever shall be concerned with any part of my Estate or cause my Executrix or Executor to give security or anywise be concerned therein. It is likewise my Will that the Crop which shall be made upon my Plantations this next ensuing yeare be at the disposall of my Executrix and Executor for the payment of my debts and supply of my family.

Wit. Christopher Hargill, Dennis Conniers, Tho: Edmondson.

Page 118.

Note. The witnesses called the testator "Col. Thomas Goodrich."

16 September, 1677;
ENGLISH, JOHN,   7 May, 1679.

To Henry Johnson one cow and 100 acres of land lying upon the head of Chiccocone. To Thomas Elvert 100 acres of land lying at the head of Chicchocone. To Richard Rice a pocket Pistoll and a holster Pistoll. To William Barber one Tenant Saw. To Wife Elizabeth English all the Rest of my Estate and doe make her my sole Executrix.
Wit. Peter Ellis, Thomas Naylor, Wᴹ: Barber.   Page 122.

25 March, 1679;
7 May, 1679.
ROBINSON, JOHN, of Farnham in Virginia.

To my deare Mother and my Brother Samˡˡ: Bayly all my Cattle at Rappᵃᶜ to be Equally Divided betwixt them the one Moyetie being for the use of my Coz: Joyce Bayly my two young Colts and one small Iron Pott and one great Chest five pewter dishes and one pewter flaggon. To my Mother (who I hereby make Executrix) one feather bed and all things thereunto belonging one great Iron Pott two Little Chests all my plate Spoones Tongs all my Linnen and all other the household lumber. To my father-in-law Wᵐ Thornbury a Spitt Table two Chairs, AndIrons and all my Cattle at Potomack. To my Bʳ Samˡˡ Bayly all my Nailes and two Gunns. To my Uncle Samˡˡ: Parrey my Mare.
Wit. John Stratton, Samᴸᴸ: Bayly.   Page 124.

28 May, 1678;
HOPEGOOD, PETER,   7 May, 1679.
Intended for England.

My whole estate (after my debts are Satisfied) to be equally divided between my daughters-in-law Frances and Elizabeth Godson and that they may be joint Executrixes in Case of Either of their Mortality before they Attaine the age of sixteen years or the Day of Marriage then the Survivor to Inherit the whole at the age or time aforesaid. I desire that my daughter Elizabeth Godson doe Continue with Thomas Roberts untill the yeare 1680 to be kept at Schoole at the Expiration of which Time (if she be willing) to be transported home with the said Roberts and to be left to the tuition of their Uncles Mʳ Paule Allistree and Mʳ John Hopegood or either of them, and that part of her Estate to be paid unto them or Either of them, for the use and benefit of my said daughter Elizabeth and in Case she be not Willing to goe home then to Remaine in the Custody of her Overseere (which she liketh best) and that part of her Estate to Remaine in the hands of the overseeres which hath her in custody to be Converted (with the advice of the two Overseeres) to the best Use for the benefit of my said daughter Elizabeth. My will and desire is that in

Case I do not Carry my Daughter Frances home with me that she Remaine in the custody of Mr Henry Smith untill the year 1680 then (if she be willing to be transported home as aforesaid and that part of her estate which belongeth unto her be paid to her Uncles or either of them for the Use and benefit of my said daughter Frances And in Case she be not willing to goe home to her Uncles then to Remaine in the custody of one or Either of her Overseers which she liketh best and that part of her Estate which belongeth unto her remaine in the custody of the respective overseeres which hath her in Custody and to be Converted (with the advice of the other two overseeres) to the best use for the benefitt of my said Daughter Frances And in Case I doe Carry my Daughter Frances home with me then all my Estate which remaineth in Virginia I doe give unto my daughter Elizabeth to be disposed of as aforesaid. My will and desire is that the Charges of my Daughter's Maintenance be paid out of my Estate. He appoints as Overseers of his Will his trusty and well beloved friends M^r: Henry Smith, Mr William Young and Thomas Roberts.

Wit. Tho: Grahame, Alex^r Wetherstone, aged 27 years or
thereabouts.   Page 126.

                                                    22 April, 1679;
                                                    21 May, 1679.
EVERIST, (EVEREST), JOHN,

To Cozen Margaret Everist one bay mare with the female increase to her and her heirs forever, also one dark gray mare about two years old with the female increase to her and her heirs forever. I will also that my Cozen Margaret Everist shall at the day of Marriage have both Male and Female increase to her and her heirs forever.

Wit. Tho: Everest, aged 30 years or thereabouts,
     W^m X Creswell.   Page 129.

                                                    22 March, 1678/9;
TAYLOR, RICHARD,   21 May, 1679.

To sons Richard and Symon my plantation and lands thereunto belonging being 200 acres and if my son Richard when he comes to age will sell unto his Bro. Symon his part then his brother shall give him 5000 pounds of Tob. and if not then the Land and Plantation to be equally divided and to cast lots both of them for their shares and I give to each of them two Cows with all their increase both male and female to take their Choice. To daughter Constance seven head of Cattle five female with all their increase both male and female and two steeres one mare and to my son Richard one mare and to my son Symon one mare and if any of them miscarry betwixt this and the last of May then what of them remains to be equally divided amongst my three Children. I understanding my wife to be in a weak condition that my loving neighbors John English Peter Ellis and Edward Friar would one a week give my children advice and that they may be kept upon the plantation with my servant and in case my wife die I appoint my loving friend Coll⁰. Leroy Griffin sole Executor.

Wit. Eliz^B. X English, aged 48 years or thereabouts, Eliz. X Wood, aged 35 years or thereabouts, John English.

Page 131.

17 March, 1678/9;
BOWLER, THOMAS, Esqr.,   2 July, 1679.

All my just debts both here and in England to be satisfied within a year after my decease. It is my will that my Tobacco which is shipt for England be consigned to Major Robert Bristow. To son James Bowler all that parcell of land more or less where the Manor House Standeth and all other houses belonging to the said quantity of Land being about 940 acres. Also to son James Bowler 500 acres of land called by the name of Mary Gold. I desire that all the said houses at the Manor House and the Quarter be kept in good repaire till the said Orphan James Bowler come to the age of twenty one. To daughter Elizabeth Bowler 500 acres of land part of it being in the plantation that was John Webbs and the rest of it to be laid out for the quiet possession and enjoying of her and her heirs forever. Also to daughter Elizabeth six cows with calves or with calf one bull two young mares and a young horse which my deare wife shall think convenient for her and six sows and one bore her mother's gold wedding ring and her embroidered looking glass. To my deare child Anne 500 acres of land Joyning upon my son James Bowler's land called by the name of Mary Gold. All the rest of my personal estate I give equally to be divided after my debts are paid to my deare and most excellent wife Tabitha Bowler and to my two good children James and Anne Bowler to them and their heirs forever. But if my said deare wife should please to marry it is my Will that then the personall Estate may be equally divided either by out cry or otherwise as my overseers shall think it most convenient for the securing of it into Tobacco or money against they shall come to age. Requests that his two most Honored and worthy friends Coll Nicholas Spencer and Capt Thomas Gouldman to be overseers of his Will and be assistant to his wife.

Wit. Robert Barrett, aged 29 years or thereabouts,
Nich⁰ Franklin, aged 31 years or thereabouts.   Page 133.

12 June 1679;
HUDSON, THOMAS,   5 November, 1679.

To daughter Mary Yates all my Lands and right to Land in Virginia after my and my wives decease. To daughter Mary Yates one young Mare two cow yearlings and four sow shoats about six months old with all their increase. Desires that all his just debts be paid and then the remaining part of his Estate to be equally divided between his loving wife Mary and his son-in-law Elias Yates and it is my Will that the mare yearlings and shoats above mentioned with their Male and Female increase may remaine to my said daughter and her heirs forever. Executor my son-in-law Elias Yates.

Wit. RICHARD GLOVER, W^M THORNTON.   Page 140.

28th January, 1668/9;

Recorded XX9° Die X^{bris} 1679.

WALKER, SARAH,

28th: January, 1668/9.

I Sarah Walker Doe give and bequeath unto Coll John Walkers Six Daughters as followeth, IMPRIMIS Six Young Negroes Item I give to Anne Paine the Negro Boy Cald Richard, Item Given to Francis [Frances] Walker the Negro Boy Cald Peter—Item I give unto Jane Walker the Negro Girle Cal'd Deborah, Item I give unto Elizabeth Walker the Negro Girle Call'd Suzanna Item I give unto Sarah Walker the Negro girle Cal'd Mareay at my decease Item I give unto Easter Walker the Negro Boy Cal'd Palmar when she Marrieth, Item I give unto Anne Payne one Young Filley allmost a Yeare Old and to the Rest of her five Sisters every one a mare Foale as Soone as it pleaseth God to send them—Item I give unto Francis [Frances] Walker five Cows when she marrieth, Item I give unto Jane Walker five Cows when she Marrieth, Item I give to Elizabeth Walker five Cows when she marrieth Item I give unto Sarah Walker five Cows when she Marrieth—January 28th: in the Yeare of our Lord 1668, Item I give unto Esther Walker Five Cows when she Marrieth, Item I give to Anne Payne, Francis [Frances] Walker Jane Walker and Elizabeth Walker all the plate that was their Fathers to be Equally divided amongst them. Item I give to my sonne Henry one Silver Beaker, and a Silver Spoone at my Decease, Item I give unto my Daughter Mary Burden one Silver Tankard & one Silver Spoone at my Decease Item I give unto my Daughter Sarah Walker, one Great Silver Salt Cellar & one Silver Spoone at my Decease Item I give unto my Daughter Esther Walker one Silver bason & one Silver spoone at my Decease Item I give unto Francis [Frances] Walker when she marrieth ten pewter Dishes Item I give unto Jane Walker when she marrieth ten pewter Dishes Item I give unto Elizabeth Walker when she marrieth Ten pewter Dishes Item I give unto my Sonne Henry when he Cometh to age one Feather Bed and Boulster, one Rugg, one paire of Blankets, one paire of pillowes & pillowbeeres, and one paire of Sheetes, Item I give to my Daughter Mary Burden one Feather bed one boulster one paire of Blanketts Item one paire

of Sheats with a Couple of pillows and pillowbeares at her Marriage
AS WITNESS my hand and Seale the Day and Yeare abovesd

FRAN^s: SETLE   SARAH WALKER   Seale

RICH^D: FOX
                    Recordat: xx9º. Die x^{bris}. 79
                         Test
                    EDM^o: CRASKE Cl Cur   Page 142.
                         Ex^a.

                                        1 March, 1678;
LUNN, WILLIAM,   21 January, 1679.

To son Roger the plantation I now live on and to his heirs forever
if he lives to be at age and if he dies before he attaines the age of
twenty one then to my daughter Mary and if my wife be with child
at this p^rsent time and lives to be delivered of a Boy that he shall
heire my land before my daughter and if a Girle that she shall inherit
halfe the land with her sister Mary and in case they all dye and my
wife Alicia Lives to Have any children then to them and their heires
for ever and if not to Giles Webb the sonne of John Webb onely my
wife her life excepted in it. Wife to be Executrix of all my goods and
chattels moveables and unmoveables conditionally that she gives out
of the Estate to my Sonne Roger and Daughter Mary each of them
three Yeares old heifers to be Delivered within twenty six months time
after the date hereof with their Increase Untill Such time as they
Shall Come to Lawfull Yeares of Age and in the meantime my wife
to have the whole managing of all.

Wit. THOMAS TAYLOR, aged 27 years or thereabouts,
    EDWARD JONES, aged 27 years or thereabouts.
                                        Page 144.

                                        20 November, 1678;
SMITH, THOMAS,   25 November, 1679.

To Sonne John my Long Gunn and Shot Bag two cows two heifers
and two Calves which are his own property and two sows which are
his own and half my Devident of Land Lying on the South West Side.
To sonne Thomas the other ½ of my land on the North East Side
of my Devident and my Short Gunn and a sow and one pied Heiffer
and her Calfe. To daughter Elizabeth one heiffer. To daughter Sarah
two sow shoates. To my two daughters one black Stone Horse to be
sold to buy them Cattle and each of them one Iron Pott. To wife one
feather bed two blankets a rug one boulster and two pillows one iron
pott and all the rest of ye household goods which I have not already
disposed of. Appoints as Overseer friend John Cheyney.

Wit. RICHARD BROOKS, aged 41 years or thereabouts,
    FRANCES X STAFFORD, aged 45 years or thereabouts.
                                        Page 147.

3 September, 1673;
WEIRE, WALTER,   5 May, 1680.

To wife Mary Weire my Land Cattle household stuffe moveables
and immoveables and whatsoever Worldly Estate unto mee belongeth
my debts being first satisfied. Wife Mary Executrix.

Wit. THOMAS ERVIN, WILL SARGENT.   Page 149.

3 March, 1679;
WAIGHT, JOHN,   3 September, 1679.

To daughter Mary Waight the upper part of my Land on the
upper Side the Creek and 100 acres of Land more I give to Elizabeth
Vickers w^ch: lyeth Back of That I formerly Sould to James Jackson
and my Sonne Robert Waight the Remainder of the Seate the whole
being 700 acres and my Daughter Mary to have Timber of her Brother
Waight's Land for her use in building and what moveable Estate I
have to be Equally Devided betwixt my Sonne and Daughter John and
Mary and my Sonne Robert to be at age at eighteen years and I doe
make John Vickers and William Griffin my Overseers to Look after
my Estate untill the one is Married and the other at age and the Estate
to remaine in the hands of John Vickers.

Wit. GEORGE LODGE, STEPHEN FUELL, aged 26 years or thereabouts.
                                                        Page 151.

3 March, 1674;
JONES, RICHARD,   15 May, 1680.

To eldest son John Jones the land I now live upon being upwards
of 200 acres 1 cow and heifer. To my young son Richard Jones & my
daughter Jane Jones 500 acres of land to be equally divided between
them this land lies betwixt Coll° Goodrich & Mr Brewerton's land &
bounds upon them. To Richard 1 cow and heifer. My two sons shall
be at age at 18 years to receive their estates into their hands & my
daughter Jane for to have her Estate when she is married And my
Childrens Cattle shall Runn upon the Eldest Brothers Plantation &
my Children shall have their Increase of their Cattle. Next I give &
bequeath to my loving Wife Avis Jones my mare & the Increase to my
Children from the Eldest to the Youngest till they have Every one one
& if the Eldest Dies to Fall to the other & so From one to the Other
And All the Rest of my Goods & Cattle to my Wiffe & two maide
Servants those Children shall receive their Cattle in the yeare 1676
the Aprill following & for to Runne upon the Plantacon as before
mentioned Next I give to a child which is my servant which is called
by the name of Susana Barance one two Yeare old Heifer & her
Increase & this heifer & her increase to be Delivered at 12 Yeares of

Age & if any of the said Richard Jones his Children dies their Estate for to Fall From one to the other. Wife Executrix & Mr George Morris & Mr Thomas Cooper to be Overseers.

his mark

Wit. JOHN M PRICE, JOHN SOPER, aged 40 years or thereabouts.

Page 153.

HOLLISTER, WILLIAM,
18 August, 1680;
3 die 7ᵇʳˢ, 1680.

To Elizabeth Bayly Junior my Chist. My Executor Robert Baylie Jr. to receive all such Debts as are due to me Either by Bill or Accompts or any other means and to take an Account of ye Tobacco I have shipt Home whether to Plymouth or Elsewhere and after my Debts paid to be accountable for all ye Remaining Part of my Estate to my loving Brother Thomas Hollister Living in Temple parish in Bristoll.

Wit. GILES WEBB, THO: TAYLOR, aged 30 years or thereabouts.

Page 155.

LOVE, JAMES,
"Rappᵃᶜ: River in Virgᵃ: Aprill 4ᵗʰ: 1681";
6 April, 1681.

To Mr. John More Living in the parish of Sᵗ. James in the Citty of Bristoll Comander of the Shipp Alexander all such Tobacco that shall arise Due to me from Mʳ Richard Farrington Living in Great Wiccocomacoe being my Aturney And Mʳ: John Hawkins Living in Deep Creek in Rappᵃᶜ River and as alsoe what Tobacco or Tobaccos shall arise from his being my Aturney. To my aforesd Commandʳ one Horse Bridle and Saddle and one long pare of Fetters a large Sedar Chest full of Books the Catalogue of which books will be found in my Little Chest in a pocket Case. Another Sea Chest with a black Coate and a paire of Breeches a large bell mettle morter weighing about sixty pounds a back Rapier a large Desk full of Drawers and many other papers and books in it all which is in the hands of the aforesaid Richard Farrington. To my aforesd Comandʳ my Wages Surgery Chest and other Chest and Cloathes and all Triffling things Either a board or a shore that may be Called mine. To my aforesd Comandʳ all the Tobacco left in my Atturney's hands in Maryland in Little Choptank.

No witnesses. Not signed.

Proved by the oaths of Richard Hobbs (he signed as Richard *Webbs*), aged 37 years or thereabouts, Morgan Thomas, aged 19 years or thereabouts.   Page 165.

29 January, 1675;
BROOKS, THOMAS,   8 die 7ᵇʳⁱˢ 1681.

After my debts are paid I give to Wᵐ Barber all yᵗ I have and
doe make him my sole Executor together wᵗ is due to me and pay
what I owe as farr as it will goe and yᵉ Remainder to take to himself.
Wit. JOHN ENGLISH, THOMAS X COLLY, aged 47 years or thereabouts.
Page 167.

4 March, 1680;
HOWELL, GEORGE,   2 November, 1681.

To son George my young mare and the rest of my estate to my
wife.
Wit. ROBERT CLOSKE, RICHARD X PEACOCK, aged 50 years or thereabouts, JAMES X PRICHARD (or PRITCHARDS), aged 53 years or
thereabouts.   Page 169.

25 November, 1681;
GRIFFIN, WILLIAM,   1 March, 1681.

His land to his son William Griffin. To daughter Anne a cow
named Rose with all her increase. To daughter Elizabeth one cow
named Browning with all her increase. To daughter Joyce one cow
named Blackface, with all her increase. To son William Griffin one
cow named Madam. To each child a horse or mare or Either of them
that shall be the produce of Two Mares one called Bess the other two
year old. To wife my horse with all other stock that belongs to my
plantation. To son William a Copper Kettle and two Guns when he
is of age. To Mʳ William Moss and Mʳ Wᵐ Sergant each one pair of
gloves each and he appoints them Overseers of his Will.
Wit. Wᴹ LATHOOPE, THOMAS X JAMES, aged 36 years or thereabouts.
Page 170.

27 September, 1680;
GOOSE, THOMAS,   3 May, 1682.

To Bridget Eale all my lands and right to Lands in Virginia
during her life also to her all my other estate both moveable and unmoveable only During her life and after the Decease of the said Bridget
Eale my lands and estate shall be equally divided between George
Eale Wᵐ Eale Jr., and Charity Eale Bridget's Children to them and
their heirs forever. Also to Charity Eale a young mare about two
years old and · all her male and female increase forever. The said
Bridget Eale to have only the use of the said estate during her Life
for her Maintenance but not to convert the said Estate to any other
use whereby to Deprive the abovesaid Children. Executrix Bridget
Eale.
Wit. RICHARD GLOVER, aged 44 years or thereabouts, HENRY CLARK,
MARY GLOVER, THOMAS LEWIS.   Page 171.

19 April, 1676;
KIRK, ELIZABETH,   2 January, 1677.

IN THE NAME OF GOD AMEN I Elizabeth Kirk Sick in body
but in good and perfect memory Blessed be God doe now appoint
Constitute and ordaine this my Last Will and Testam^t: First I bequeath my Soule into the hands of the Almighty God the Father
Everlasting and my body to be buried At the Disposing of my Friends
and my Worldly Estate in man^r: and Forme Following Imp^{ris}: For
my Land I give with what housing is Upon it to my Sonn John Kirk
his heires for Ever And the Rent I give to my Two Daughters Mary
and Elizabeth that is to say the Rent of my Land till such time as
my Son John shall Attaine to the Yeares of Eighteen, then the Land
to Come into the hands of my Son as abovesaid and I give my Wearing Cloathes with my Stock being two Cows and one Sow to my
Daughters as above mentioned with their Increase, And for my Sonn
I Freely Give him to the Tuition of my Wellbeloved friend Henry
Lucas till such time as he shall Attaine to the Age of Eighteen Yeares
And Further I doe Intrust the said Henry Lucas to Receive the Rent
of the abovesaid Land and to keep it in his hands till such Time as
my Boy ataine to the Yeares abovementioned and then to be Account-
able for the same IN WITNESS whereof I have hereunto Sett my
Hand and Seale this 19th: Aprill Anno q^r:dom 1676

SIGNED Sealed   ⎫   the Marke & Seale of
and Delivered in the p^{r}sence ⎬   ELIZABETH X KIRK   Seale
Of us ——————   ⎭

THOMAS TAYLOR
HENRY LUCAS

I Henry Lucas witness hereto doe Declare Upon my Oath that
I saw the Testator Sett her hand and Seale to the above Written Will
and also Doe Testifie that I saw Thomas Tayler WITNESS hereto
Sett his hand Likewise This I Testifie on my Oath

P^{me}: HENRY LUCAS

Juratus Est Henry Lucas in Cur Com Rapp^{ac}: 2do: Die Januarij
Anno 1677   Test
                                   EDM^o: CRASKE Cl Cur
Recordat^r: 1mo. die Junij Anno 1682
                        Test EDM^o: CRASKE Cl Cur
            Ex^a.   Page 174.

26 March, 1679;
BAGWELL, (BAGWILL), ROGER,   6 July, 1679.

To friend John Alloway my horse that is in the Country Services.
To friend Samuel Samford my horse called Lawrence. To Giles
Webb, J^r. son to John Webb my young horse on the South Side of
Rapp^{ac}: River. To friend Thomas Taylor my mare that is at my
Land Lords Samfords. To my Executor my two Chests that is at my

said Land Lords house and all that shall be found therein Debts obligations and papers excepted. Also to my Executor my gun. To friend Edwin Conway twenty shillings in money to buy a Ring. All my debts that I justly owe to be paid. All the remainder of my estate to my deare brother Andrew Bagwell in Apson in the County of Devon in the Kingdom of England. Executor my friend Edward Jones.

Wit. JAMES SAMFORD, aged 55 years or thereabouts,
EDWIN CONWAY, age 25 years or thereabouts.   Page 176.

COLE, ROBERT,	7 February, 1681; 6 September, 1682.

IN the Name of God Amen I Robert Cole being now at this present time very sicke and weake but in perfect memory for the which I doe give praise unto Almighty God I do hereby make my Last will and testament as followeth

Imprimis I do bequeath my soule unto Almighty God hoping and trusting through the meritorious death and passion of my only Saviour Jesus Christ to receive everlasting Life and my body to be buried at the will and discretion of my Executors if it shall please God to call me out of this life.

2ly I do hereby give and bequeath unto my sonne Robert Cole three cows being young cowes and my mare and all her increase that shall happen to come of her only the first fold and that I do give unto my well beloved wife my sonne to have all the female increase of the above said Cows.

3ly I do give and bequeath unto my well beloved wife Mary Cole all the rest of my personall Estate my debts being paid my wife having the charge of my sonnes Cowes and his mare during her life or till my son comes to eighteen years of age & then he to have the whole disposal of them himself & if my wife shall happen to dye before my sonne comes of eighteen years old then my will is that my friend William Davis shall take my sonne and all that he has or doth belong unto him & keepe him and what he hath until he comes of age.

4ly I do make my wife Mary Cole my whole & sole Ext\rx.

In confirmation I have hereunto set my hand & seal anno domini one thousand six hundred & eighty & one february the 7th Day.

Signed Sealed & declared
in the presence of us
NICHOLAS YEATES
the marke of
MARY X YEATES

ROBERT R COLE   Seale
his
mark

Proved by thee oaths of the witnesses, Nicholas Yeates, aged 33 years or thereabouts and Mary his wife about 19 years of age, in Rappahannock County Court 6th die 7bris 1682 and probated same date

Recorded 21 September, 1682.
Test EDMᵒ CRASKE Cl. Cur.   Page 178.

Wills in the Record Book entitled Deeds, &c., No. 6, 1682-1686.

Dated————————, 1675,
Sworn to 6to die 7bris 1682,
Probated 26 January, 1682.

ASHTON, JOHN, of Stafford County,

To loving wife Elizabeth if she will come and live here all my whole estate both personall and real during her life but if she will not then I doe bind over my Estate to pay her twenty pounds Ster. p. year or one hundred and fifty Ster. which she would rather have. To Thomas Bunbery and his wife five pounds Ster. To Capt. John Aston twenty shillings. I doe make my Brother James Ashton my whole Executor and the heires of his body forever but in Case he have none then after his decease to my Couzen John Ashton of Russell Street at the Adam and Eve in London and to his heires forever.
Wit. DOMINICK RICE, ROBERT MASSESE.   Page 1.

15————————;
SARGENT, WILLIAM,   14 April, 1683.

I dispose of my worldly estate as followeth after my funerall charges debts and Legacies paid. To son George all my lands in Virga or elsewhere to be delivered to him by my Executors hereafter named when he shall attain to the age of twenty years also to my son George all my personall estate together with the produce thereof to be delivered to him as soon as he shall attaine to the age of twenty years aforesaid. If my Executors hereafter named shall think fitt to bring my perishable goods to an appraisement or to be sold at an outcry then the produce thereof to be delivered to my son George at the age abovesaid. My will and desire is that one diaper table Cloath fifteen napkins a bell mettle pot And a feather bed and furniture ten breeding Cows A bull and my Mares Remaine unsold with their Encrease And that the said Cattle and Mares Remain on the Plantation and lands whereon I now live And the encrease to be delivered to my son George at the age aforesaid. What other goods my Executors shall keep and think fitt not to be sold or appraised to Remaine in their Custody And to be delivered to my son George at the age aforesaid. My will is that out of ye produce of what goods my Executors shall make sale of that it be laid out in good Non household stuff and such other necessaries as they shall think fitt for the benefit of my son George and his Plantations to be delivered to him at the age abovesaid. My will is that both my Plantations be kept employed by my Executors And that my houses and fences be kept in Repair until my son shall Attain to the age above said And that one sixty foot tobacco house be built on the Plantation where I now live about two years before he attain to his said age. It is my will that my Executors give a lease to Richard

Mathews of the land he now lives on until my son George comes to the age aforesaid he paying the quit Rents during ye time. In case my said son shall dye (wch God forbid) before he attain to the age of twenty years then I give unto Richard Mathews his heirs and assigns forever ye Plantation whereon he now lives in the fforest with a hundred acres adjoining it. In case of my sons death above said ——————— unto William Whitridge his heirs and assigns forever ——————— Son of John Whitridge one hundred acres of land of the same dividend adjoining on the dividing land between Mrs Joane Clark and mine. In case of my sons death as aforesaid I give unto Will Warren his heirs and assigns forever son of John Warren one hundred acres of land of the same divident adjoining on Will Whitridge Richard Mathews and John Bowen. In case of my sons death as aforesaid I give unto Henry Feild his heirs and assigns forever son of Abraham ffeild decd one hundred acres of land of the same divident Crossing the lines of Will Whitridge And William Warren to John Bowens line and back to the dividing line of Mrs Joane Clark and mine. In case of my sons death as aforesaid I give unto Will Griffin his heirs and assigns forever son of Will Griffin decd fifty acres of land the same divident beginning at the great Swamp of his fathers line running along the said line to the line of Henry feild afores^d. In case of my sons death as aforesaid I give unto Frances Sterne her heirs and assigns forever daughter of David Sterne and Rebeccah Wells her heirs and assigns forever daughter of Barnaby Wells the residue of the said land in the forest aforesaid to be equally divided between them quantity for quantity and quality for quality. In case of my sons death aforesaid I give unto John Deane his heirs and assigns forever son of John Deane one of my Executors hereafter named all the plantation with the land belonging whereon I now live together with ten Cattle that is to say six cows and one bull and three steeres Alsoe the hogs on the said land belonging to me. In case of my sons death aforesaid ye Residue of my Estate to be distributed among the poorest and most incapable of living of my God Children According to ye discretion of my Executors if they think fitt. To every and each of my friends here named George Jones to Honoria his wife to John Weire to Mr Daniel Gaines to Mr Thomas Perkins to Mrs. Jane Deane wife of John Deane one of my Executors to Mrs. Martha Taylor twenty shillings apiece to buy them mourning Rings. To each of my Executors hereafter named twenty shillings apiece to buy them mourning Rings. It is my will that my said Son remain with his God father and Godmother until he attaine to the age aforesaid and to be brought up to learn to Read write and Cast accounts and the Grammer Rules if possible. And last I ordaine and appoint Capt George Taylor John Deane and Mrs Elizabeth Jones Exrs. of this my last will and Testament.

Wit. ALEX. DONIPHAN, aged 30 years or thereabouts, REES EVANS, aged 30 years or thereabouts, JOHN MILLS, age 36 years or thereabouts.   Page 3.

8 March, 1682;
CLARKE, JOAN,*   3 May, 1683.

To my two daughters Ann Gower and Elizabeth Jacobus all my wearing apparel to be equally divided between them. To Stanley Gower the son of Francis and Ann Gower one cow with all her increase forEver to be delivered to the said Stanley the next Spring shall be Twelve month after my decease. To Elizabeth Jacobus daughter of Angell Jacobus and Elizabeth that feather bed I generally used to lye upon with the bolster Rugg and two feather pillows. Also to the said daughter of Angell Jacobus one cow with all her increase for ever to be delivered the next Spring shall be twelve month after my decease. To son John Clarke all my other estate (except what is above specified) as household stuff and all other Hereditam^ts and all other personall Estate as slaves cattle hoggs and a horse called Button And everything else I do possess with whether debts or otherways only what I above give to my daughters and their children excepted. It is my will that my son John remove nothing from the Plantation I now live on till he comes to the age of one and twenty. I also give to my son John a Certain Tract of Land that belongeth to me of seven hundred ninety and two and one halfe (792½) acres that lyeth upwards upon Rapp^ah River and nigh unto one William Sargent to him my said son and his heirs forever but if my said son should die without issue then the said tract of land to be divided between the heirs of the bodies of my two daughters Ann Gower and Elizabeth Jacobus. Appoints her son John Clarke her sole Executor. To Francis Gower son of Francis and Ann Gower one cow to be delivered the next Spring Come twelve month after my decease the wch Cow I give with its increase for Ever. This Cow is to be excepted from those Cattle I give my son John as well as the other two I gave my Grandchildren Stanley Gower and Elizabeth Jacobus. I desire my trusty and welbeloved ffriend Co^ll John Stone of Rapp^ac County to guide and direct and counsel my son John Clarke till he Comes to ye age of one and twenty.

Wit. ISAAC WRIGHT, EDMUND NORTHEN, aged 30 years or thereabouts, THOMAS X HART, WILLIAM WARD, aged 28 years or thereabouts.

Page 4.

5 March, 1682/3;
MILLS, JOHN,   26 June, 1683.

Very sick and weak of body but perfect of sence.

To sonn Robert Mills one hundred and fourty acres of land bounding upon a deep Swamp Joyning upon Anthony North excepting the mount valay and ye North side of the Valley which I doe reserve for my two younger Sonns for timber. To Sonn John Mills one hundred and fourty Acres of Land bounding upon his Brother Robert. The remaining of the said Divident to Land to be equally divided betwixt

───────────

*Signed *Jone* Clarke to original will.

the two younger Brothers Henry and James Mills and if either of them die without issue ye Survivor of either of them to have all the Land to himselfe. To my two daughters Martha and Jane one heifer apiece and if either of the said heifers should dy without Increase they are to be made good out of the stock. To my son James Mills one yearling Cow Calf of the breed of the Cow called Cherry. To my son Henry Mills one cow his Choice out of the Stock. To the two younger Brothers one Mare and her Increase betwixt them both also to them one ffeather bed betwixt them but they are not to take it out of the house as long as the aforesaid James Mills doth Stay with his Mother. To my son John Mills one long gun. Wife Executrix.

Wit. JOHN KINGE, aged 26 years or thereabouts,
    JOHN ROBERTS, aged 35 years or thereabouts,
    WILL X MACKENNY, aged 60 years or thereabouts.

Page 6.

                                        20 July, 1683;
CRASK, EDMUND,   1 August, 1683.

I will that all those debts that I Shall happen to Justly owe at ye time of my decease be paid & satisfied by my Executors hereafter named.

I will that Elizabeth Moss and ffrances Moss be paid their equall shares of their deceased fathers estate According to the tenn^r. of the Inventory & appraisement of my estate by my Executor hereafter named. I give unto my well beloved wife Elizabeth one Negro woman Called fflora and my mourning ring to her and her heirs forever I give unto my son John Crask one young negro boy called Michall & my sword and belt unto him and his heirs forever. I give to my Daughter Ellen Crask one young Negro girl called Jenny and her own Mothers Cabinett to her & her heirs forever. I give to my son John six hundred and fifty acres of land being part of the dividend formerly belonging to M^r. Thomas Button deceased Called the Range wch was lately granted to me by Escheat to him and his heirs forever. I give to my Daughter Ellen a Tract of Land Containing three hundred acres Lying near to the said Range land wch I purchased of Robert and George Pley to her and her heirs forever. All ye rest of my psonall estate of what nature or kind soever it be I give to my well beloved wife Elizabeth to my son John and to my Daughter Ellen to be equally divided between them.

Wife to be Executrix and son John Executor of this my last Will & Testament and I do desire my honoured friends Lt. Col. Wm Loyd & Mr Henry Awbrey to be assisting to them in advising them in the management of my Estate & I do give to each of them A Mourning Ring of fifteen sh. price for their pains & Care and Likewise I desire the Worthy Court of Rapp^ak to be Aiding & assisting to my wife and Children for the procuring what Clerks fees shall be due to me in this County of Rapp^ac or Elsewhere And what the Sheriff shall be deficient in Collecting I humbly desire they will give a power to Thomas New to Collect the tob. that shall be found due to me and pay the debts And use all means possibly he can for the Recovery of them And for what Tob he shall so Collect and pay he to Receive his full Sallery for the same he paying to my sd. Executor the Remainder in ye County of Rapp^ac.

Wit. HENRY NEWTON, aged 29 years or thereabouts,
        THO: NEW, THOMAS HERBERT.   Page 9.

16 February, 1679;
22 May, 1684.

MILLER, SYMON, of the ffreshes of Rapp^a aged seaven and thirty years or thereabouts of true and perfect memory.

To son Symon Miller ½ of the divident of land I now live on to him and his heirs forever. And my son Symon to clear and plant as he shall think fitting in his Mothers lifetime upon the said dividant excepting the Plantation Also to son Symon a sorrel Mare with a white blaze in the face and all her increase to him forever. In case I dye it is my will that my son Symon be sent home the next yeare for England. To son William the other ½ dividant of Land to him and his heirs forever and a chestnut Mare with her increase forever and full power I give to my son William to Cleare and plant as he shall think fitting upon any part of the said dividant. To son John Miller two hundred acres of land adjoining to Dr Reynolds to him and his heirs forever and a black mare with a hook brand on the near buttock and her increase forever. To my daughter Susanna Miller fower hundred eight acres and a halfe (408½) the land being the ½ dividend of land adjoining to Co^l Cadwallader Jones on the head of Pumansinn to her and her heirs forever and my old mare with her increase forever. To my daughter Isabella Miller the other halfe of the dividend at Peumansinn to her and her heirs forever And a black mare about two years old branded with SM on the near buttock. To daughter Margaret Miller two hundred acres of land on ye back of my land Adjoining to Doctor Reynolds to her and her heirs forever and a brown mare branded SM with her increase forever. Lastly I leave my wife full executrix and the rest of my Estate I give to my wife to bring up my Children and to be at her disposing after my decease my debts and other necessary Charges being paid. And in case my wife dye before she marryeth the rest of my Estate to be divided equally betwixt my children. It is my will that the three mares given to my son Will and my son John and my daughter Susan that the foales they go withall shall go into the stock and if any of them be a mare foale it is to be given to my wifes son Anthony Prosser and if they do not bring a Mare foale my wife as she thinks fitting is to dispose of soe much of the stock to purchase her son Anthony a Mare foale and all the male increase of all the Mares except my sonn Symons to goe into y[e] former Stock till my Children Come to y[e] age of fourteen then male and female the children to have y[e] full increase and if any of these Children dye before they Come of lawfull age that then that Estate land or Mares to be equally divided among the survivors and if any of the Childrens Mares dye Then my wife is to buy out of the said stock to make good the same And the sons of M[r] Prosser are to have every one of them a heifer delivered to them one after another by my Executrix after my decease. To wife Margaret the Plantation and houses I now live in during her natural life and in case my wife should marry one that should lett the house and Orchard goe to ruin Then she is to return to her thirds according to law. I make M[r] James Ashton overseer of my estate and children and the said M[r] Ja: Ashton to dispose of the said Children at sixteen years of age as he thinks fitt and in case the said M[r] James Ashton dyeth then the children to be at their own disposing if they like to go to any handy craft they have a mind unto.

Wit. NATHANIEL TOMLIN, FFRANCIS THORNTON, JAMES TAYLOR.

Proved by Francis Thornton, aged 32 years or thereabouts, 5 7[bris] 1683, who calls him Cap[t]. Symon Miller, and James Taylor, 7 May, 1684.   Page 10.

GEORGE, THOMAS, Gent.,   17 August, 1683; 7 die 9[bris] 1683.

IN THE NAME OF GOD AMEN the seaventeenth day of August Anno Dom 1683 I Thomas George of the County of Rapp[ac]. in Virginia Gent. being Sick and weak in body But of Sound mind & memory (praised be God) Doo Therefore make and Declare my last Will and Testam[t]. in maner and fform following (Viz[t]) ffirst & principally I Recomend my Soul back into the hands of the Almighty and my body I Comitt unto the earth to be Decently buried at the Discretion of my Deare Wife Trusting and Assuredly believing it Shall partake of that Glorious Resurection purchased by that precious Blood & meritts of o[r]. Dear Lord & Saviour Jesus Christ And for that worldly Estate God of his goodness hath Blessed me wth. after my debts paid and funerall Charges Discharged I Dispose Thereof as is herein expressed (That is to say) I Give and bequeath unto my s[d] Deare and welbeloved Wife Elizabeth George my white horse called Swan and another pacing horse w[ch]. I exchanged wth. m[r] Bray for another on Condition that she Deliver unto my Daughter Margarret a horse when she Attaines the age of twelve years Item I give and bequeath unto my Son Leroy George my horse Called Spiff with all the furniture I have belonging to a mans horse Togeather with all my books Item I give and bequeath unto my Said Daughter Margarret Twenty Thousand pounds of tobacco & Cask to be paid her by my Executo[rs]. hereafter Named Or the Land I purchased and bought of Edward Lewis Scituate in ffarnham parish in the said County near Totaskey Creek to her and her heires forever to be at her Choice and Election when

she Attaines to the age of twenty one years or Day of Mariage w^ch.
shall first happen Item I give and Devise my Plantation Land &
housing whereon I now live And ye Plantation In Case my Daughter
Shall make Choice of the Twenty thousand pounds of Tob as aforesd
which I bought of Edward Lewis unto my Sd Sonn Leroy George and
my Said Wife to be held by them During her natural Life and after
her Decease to the heires of the body Lawfully to be Begotten of my
Sd Sonn and for want of such Issue to my sd Daughter Margaret and
the heires of her body Lawfully to be begotten And for want of Such
Issue to the heires & assignes of my said Wife Elizabeth for Ever And
my True Intent and meaning is that in case my said son dye Leaving
yssue of his body before my said wife Then She to have no benefit
by Right of Survivo^rship but that part and portion in the sd Land
and premises Decend on Such yssue of my said Sonn as might belong
unto him Liveing Item all the Rest & Residue of my said Estate be
it Ready mony, Goods, Cattle Servants horses Mares or other Cattles
I give and bequeath unto my said Wife and Sonn Equally to be
Devided between them part and portion alike but my minde and will
is that my wife Shall and may Enjoy the male Cattle belonging to
my Son & benefitt of the Servants for the better maintenance & bringing up of my said Children until my sd Sonn Attaine the age of
Seaventeen years Att wch. Time I doo hereby appoint That what is
hereby given to him be at his own dispose and to be Invested therein
as in Case he had Attained the full age of Twenty one yeares And to
p^rvent appraisement That

                                        Tho. George   Seal

Comonly Viperously Eats out the Sides of Orphants Estates my
Request is that my trusty and welbeloved ffreinds m^r. Edwin Conway
m^r. Arthur Spicer and Jno. Taverner take on them the Charitable
oversight of this my Will And to be Aiding And Assisting in the
Execution thereof unto my Executo^rs. And that they would Inventory
my personall Estate And to the best of their Judgm^ts. Devid the
Same in Specificall goods and Chattles as they Shall then be And to
take a particular acc^t. of what Shall fall to my Sonns part (the Goods
& Chattles being Delivered to my wifes Custody again) And the
same Acc^t. being signed Receipt wayes to putt upon Record But if my
wife remarry Then Such husband to give Security for my Sonns part
to be Delivered him as aforesaid Item I Give and bequeath unto my
sd three ffreinds twenty Shill. apeice to buy them Rings to wear in
Remembrance of me and twenty Shillings more to Each of the wifes
of the sd m^r. Edwin Conway & John Taverner for the same porpose
And I Doo hereby Constitute and appoint my said Loving wife and
Son Exec^rs. of this my last Will & Testam^t. Provided and Upon this
Condition the Bequest and Devize of my Land made unto my Wife
Joyning her in Joynt Tenancy with my said Sonn as aforesaid be in
Leiu and full Satisfaction of her Right of Dower of all and singular

my Estate Real and Personall And that she Seale a Release thereunto
if occasion be or Require And I doo hereby make void and Revoak all
former Wills by me Wrott or Spoake In Witness whereof to this my
Will Consisting with this of two Sheets of paper I have affixed my
Seale att the Topp & Subscribed to each Sheet my Name the Day in
the first Sheet first above written,

THO. GEORGE   Seale
83

Signed Sealed delivered
and by the sd Testat^r. published
as his last will & Testam^t.

M^r. John Taverner & m^r Denis
Carty Doth Depose and say that
they did see the Testato^r. Signe
Seale & publish this above men-
tioned Will as his last will &
Testam^t. And that he was then in

DENIS [M^A] CARTY*
PHILLIP HUNINGS†
JO: TAVERNER

perfect Sence at the signing & sealing thereof And further say not

JO: TAVERNER
DENIS [M^A] CARTY*

Probat^r P Sacrament in Cur Com Rapp. 7° die 9^{bris} 1683 Et Recordat xx6° die ejusd mens An°. Sup. dicto

Test THO: NEW Cl Cur P temp^{ed}   Page 13.

14 September, 1682;
6 September, 1683.

MORRAH, (MORROUGH), JOHN,

To Godson Thomas Warden of Barbadoes 1000 pounds of Mus-
covada sugar which sugar is in the hands of Joseph Warden of Barbadoes father to the said Thomas. To Thomas Chitty Jr. 1000 pounds
of good sound Tobacco. To John Jacob my Broad Cloath Coate and
breeches. To my good friend Grace Bedford 1000 pounds of sound
and good Tobacco. Executors my good friends Thomas Chitty Senr
and John Bayley and do give the remaining part of my Estate to them.

The deposition of Mr Dominick Rice aged aboute 33 years or thereabouts Sworn saith That being sent for from my whom (*home*) to
the house of John Jacob I found John Morrah* very Sick and lying
on a couch I asked him how he did the said John Morrah gave answer
that he was very Ill at wch time Mr John Bayley brought to the
said Morrah his will in writing and read the same to ye said Morrah
distinctly and deliberately word by word and the said John Bayley
asked the said Morrah if he approved of it who answered very well
and said he was ready to Signe it and Accordingly endeavoured to
rise up and sign the same but was at that time advised to the Contrary

---

*Denis Mª Carty in original will.
†Phillip Hunnings in original will.

by his nurse he being then in a great sweat wch said will to the best of yor depon^ts memory the very numercial paper now exhibited to this worshipful Court by Mr John Bayley and Mr Thomas Chitty and farther this depon^t saith not.

DOMINICK RICE

Nicho: Constable aged 44 years or thereabouts sworn and examined Saith that being sent for to the house of Mr John Jacob did hear the said above mentioned Will Read distinctly to John Morrah who approved of it in every respect above mentioned And deposeth the same above written and further saith not

his

NICHO O CONSTABLE

mark

The deposition of Roderick Jones aged about 35 years Saith That John Morrah being at my house about ye middle time of June last said he had a will made wch wanted nothing but signing And that it was his last will and testament And further saith not

RODERICK E JONES

Sworn to in Court September 6, 1683.   his mark

Recorded September 26, 1683.   Page 13.

18 November, 1683;

CRASK, ELIZABETH,   proved 3 January, 1683/4.

probated & recorded 23 January, 1683/4.

To ffrances Moss daughter to my former husband Thomas Moss one negro woman fflora and the first and second child that the Negro woman shall bear I bequeath unto Elizabeth Moss daughter to my former husband Thomas Moss. I will that ffrances Moss have the third child that the said Negro woman shall bear. I will that the two children that the said Negro woman shall happen to bear to the use of Elizabeth Moss be and remain with the mother until they shall be one years old and that then they be taken away by the said Elizabeth Moss. I give to Elizabeth one hoop gold ring And I give unto ffrances Moss my hoop gold ring that I wear on my hand. I give unto Elizabeth Moss and ffrances Moss all my Cloaths and apparel that I leave to be equally divided between them. I give to my God daughter Elizabeth Moss daughter to William Moss one silver box and one gold ring with a stone in it. I give unto George Murrill one two year old heifer. I give unto my sister Rebecca Moss one seirg gown. I give to Ellinor daughter of Richard Stoakes one two yeare old heifer. I give my chest of drawers to the above said ffrances Moss. I give the said Elizabeth Moss daughter of Thomas Moss one feather bed boulster red rug and

---

*Morrough in the original deposition.

one pair of sheets. I give to the above said ffrances Moss one sack cup of silver and one small silver bodkin. I give unto Elizabeth Moss one silver spoon and one silver bodkin. To Robert Parker son of Thomas Parker one two year old heifer and if Robert die then the said heifer to go to any of the other sons of Thomas Parker as he shall think fitt. And of my estate that remains when my legacis are satisfied I will that my debts be fully paid and satisfied. Executor Thomas Herbert of the Parish of Sittingborn and Executrix Elizabeth Moss daughter of my former husband Thomas. I will that when my debts and legacies are fully paid and satisfied that what of my estate doth remain to be equally divided between my executor and executrix and ffrances Moss. I will that my executor and executrix doe call Thomas New to accompt for all the concerns of my husbands Captain Edmund Crask or of mine that are hath been or shall be in the hands of the said Thomas New or in his management. I will that out of my hoggs there be paid to ffrances Moss six sows one boar and three barrows. I give unto my brother Robert Moss one boar barrow of two years and a half old and another barrow of that age and one purple rug. I give to Rebecca Stoakes wife of Richard Stoakes my Pallmata hat and one whole suit of linen throughout shift and all. To Elizabeth Newton wife of Henry Newton two pewter dishes two plates and one dutch iron pott. I give to my God child Ann daughter of Alexander Robbins one silver whistle with bells and tassel. I give unto ffrances Moss my feather bed with Red Curtains and vallence Red Rugg and boulster two pillows and one paire of sheets. I give unto Elizabeth Moss one blanket and two pillows. I will that all my table linen be equally divided between the two sisters Elizabeth and ffrances Moss. I give unto Thomas Herbert my great chest. I give unto John Crask a mourning ring that was his fathers and one pair of silver buckles. I give unto Ellen Crask two pairs of shoes and one pair of slipps. I give my little table in my room to Rebecca Stoakes above mentioned and one pewter dish and two sawscers and one spitt. I give unto Thomas Herbert one heifer big with calfe of three years old called Mayden. I give unto Martha the daughter of Abraham Stapp one heifer of two years old. I give unto Dr Greine that was with me in my sickness two hundred pounds of Tobo. I give unto Thomas Parker Sr. two Dowlis shirts. I will that Thomas Herbert have to his own use my negro woman fflora to serve him one year and that he also have my servant boy to make one crop to his own particular use and service and what time the said servant boy hath longer to serve I will he lend it to Elizabeth Moss. I will that what remains of my pewter I give between the two sisters Elizabeth and ffrances Moss. I will that I be interred with my husbands and that my burying place be inclosed with a decent pale. I give to my brother Wm Moss one silver seal.

Wit. HENRY TANDY, THOMAS PARKER, HENRY X NEWTON.

Page 16.

4 December, 1683;
JOHNSON, PETER,   2 January, 1683/4.

My will is that my son-in-law Jn⁰ Martin go free and be for himself and that he have the tuition of my son Peter Johnson until he be twenty years of age alwaies Provided that the said John Martin give my son Convenient Education and Maintenance and take no Ill Courses wherein if he falters in any Respect my will is that my executor James Jackson to take my son Peter into his Guardianship and that he remains with my executor the terme aforesaid. All my estate to my son Peter Johnson to remaine in the custody of he that keeps my Child Care being taken to pay my debts. Executor my friend James Jackson.

Wit. JAMES HARRISON, SUSAN X HAMMOND.   Page 17.

7 February, 1683/4;
MATLIN, JOHN,*   5 March, 1683/4.

In the name of God Amen I John Matlin of the pish of Cittenburn in the County of Rappahannock being sick & weak in body but of sound & pfect memory doe hereby make & ordaine this my Last will and Testamᵗ. in manner & forme ffolowing hereby Revoaking all former wills by me made & this to be my Last will & Testament.

Impʳˢ I give & bequeath my soule into the hands of Almighty God hoaping & trusting through the Merritts of Jesus my saviour to obtaine full & pfect Remission of all my sins and as for my body to yᵉ Earth from whence it came to be buried in decent manner by my Executoʳ hereaftʳ named, and as for my worldly Estate God hath bin pleased to bestow upon me I bequeath as followeth

Item : I give and bequeath unto my two sones William Matlin & Henry Matlin all that Tract of Land I am possessed of to be equalie divided between them when they come of age the sd William to have his first Choyce

3ᵈˡʸ My will is that the rest of my psonall Estate be equally divided between my three sons William Matlin Henry & John Matlin

4ᵗʰˡʸ I give & bequeath unto Elizabeth Richardson one black heifer which comes of the Cow called Black Eyes to her & Her heirs forever.

5 My will is that my psonall estate be inventoried by David Starne & James Trent & according to quality & quantity to be delivered by my executoʳ hereafter named unto my three sons when they shall come to the age of one & Twenty years.

6 My will is that if either of my sones die without Issue of their body, Lawfully begotten that then the reall & personall estate Returne unto the next survivor and in case that all Three decease before they come of age, that then one third pt be delivered unto my son in Law

*Copied from original will. John *Motlin* in Record Book.

John Spicer And the Rest of my estate to my executo^rs hereafter named

Ite I give to Knight Richardson my sarge suite to be delivered to him presently after my Decease.

8^thly My will is that David Sterne have the care of my two sons Henry Matlin and John Matlin and theire pte of the estate & to deliver it in Kinde to them when they come to the age of one & Twenty years & as for my son William my will is that he Chuse one of my executo^rs to be his Guardian which he please

9^thly My will is that David Sterne & James Trent be my ffull & Reall executo^rs to see this my last Will & Testament pformed

Ite I give to Ric^h Mathewes my osenbrigg suit

I give & bequeath to Mr Arthur Spicer my seale Ring

I give unto Nathaniell Allen one Gould Ring

I give unto Alice Trent one Gould Ring

I give unto Elizabeth Knight one Gould Ring

My will is y^t Knight Richardson have house & ground ffor ffower years and Cleare uppon my Land except the Iland & Calfe paster

In wittness whereof I have hereunto set my hand & seale this 7th day of ffebruary 1683/4

his

JOHN X MATLIN

mark

Sealed & delivered in the prsents of
NATHANIEL ALLEN AND MARTIN MIDLETON

his

KNIGHT K RICHARDSON   O
    his mark   mark

Proved in Rappahannock County Court by the oaths of Knight Richardson & James Trent quinto die Martij 1683/4.

Test W^M COLSTON Cl. Cur.   Page 18.

WHEELER, WILLIAM,* (Nuncupative Will),

The Deposition of Thomas Searle aged 50: years or thereabouts Sworne Saith that yor. depon^t. Came to the house of Jno. Linckhorn to demand some tobacco of m^r. William Wheeler which was owing to yor. depon^t from the said Wheeler who then lay very Sick at the said Linckhorns of wch. Sickness he the said Wheeler some small time after dyed And at that time when yor. depon^t. was with him demanding his debt, said Wheeler declared that he has ordered John Linkhorne to pay the said tobacco to yor. depon^t. (if he should die) on wc^h. answere yor. deponent was well satisfied and took leave of the said Wheeler and going to depart the Roome m^r. Wheeler Called to yor. depon^t. Saying that if he died Jno Linckhorne Shold Certainly pay me, for that

*Not in Torrence's "Virginia Wills and Administrations."

his full purpose and Designe was to give all his Estate to the said John Linckhorne who was to pay all his debts after his decease And the overplus wch. Remained the^{r}eof he freely gave to the said Linckhorn further yor. depon^t. Says that at the same time to the best of yor. depon^{ts}. Knowledge and Judgm^t. the said m^r. Wheeler was in perfect sence mind and of a disposing memory.

And further Saith not

ye marke of

Sworn the 28th xber 1683   THO: T SEARLE
LEROY GRIFFIN
83

The deposition of Abraham Bush aged 61: years or thereabouts Sworne Saith, That yor. depon^t. was wth. m^r. W^m. Wheeler when he lay sick at the house of Jno. Linckhorn to demand a debt due from the said Wheeler to yor. depon^t. And that then he the said m^r. Wheeler declared to me that Jno. Linckhorn Should pay to yor. depon^t. that was due for that if he should dye his full Resolves was that the said Linckhorn should have all his Estate to pay his debts after his decease At wch. time the said m^r. Wheeler was to the best of yor. depon^{ts}. Judgm^t. in pfect sence & memory.

And further Saith not

ye mark of

Sworn to before me y^e. 28th ABRAHAM X BUSH
xber 1683

LEROY GRIFFIN

Probated and recorded the 24th day of Januarij, 1683/4.

Test W^M. COLSTON Cl. Cur.   Page 17.

2 April, 1682;
Sworn to 6 March, 1683/4 & 7 May, 1684.

HENLY, ELIZABETH,

Now wife of Robert Henly and formerly relict of John English.

To my husband Robert Henly all the land given me by my former husband John English in his will which before the publication of matrimony to my last husband I made over to myself by deed indented and recorded in the County Court of Rappahannock and I do now freely give it to him forever.

Wit. ALEXANDER DUDLEY, W^M BARBER.   Page 18.

6 February, 1683;
WATSON, JOHN,   2 April, 1684.

IN THE NAME OF GOD AMEN I, John Watson of Sittingborn Parish in the County of Rapp^a In Virginia Planter, being very Sick in body, but of Pfect memory in minde, praised be God therefore

Considering that it is appointed for all men once to dye And after Death to Judgment Doe Constitute & appointe this my last will & testament in manner and form following (that is to say) Imp^{rs}. I give my Soule into the hands of Almighty God my Creato^r. hoping for Salvation only by the meritts of my Redeemer Jesus Christ, whom I trust by his mighty power Shall unite my body & Soule being Raised at the last Day And to Enjoy the blessed p^{r}sence of Almighty God to all Eternity, my Body I Ord^r. to be buried decently at discreation of my Executrix hereafter named, And for my Estate both Reale & personal and all such worldly goods Cattles & Chattels, As it hath pleased God to bestow upon me in this mortall life I give and bequeath them in Manner and form following—Item I give and bequeath all the Land that I am possessed of unto my two Sones Jno. Watson & Thomas Watson Alsoe I ord^r. that my two Son's shall live and bide with their mother untill they shall Come to the age of one and twenty yeares each of them I Alsoe doe Ord^r. that my wife Shall have the priviledge of the Plantation whereon I now live untill my son Jno. Watson shall Come to age and fulfill the years of one & twenty, As alsoe after my Son Shall Attaine the age of one & twenty years I doe give my wife Pricilla Watson the one halfe of my Land Orchard & Plantation whereon I now live and the benefitt thereof During her life As alsoe I doe ordaine and bequeath unto the Child wherewith my wife now goeth with that if it Shall please God it be a man Child it Shall be equally Concerned in the land with my Son's Jno. Watson & Thomas Watson, As alsoe my will is that if either or any of my sons Shall dye without lawfull Issue that then the Survivo^r. or Survivo^{rs}. Shall Inherit But if my Son's Shall dye all of them without Lawful Issue That then my land Shall be devided between my two Daughters Susan Watson & Eliz^a. Watson be equall division. Alsoe my will & Testament is that if my Children shall be any way abused that then it Shall be at the discretion of my freinds hereafter named to Remove them untill they shall be of age to Chuse their Guardian. Item I give unto my well beloved Wife Priscilla Watson a gray Mare with her Increase as alsoe my black Rideing horse as alsoe the old horse I give my wife to be for the use of the house Item I give and bequeath unto my son Jno. Watson a sorrell Mare with her Increase and a gray horse aboute fower yeare old Item a black mare Colt about two year old with her Increase unto my son Tho: Watson Item I give the bay Mare with a Sprig tayle with her Increase I give to my Daughter Susan, Item I give and bequeath the bay mares foale if it be not otherwise disposed of I give with her Increase to my Daughter Elizabeth Item I give and bequeath unto my welbeloved wife Priscilla Watson I give and bequeath the bed whereon I ly togeather with the furniture

JOHN JW WATSON
his marke

Item I give and bequeath unto my son John Watson the bed and furniture that is in the Chamber Item I give unto my daughter Susan

Watson the bed that is in the out Room Item I Order that the yellow
Steere with wide hornes be Killed and used for the use of housekeeping according as my wife shall appointe Item all the Rest of my
goods and Cattell my Chattells Horses Mares or whatsoever else of
Estate belongs to me I Order to be Equally devided between my welbeloved wife Priscilla Watson and my Children Jnᵒ Watson Thomas
Watson Susan Watson and Eliz: Watson as alsoe the Child or Children
wherewith my welbeloved wife Priscilla is now with Child Item I doe
Order that the hoggs wherewith I am possessed I ord. to be killed &
used for the good of housekeeping, Item I doe hereby Constitute give
& bequeath unto my loving freind Henry Garman my back sword &
belt Lastly I doe hereby Constitute and appoint my welbeloved wife
Pricilla Watson & Jnᵒ. Watson to be Execuʳˣ. & Executoʳ. to this my
Last will and Testament he Entring upon the executorship when he
Comes to the age of twenty one years And I doe hereby appoint my trusty
and welbeloved friends Capt. Daniell Gaines, mʳ. ffrancis Slaughter, mʳ.
Jnᵒ Catlett and mʳ. Willᵐ. Underwood as overseers of my will soe far
as to see an Equall division made of my goods & Cattle & other estate
According to my will & Testament As alsoe I doe hereby Impower
them to look after my Children, And in Case they shall think fitt
upon Just Complaint to Remove them as they shall See fitt According
to their discretion Item I Order and appoint my Daughters Susan
Watson & Elizabeth Watson to abide with their Mother till they are
married or Attaine to full age, In witness whereof that I doe Declare
this to be my last will and Testament Contayning two Sheets of paper
writ on the one Side And So wed togeather Revoaking all former
wills wtsoever As witness my hand and seal this sixth day of ffebruary
one thousand Six hundred and eighty three.

                         by me affixed
                                        Jnᵒ JW Watson   Seale
Signed sealed & pronounced   his marke
to be my last will & Testamt.
in the presence of us
        David Hoomes
        Samuell Henshaw
        Will Heather

   I William Heather within mentioned aged about fourty years Doe
Attest upon oath this within written to be the Last Will and Testament of the within mentioned Jnᵒ Watson And hereunto have Sett
my hand this 2ᵈ of Aprill 1684
                                          Will Heather

   I Samˡ Henshaw within mentioned aged about three & twenty years
Doe Attest upon oath this within written will to be the wthin mentioned Jnᵒ. Watson And hereto sett my hand the 2ᵈ of Aprill 1684
                              Samˡ. Henshaw

Probator P Sacrament Eorum in Cur Com Rapᵃ. 2º. die Aprillis
Anº. 1684: Et Recordatʳ. ejusd mens Anº Supʳ dicto
Test Wᴹ. COLSTON Cl Cur   Page 19.

16 February, 1683;
ROBINS, ALEXANDER,   16 April, 1684.

To daughters Rebecca, Eliza, Judith and Ann Robins 650 acres
of land on the branches of Gilsons and Hodgkins Creeks viz. to my
eldest daughter Rebecca 200 acres; to daughter Elizabeth 150 acres;
to daughter Judith 150 acres; to daughter Ann 150 acres which makes
the sum of 650 as by Pattent will appear but if all or any of my
daughters die without lawful issue then to go to my son Alexander.
To son Alexander land I bought of Wᵐ Berry containing 133 acres.
All my cattle to be divided between my wife and children share and
share alike. To daughter Rebecca two pewter dishes that were her
grandmother's. To wife all household stuff goods and chattles and all
moveables. To John Cook my wife's son my wearing apparel my Kane
with the silver head. To daughter Rebecca one silver sack cup. To
son Alexander my great gold ring and set of silver buttons. To daughter Rebecca my silver seal. To daughter Elizabeth one gold ring. To
son Alexander one pair of breeches buttons of silver. To John Cook
my gun that I had of James Black. To son Alexander my left handed
gun my horse and horse cloth to be sold to pay my debts. My son to
be kept at school the charge to be defrayed by the increase of my
cattle. Wife Judith Executrix and friend Thomas Parker Executor.
Wit. THOMAS PARKER, SUSAN X WILLIAMS.   Page 21.

18 February, 1683;
PETERS, RANDOLPH,   2 April, 1684.

To Margaret Curtis and her heirs forever 142 acres of land lying
upon Barbara Goldmarsh also one cow and two yearlings marked with
two crops and two holes and also my working tools. Executrix Margaret Curtis.
Wit. GEORGE COLECLOUGH, aged 29 years or thereabouts,
    ANTHONY SMITH, ANN SMITH.   Page 21.

18 December, 1683;
PERKINS, THOMAS,   2 April, 1684.

To Thomas Parker my wearing gould ring. To Elizabeth Blomfield my Ring that is due me from the Estate of William Sargent. To
all my God children a hhd of toba apiece. All the remainder of my
estate (my just debts first satisfied) I give to Capt. Samˡ. Blomfield
whom I make my Executor.
Wit. MARTIN JOHNSON, aged 48 years or thereabouts,
    MARY X JOHNSON, aged 50 years or thereabouts.   Page 21.

12 March, 1682/3;
FLOYD, SAMUEL,   Recorded 24 May, 1684.

To Andrew Boyer all my worldly goods wherewith it hath pleased
God to bless me withall as well what is in my own custody as what is
in the custody of any other person whatsoever as all debts which are
by any manner owing unto me whether by Bills or otherwaies and all
dues in Generall.

Wit. BRIDGETT X SOUTHWELL, JOHN BEATSON.

The Deposition of John Beatson Aged 39 years or thereabouts
Saith That whereas Samuell ffloyd deceased the last year now past
before the Date hereof was Resident in the house of one ffrancis
Taylor And there being in an exceeding weake and decrepit Condition
by Reason of a sore legg which pleased Almighty God to vissit him
with Insomuch that he was not able to help himself was brought by
the said Taylor to the house of Andrew Boyer and immediately after
his Coming thither the said Andrew Boyer demanded of him where
his Chest was and what toba he had Due unto him whereupon the said
Sam: ffloyd told him of severall parcells of Tob which was due unto
him as alsoe of Corne which was due unto him for worke and the said
Andrew Boyer Did owe at that time unto the said ffloyd two Barrells
of Corne for work And likewise the said ffloyd told the said Andrew
Boyer of two Bills wch. had for tob Due unto him (viz) Joshua
Lawson Bill and Danl. Jackson bill the wch. Bills the said Boyer
without delay got into his Custody And further the said ffloyd told
him that his Chest was at the house of the said ffrancis Taylor aforesaid And the said Taylor Did owe unto him Severall goods expressing
what goods they were which he had lent unto him And the said Taylor
had promised to pay ye like goods in Kind the next yeare following
And also the said ffloyd told him that Charles Snead did owe him a
Considerable quantity of toba But yor. Deponent Cannot positively
declare the Just sume But According to the best of his Remembrance
it was well towards (if not *altogeath*) a Thousand pounds of tob
whereupon yor depon^t being then a Servant to the said Boyer was
Commanded by his said Master to write a Will and thereby to bequeath unto him the sd Boyer All and whatsoev^r. the said ffloyd was
possessed with Also whatsoever was due unto him by any means whatsoever The which when yor. depon^t. had writt he Read to the said
ffloyd And the said Boyer Commanded him to Assigne it But the said
ffloyd Refused to Doe the Same Saying he did not Know what it was
whereupon the said Boyer fell into a Passion And Did Inhumanely
Revile the Said ffloyd with many Opprobrious and Ignominious words
and Divers Threats Saying that if he would not Assigne it he would
turne him out of doores and therefore (as yor. deponent. Doth Im-
agine) more out of fear than Love he did Assigne the same And thereupon Immediately the said Boyer sent yor. depon^t. to the aforesaid
Taylor to fetch his Chest But the said Taylor would not deliver the

Chest to yor. depon^t. saying it was not paid for But gave yor. depon^t. Lycence to take what was in it and it was full of Cloaths and very good goods the which yor. depon^t. brought home to his Master Now Immediately after this the said Andrew Boyer himselfe went to the said Taylors house And at his Returne from thence Shewed yor. depon^t. a Bill wch the said Taylor had assigned unto him for the payment of the goods aforesaid & also the said Taylor had oblidged himselfe to bring the Chest to the house of the said Boyer And According to the best of yor. depon^{ts}. Remembrance he had likewise a bill from Charles Snead for the tob aforesaid And finally the said ffloyd lay in a sad and deplorable Condition in the hogghouse of the said Boyer and when it was any quantity of Raine the water ran under him and there he Remained in this lamentable & disconsolate Condition when yor. depon^t. was free from the said Boyer wch was the 7th day of October last past And further yor. depon^t. Saith not.

JOHN BEATSON

May 7th 1684

John Beatson maketh oath In open Court to the truth hereof Test W^m. Colston Cl. Cur.

Recorded 24th day of May 1684 Page 26.

4 December, 1683;
2 April, 1684.

HARPER, THOMAS, of the County of Rapp^a in the Parish of ffarnham.

All my debts being honestly satisfied & paid then it is my desire that my welbeloved wife Mary Harper and Jno Harper my eldest son be Joyntly Executo^{rs}. of all my personall estate moveable & Immoveable & furthermore it is my desire that all my land be Equally Devided between my three sonns Jno., Solomon and Thomas Harper Then my desire is that my wife and other son Jno. Harper be posest with the aforesaid Land untill my two youngest sons doe Come to age Provided my wife should Marry any such pson who may by his prodigallyty wast Consume & destroy ye aforesaid Land then my son Jno. Harper to take it into his Custody untill they Come to age furthermore I doe bequeath unto my son Jno. Harper one servant boy named W^m. Cassaulough And one gun.

Wit. HENRY WATKINS, JN^o. BONNER, JOHN X STEWART.

Page 22.

26 February, 1683;
GULLOCK, ROBERT, 23 May, 1684.

All my lands and tenements to be equally divided between my daughter Jane Gullock and the unborn child of my wife whether boy or girl. My will is that all my sheep shall be kept upon the plantation till my daughter Jane and the child with which my wife is bigg arrive at twenty one or marry and then to be equally divided between them except one third part of the wethers I give to my wife during her life. It is my will that none of my hogs shall be removed of the plantation but shall be and remain all for the good of the above said Children except my wife live upon the plantation then my will is that she shall have one-third. I will that two-thirds of all my cattle shall be and remain for the good of the said Children equally to be divided between them and the other third to my wife. To the abovesaid children all my linen plate and three feather beds and furniture curtains and vallence and do leave the whole tuition of my daughter Jane Gullock to my wife and sister Vaulx. To Robert Payne one young sorrel horse branded with IG. To Elizabeth Rowzee one young mare aboute four years old wch said mare commonly useth about John Williams Plantation. To wife my horse Dick with side saddle bridle halter and whip. My will is that all the rest of my horses and mares except the two old cart horses shall be and remaine to my above said children to be equally divided between them at twenty one years of age or Marriage which shall first happen. I request my cousin Edward Rowzee to be careful to look after everything bequeathed to my two children and to brand the colt and marke the sheep and hogs for their use and for his care and pains I give him out of my stock every fower years a mare or horse colt. To wife two feather beds with furniture. My will is that after Mr Deans lease is expired for the plantation he now lives on I will & bequeath the use of it unto my loving friend Robert Brooke until my daughter Jane Gullock shall attain the age of one and twenty years making no waste of the timber for the use of the plantation and fencing and leave it tenantable and if my daughter Jane or other child shall happen to die before they attain twenty one I will the said Plantation to the said Robert Brooke and his heirs forever not exceeding above 100 acres of land. To Robert Brooke my old horse Puppy. To my cousin Edward Rowzee my old horse Jack with all the harness. All the rest of my psonall estate after my debts legacies and funeral expenses are discharged I give to Mr John Foxhall and Mr Robert Vaulx whom I make my Executors.

Wit. EDWARD ROWZEE, TOBIAS INGRAM, RO: BROOKE.

Codicil. The use of his maid servant Mary Therdford to go to his wife the time she has to serve. Leaves to his loving friends Mrs Mary Vaulx Mr John Deane Mrs Jane Deane Mr Wm Clapham Mrs Mary Clapham Mr John Foxhall Mr Robert Vaulx each of them a gold ring of 10 shillings price.   Page 23.

24 August, 1683;
5 May, 1684.

MORGAN, EVAN, of the ffreshes of Rapp^{ac} River in Virginia.

To my Godson Maxfielde Browne my wifes youngest son two able men servants sound in their limbs and well in health each of them having five or six years to serve to be delivered to my said Godson at the age of eighteen years in the Roome and stead of my two men servants wch now I have (vizt) Thomas Hamons and John Robinson. I do order and appoint that in case my wife Elizabeth do alter her condition by marriage any time before the said servants Thomas and John be free that then my loving friend Mallachy Peale to take the said servants into his care and custody for the good of my Godson and also my Godson if he thinks fit so to do. To my said Godson 120 acres of land being part of a tract of 220 acres on which John Rose is now living also to my Godson two good cowes of the age of five or six years old being with calf or calves by their sides also one good feather bed and boulster with a good rugg and a pair of blanketts at the age of eighteen. To my wifes youngest daughter Elizabeth Browne two good cowes with calf or calves by their side of the age of five or six years old also one good feather bed and boulster with rugg and blanket at eighteen years of age or day of marriage also one young mare of one or two years old to be delivered as aforesaid. To my wifes son John Brown one good cow with calf or calves by her side and a young mare of the age of one or two years at twenty one years of age. To my wifes son William Brown one good cow with calf, &c., (same as above) when he keeps house and all my carpenters tools. To my boy Thomas Booth the time he hath to serve me by indenture or otherwayes and one hhd of tobacco to pay his passage for England alwaies provided he returns there but if not that he serve his time with my friend Mallachy Peale he paying my wife twelve hundred pounds of Tob. All the rest of my estate real and personal (after my debts are paid) to my loving wife Elizabeth and my loving friend Mallachy Peale whom he appoints Executrix and Executor.

Wit. JOSIAH MASON, THOMAS X JONES, aged 33 years or thereabouts, THOMAS BOOTH. Page 24.

23 January, 1683;

BARRATT, MAGGUE,   Recorded 28 May, 1684.

To daughter Sarah Barratt 425 acres of land lying at Potomack Creek joining upon Dr. Elder and my own feather bed and furniture and one pott of fower Gallons a frying pan and two cows Brandy and Cherry and Brandys heifer and a steere two years old and ten barrows of two years old besides her own stock of hoggs. The remainder of my estate real and personal to my daughter Patience Marks. My will is that Frances Irell should have two or three barrows.

Wit. HENRY LAWRENCE, JAMES X BLANN. Page 25.

Proved in "ye County of Sn^t Maries," [Maryland] 14 February, 1683/4. Recorded in Rappahannock County, 28 May, 1684.

15 April, 1684;
SMITH, HENRY,   4 June, 1684.

To my sons Toby and Henry Smith my whole tract of land to be equally divided between them and their heires forever but if in Case there be a valluable seate Land Cleared in the Matrums Neck and is Justly found & surveyed my will is that my son Henry have it. And then he have only ye land that is above the Creek Called the great Creek where on George now liveth to him and his heirs forever. To wife one Sorrel pacing horse with a side saddle to her and her heirs forever. I give and bequeath all the Rest of my goods & Chattles to be equally divided between my wife and my two sons share & share alike. Wife Executrix and Edward Adcock Executor of his will for the performance and managing hereof. I bequeath Col^l. W^m. Loyd & M^r. Saml. Peachy overseers to see this my will pformed.

Wit. GEORGE COLCLOUGH, ROGER WATERS, JOHN WEBB.   Page 27.

12 March, 1683/4;
SKELDERMAN, HARMAN,   3 September, 1684.

To wife all household goods and cattle hogs and horses and young mare and if said young mare lives to Increase that then each of my children to have a Mare foal out of the said mare's increase. To my children six hundred acres of land where now I live to be equally divided between them when they come of age and if any of my children should die before that they should come to age the said land to go to my wife. Wife Executrix.

Wit. ALEX. DONIPHAN, JOHN X GARTON, SUSANNA X HAMMON.

Page 32.

18 August, 1682;
1 October, 1684.

GAINES, DANIEL, of the parish of Sittingburne in the
    County of Rapp^a.

The orphans of Col^{ll} John Catlett Decd. to be paid out of the Negroes and goods that did belong to the sd Coln^{ll} Catletts Estate the Negroes and goods to be as they were appraised to me as may appear by Inventory. To son Bernard all my land that I now live upon to him & his heirs lawfully begotten &c. and that he shall not let sell or mortgage any part or parcel of the same so long as his Two Sisters Margaret and Mary or their heirs be alive. If all my children die without heirs then my land to fall to my Grandson John Smyth and his heirs forever. To daughter Mary the Mare Colt that now sucks on my mare Betty and all her increase to her and her heirs for ever. The Mare Heyfer and Hogs that I have given to my grandson-in-law John Smyth to be and remain to his proper use forever. The first child that my negro Cate doth bring to be given to my daughter Margaret and her heirs forever and if it live to the age of three years to be in lieu of a man Servant otherwise to be in no stead. To son Bernard my silver hilted sword and belt and my Seale Ring. To wife Margaret one third of my estate in lieu of dower. My will is that the other two parts of my Estate be divided between my three children Bernard Margaret and Mary and no part of it to be appraised but to be Inventoried and delivered in kind. To daughter Margaret a good feather bed and furniture at my death in full of her part of my bedding. My daughter Mary to have the use of so much housing and land as she needs so long as she continues unmarried. My will is that as soon as it can a Man servant be bought with tobacco for my daughter Margaret in part of her Porcon. It is my will that my wife son Bernard and daughter Mary keep their shares together for their Menteynance doing their best by their endeavours to Encrease the same as long as my Wife Continues a Widdow or so long as either of my Children Continue unmarryed and at the day of Marriage of my Wife or of either of my Children then my Childrens part to be delivered to them in Kind. My Two Children Bernard and Mary to have as many things apiece out of my Estate as my Daughter Margaret hath had already and the rest to be divided between them equally by my loving Kinsman John Catlett and sons-in-law John Smyth and Ralph Rouzey and not to goe to Law one with the other. It is my will that my estate be Inventoryed within ten days after my decease. To wife Twenty shillings to buy her a Mourning Ring to ware for my sake and to my Two daughters each of them a Ring of Ten shillings price. If I die having no Tobacco in house that then my servants be and remain together till they make a good crop of Arenoco Tobacco out of which my wife having first taken her Third then my son Bernard and daughter Mary have out of the rest each of them as much as my daughter Margaret hath already then if any be remaining over and above to be divided equally between them all three. It is my Will that my Children have their Estate at the death or day of Marriage of my Wife whether they be of age or not. The children of Coln⁰ John Catlett to remain with my wife till they come of age if my wife continues unmarried. Wife Executrix and guardian of my children so long as she remains a widow.

Wit. Wᴍ. X Mᴜʀʀᴏᴡ, Jᴏʜɴ Cᴀᴛʟᴇᴛᴛ, Wᴹ. X Bʀᴏᴡɴᴇ.

Note: The witnesses called the testator "Capt. Daniel Gaines."

Page 35.

28 December, 1683;
STALLARD, WALTER,   1 October, 1684.

To son Samuel and daughter Sarah all my land housing and orchards to be equally divided my son to have his choice and if one of them die without issue the other to enjoy the whole. To each of them two cows and all their female increase to be divided at the age of twenty one or day of marriage which shall first happen. Also one heifer two cow yearlings and the first cow calfe that any of my cows bring together with their female increase to them and their heirs. Also my three mares Betty Jenny and Pegg the last two to my son Sam^ll and the other to my daughter and all their female increase to them and their heirs forever. To daughter Sarah my black horse Ball. To my son one Pottanger and one pewter dish when he comes at age. To my daughter one Pottanger and one pewter salt when she comes of age. To my loving wife the rest of my estate together with the male colts bull calves that came from my childrens mares and cows for the paying of my debts and bringing up my children. Wife Winefred Executrix.

Wit. John Evans, Geo. X Peachy, Geo. X Andrews.

Page 35.

29 January, 1683;
1 die 8^bris, 1684.

EVANS, JOHN, of Sittingburne Parish in the County of Rapp^a.

All the land I am possessed of to my two sons John Evans and W^m. Evans to be equally divided between them both for quantity and quality the division to be made when my son John is twenty one but in case the one shall decease before his full age the other shall succeed to his inheritance. To each of my children a mare and all their increase the youngest mare to my son John the other to my son William also to each of them a cow and its increase my son John to have a cowe called Mealy Nose William to have a black cow called Slow. Desires his children shall stay and live with their mother until they each of them attain the age of nineteen years. To father-in-law M^r. Wm Veale a case of pistols and holsters. To my loving brother Martin Johnson a chest which I had of him also a gun I had of him and a Caster hat. To my Godchild Margaret Ward daughter of Bryant Ward a cowe calf. All the rest of my goods and chattles after my debts are satisfied to my well beloved wife Elizabeth Evans. Wife Elizabeth to be Executrix and to be guardian of the children.

Wit. Rich^D R West, Thomas Johnson, Will^M. Heather.
      his mark   Page 36.

14 February, 1683/4;
WHITE, HENRY,   5 November, 1684.

    To daughter Arabella all my plantation I have and do enjoy in this County and elsewhere and if she die without issue then to my beloved wife Dorcas. To wife Dorcas all my personal estate. Wife Dorcas Executrix.

Wit. Robert Moss, John Googe.   Page 38.

26 March, 1682;
5 November, 1684.

WASSITT, JOHN,* of the Parish of Sittingbourne in the
County of Rappᵃ.

His land to be divided into three parts one part to his wife during
her life and after her decease to his son. Likewise my daughter to
have a part during her life and after her decease to my son aforesaid
or his heirs forever but he having no issue to the longest life of them
all. But as for my stock and goods to be equally between them my
wife to be Cheife and Executrix and manager of all as long as she
remaines a widow but if she be changing her condition in marrying
then for each to have their shares if they demand them.

Wit. MARY MASON, JOHN MASON, THO: WEBLEY.   Page 38.

1 January, 1683;
5 November, 1684.

GRIFFIN, WILLIAM, of Cittingborne Parish in the County
of Rappᵃ Planter.

To son William 225 acres of land I bought of Mr. Mott and to
have it next the River and the rest of that tract being 125 acres to
son John. Also to son John 75 acres bought of James Jackson which
makes the number of acres given to my son John equal with my son
William. If either of my sons die without issue the survivor to enjoy
the whole estate. To sons John and William two-thirds of my
personal estate and the other third to my wife. My sons to remain
with my wife until they are twenty one if she remains a widow but if
she remarries my will is that they be free at the age of eighteen. Wife
Jane Griffin Executrix.

Wit. JAMES HARRISON, JAMES JACKSON.   Page 37.

28 October, 1683;
RICE, DOMINICK,   4 March, 1684/5.

To Wᵐ Castor, John and Ann Tune the children of James Tune
each one young Ewe and to the said Wᵐ: my broad Cloth suit. To
Son-in-law Tho: Due my stuff Coat & Breaches & my Rapier. To
my son-in-law Marke Toone my Gunn. To my son-in-law Andʷ: Due
twenty Shill. to buy him a Ring. To my Wifes Neice Jane Duncombe
one young heifer Three years Old and her encrease to be allowed her
in May next. To my well beloved Wife Ann Two small Gold Rings.
To the overseers of my Will Twenty shillings each to buy each of them
a Ring. To son Stephen Rice all my Lands five hundred acres being
upon Sᵗ. James Point in Choptank in Maryland Three hundred and
fifty acres more wᶜʰ I bought of Mathew Kelly and Ignatious White

---

*Not in Torrence's "Virginia Wills and Administrations."

called Hony Hill and Three hundred acres Lying neere ffarnham Creek where John Peacock now liveth and Joyning to it wch I have entered in the Secretarys Office and desire that over-seere of this my Will to Escheat the sd Land to my son Stephen. All the remaining part of his estate to his wife Ann and son Stephen and appoints them Executrix and Executor of his will. I do order and appoint my son Stephen be sent to Ireland to my father when he is five years old there to be Educated so long as his Grandfather shall think fitt and what I have given him to remaine in the hands of his mother untill he comes to the age of seventeen security being given for it but in Case the said Stephen should dye before he comes to the age of seventeen what I have here given him to Come to his mother if she be then living but if not then to fall to my Eldest sisters Eldest son in Ireland. I do order and appoint my good friends Colon°. W^m. Loyd, Capt. Tho: Matthews and John Bayly to be my overseers in trust and to do their Endeavour to see that neither my Wife nor Child be wrong'd or abused either in Body or Estate.

Wit. J°. BAYLY, W^M BROCKENBROUGH, AND^W: DUE.   Page 42.

                                        25 January, 1684/5;
PRITT, (PRID), ROBERT,   4 February, 1684/5.
                  January 25th : 1684/5

    In the Name of God Amen. I Robt: Pritt of the County of Rappa in the Goverm^t: of Virginia through som distemper in Body but of sound & perfect memory praised be to God for it do here make & ordaine this as my last Will & Testam^t:
    Imp^s: I give & bequeath my Soule to God Almighty that gave it me & to Jesus Christ that died for me & to the holy Goste that sanctified me & my body to the Earth from whence it was taken & to be buried in Christian Buriall & my Worldly goods as foll
    Imp^s: I give and bequeath unto my well beloved friend Rich^d: Rice S^r and to his son Rich^d: Rice Junr: one seat of Land Contayning Two hundred Acres of Land w^ch: doth belong to me the sd Robt: Pritt to be Equally devided between him the sd Richard & his son this seat of Land lying in Rappa County upon Rappa Creek bounden as followeth upon the Land of And^w: Boyer Dueke Thornton Josias Lawson & ffran: Suttle.
    I^t: I give unto my Country Woman Ann Condon Widdow five hundred Pounds of Tobb. I^t. I give & bequeath unto my ffriend Eliza: Rice five hundred Pounds of Tobb. I^t. I do here here by these p^rsents make Ordaine Constitute & appoint these my friends Richard Rice Senr: & his son Rich^d: Rice to be Exec^t: Admst^rs: to take all my Worldly goods as aforemencond and to pay all my Legacyes & to defray Christian Buriall.
    I Request these my ffriends Jointly & severally to ask and to demand of the under Sheriff of Rappa Co. W^m: Tayler by Name for

January 25th, 1697

In the Name...
County of Rappa...
Distemper in Body but of sound...
do to God for it do here make & Ordaine...
& Testam...

Imprimis: I give & bequeath my Soule to God almighty that gave it me
& to Jesus Christ that dyed for me & to the holy Go[st] that sanct...
...my body to the Earth from whence it was taken
& to be buried in Christian Buriall & my Worldly goods as...

Item: I give & bequeath unto my wife beloved friend Rich: Rice
and to his son Rich: Rice Jun: one tract of land Contayning
two hundred acres of land which doth belong to me the s[ai]d Rob...
Pritt to be Equally devided between him the s[ai]d Richard &
his son that tract of land lying in Rappa County upon
Rappa Creek bounded as followeth upon the land of And:
Boyer Duke & Thornton ... Lawson & Tham: Little

Item: I give unto my Godly Woman namely Ann ...don Widdow two
hundred pounds of to[bac]co & I give & bequeath unto my
friend Eliza Rice five hundred pounds of to[bac]co. It I do Kno
Rice by these p[re]sents make Ordaine Constitute & appoint this
my friends Richard Rice sen: & his son Rich: Rice to be
cord... & exec[uto]rs to take all my Worldly goods as is afore menc[ione]d
and to pay all my Legacyes & to defray Christian Buriall.

Item: I request that my friends joyn...severally to ask and
to demand of the Sheriffe of Rappa County Taylor by
Name for in their reckoning against ... So Rob:...
two thousand pounds of Sweet ... to[bac]co & four hundred
weight ... & I also give & bequeath unto Richard
Rice sen: & to his son Richard Rice Jun: this I assigne as
my last Will and Testam: As Witness my hand & seale this
day & yeare above Written in the p[rese]nce of these Witnesses:

Geo: Thornbough Good Pate   Rob: Pritt [seal]
Virginia Thornton her Marke
           Vera Copia ... Cha: Colston ...Tho: Nathan...
                  Record March 11 169[?]

Northumberland ss
These are to Certifie that on the 4th day of february Thorn...
...good Pate & Virginia Thornton Witness of the within Will
...swore before Col: Jam: Smith that the s[ai]d Will was
the Last Will & Testam: of Rob: Pritt dec[ease]d the abovesd
being appointed for a Court for this County & no other
...appearing but the abovesd Smith
                  Teste Tho: Halton Cl:
                  Record Cl: W[illia]m Colston Cl:

and Exec^t: taken out against Capt: J^o: Rolt for Two Thousand Pounds of Sweet sented Tobb. & four hundred Weight Neet Pork These also I give & bequeath unto Richard Rice Senr: & to his son Richard Rice Junr: This I assigne as my last Will and Testam^t. as Witness my hand & seale the day & yeare above Written in the p^{r}sence of these Witnesses

Rob^T:Prid   Seale

Tes^t: Thorough Good Pate

    Jeremia Thornton his Marke

        Vera Copia Tes^t: Tho: Hobson Junr: Cl Cur Northand

Record. March 11th 1684/5

Northumberland SS

These are to Certifie that on the 4th. day of February Thoroughgood Pate & Jeremia Thornton Witnesses of the within Will did sware before L^t: Coln^{ll}: Sam^{ll}: Smyth that the sd Will was the Last Will & Testam^t of Robt: Pritt decd the abovesd day being appointed for a Court for this County and no other Gen^t appearing but the abovesd Smyth

Tes^t: Tho: Hobson Cl Cr.

Record Tes^t: W^M: Colston Cl Cr.   Page 43.

<table>
<tr><td>FRACK, WILLIAM,</td><td>7 April, 1684;
5 March, 1684/5.</td></tr>
</table>

All my Estate real and personal to my beloved Wife Martha Frack to be at her disposing my debts and Legacies being paid. To my Man Robert Vincent house and ground to work upon for the term of seven years if he please to work on it himself to have it rent free for the full Time aforemenconed. To my two Godsons John Browne and William Pitman to each of them a Cow Calfe.

Wit. Joseph Heminge, Rob^T. Vincent.   Page 43.

<table>
<tr><td></td><td>15 February, 1682;
4 March, 1684/5.</td></tr>
</table>

EDRINGTON, (or ETHERINGTON), MARGARET, widow, of the Parish of Sittingburne.

To my three sons John Jennings, William Jennings and Christopher Edrington all my hogs sheep and household goods to be equally divided according to quantity and quality. To sons William Jennings and Christopher Edrington all my mares & horses to be equally divided between them. To son Christopher Edrington all my cattle and if either of my sons William or Christopher die that all that I give should goe to either of them. It is my will that my sons should be of age at sixteen.

Wit. ffran: Stone, Eliz. X Stone.   Page 43.

8 January, 1684/5;
HERBERT, THOMAS,   1 April, 1685.

To cousin John Waters after my debts and funerall charges paid
all my estate moveables and immoveables and whatsoever or right ap-
pertain to me as being Executor of Mrs. Elizabeth Crask decd. only
one cow & calfe which I have att Henry Newtons, I give unto John
Waters, Jr. Executor John Waters, Sr.

Wit. Eliz. X Newton, Frances Moss, Wm. X Jones.   Page 44.

24 January, 1684;
1 April, 1685
KING, JANE,   & 2 May, 1685.

IN THE NAME OF GOD AMEN. I Jane King of the County
of Rappa in Virginia being sick & Weak in Body but of Perfect Sence
& Memory thanks be unto God for it do make & Ordaine this to be my
last Will & Testam^t. in Manner & forme following

Imprim^s: I give and bequeath my Soule to god that gave it me in
Certaine hopes of a Joyfull Resurrection at the last day in & through
the Merits of Jesus Christ my redeemer my body to the Ground from
whence it Came.

I^t: After my Debts are satisfied I give & bequeath my Estate as
followeth I give unto my Eldest son John Loflin* Two Pewter Dishes
& one Cow Called by the Name of Brownee with all her future Increase.

I^t: I give & bequeath unto my son Robert King one Heifer yearling with all her increase to him and his heirs forever and one broad
Pewter dish and one Pewter Tankard.

I^t: I do make & Ordaine John Mills my Whole & Sole Exect^r of
this my last Will & Testam^t: into whose Care & Custody I do Commit
the tuition of my Two foresd Children and what Corne & other Provision I shall be possessed off at the time of my decease I do give
towards the maintenance of them.

I^t: What other household Stuff I shall Leave as also the Tobb hang-
ing and My Wearing Cloaths I desire may be sold to pay my Debts
& defray my funerall Charges and if any over Plus there be to be
devided Between my Two said Children Equally. In Confirmation
whereof I have hereunto set my hand & Seale this 24th. day of January

An°: 1684.   Jane H King
                                                  her marke
Signed Sealed in p^rsence   Interlined before signed
    of us
        Tho: New
        Robt O Webber
            his marke

————
*"Jn°: Lofling" in original will.

I the Subscriber do depose & say that I did see the w^th :in Named Jane King Signe Seale & publish this within Menconed as her last Will & Testam^t. and that she was then in perfect sence & memory to the best of my Knowledge as Witness my hand this 1st day of Aprile An⁰: 1685

Tho: New

Proved in Rappa County Court Aprile 1st: 1685 by the Oath of Tho: New & Record. Tes^te: Wm Colston Cl Cur. Also proved 2 May, 1685 by the oath of Robert Webber.   Page 45.

3 February, 1684;
6 May, 1685.

BARROW, JOHN, of ye parish of Sittingburne in ye County of Rapp^a.

To son Jonathan all that tract of land called the Cabbin Point adjoining the land of Peter Foxon and if my said son dies without lawful issue then I give the land to my son Alex^r. Barrow. To son Moses a tract of land adjoining Roger Richardson and Peter Foxon which the said Foxon holds for the term of life and after to revert to my son Moses and if Moses dies without heirs then to my son Alexander. To son Alexander all the rest of my land reserving only to my loving wife the plantation whereon I now live with houses and orchards thereon during her natural life And further it is my will that my son Alexander shall be at his own disposall in the management of his estate at sixteen years of age and to be then possessed of his estate and if he dies without heirs then the land to go to my son Moses and if both Alexander and Moses die without heirs then to go to my son Jonathan. If all my three sons die without heirs then all my lands to be divided between my two daughters Honor and Cicily Barrow. To my two daughters one young mare and one cow a piece with two pewter dishes one larger and one lesser. The rest of my personal estate to be equally divided between my loving wife Mary and son Alexander suddenly after my decease by my overseers hereafter named. My will and desire is that my debts be paid out of my debts due to me or other my personal estate. Wife Mary Executrix and son Alexander Executor. Overseers to be my loving friends Mr William Underwood Sen. and Mr John Burkett and to each of them a gold ring of twenty shillings price.

Wit. W^M Underwood Sen^R., Joane X Underwood,
W^M X Underwood Jr.   Page 46.

8 April, 1685;
WATERS, ROGER,   6 May, 1685.

To Mrs. Ann Glascock my horse Trippillo. To Frances Glascock a ewe and a lamb. To John Ockly, Jr., a ewe and a lamb. To John Ockly, Sr., 500 pounds of tobacco. To Nicholas Clark 500 pounds of tobacco. To Michaell Scurlock all my wearing cloaths and my hatt. Executor Mr. Thomas Glascock to whom I give all the remainder part of my estate. I do desire that John Ockley do see that this my last will & Testament be fulfilled. Also it is my desire to have a funerall sermon preached by Doct^r. Dacres.

Wit. JOHN OCKLY, NICH⁰ CLARK.

Nicholas Clark, aged 40 years or thereabouts and John Ockley aged 40 years or thereabouts "sayeth we saw Doctor Roger Waters being sound of mind & memory Signe Seale & deliver the annexed will as his Last Will & Testament & further sayeth not."

Page 45.

18 February, 1684/5;
CARDEN, ROBERT,   6 May, 1685.

I Robert Carden of the County of Rappa being sick of Body but of perfect sence and memory do make this my last Will & Testament. To my son Robert Carden my Land with all the housing Orchards gardens and other appurtenances. After my decease my son Robert to go immediately to live with Humphrey Davis and his wife until he is seventeen and then to be for himself. Humphrey Davis and his wife to live in that house now in their possession and enjoy it with what belongs to it by my former agreement with them as long as they both shall live Paying 300 pounds of Tobb. and Cask as rent to my executors. To wife Elizabeth all my goods and chattels and plantation during her life. Wife Elizabeth Executrix.

Wit. THO: PARKER, WILL: X JONES.   Page 47.

10 April, 1685;
RICHARDS, BRIDGET,   Recorded 19 May, 1685.

In the Name of God Amen. I Bridgett Richards being sick of Body but of perfect Sence & memory blessed be God do bequeath my body to the grave and My Soul to god that gave it mee [in] sure & Certaine hopes of Resurrection both Soul & body to Endless happiness through the Tender mercy of god by the only Merits of our blessed Lord & Saviour Jesus Christ. Item I give unto my foure Children to them & theires all my Land to be Equally devided amongst them and this my desire is that my husband Lewis Richards should have his Life time on his now dwelling Plantacon and moreover my desire is that M^rs: Sisson shall keep my daughter Ann Pridum till she is Eighteen years of age and if she die before the Time is Expired for her to give it to Whom she will And also my desire is that M^rs: Eale have my Son Christopher Pridham whilst he comes to the age of Seventeen years and if she dieth to dispose of him as she thinks good the Will of God be don. Signed wth: my hand & seale Dated the tenth day of Aprile 1685

signum

MARIA WRIGHT   BRIDGET X RICHARDS   Seale
THO: X WALKER his Mark
W^M: SISSON

Record^r: xviiij° die May An°. 1685
Teste: W^M: COLSTON Cl Cur   Page 47.

18 April, 1685;
PUTLEE, NICHOLAS,   4 June, 1685.

To wife Mary all my estate real and personal. To one orphan boy named Peter Ganfallow a mare foale and her increase when he is twenty one. Wife Mary Executrix.

Wit. ARTHUR FFORBIS, ROBT. X MILLS, JOHN KING.   Page 50.

21 April, 1685;
MOSS, WILLIAM, Sr.,   1 July, 1685.

To son William Moss all this tract and plantacon whereon I now live Contayning 980 acres and six draught oxen now broak together with Plow and Cart and all Materialls belonging to them also one other parcell of Land contayning 600 acres which I bought and purchased of Joseph Chisell late of this County decd. To daughter Frances Moss 400 acres of land adjoining the tract of Land whereon Thomas Newman now liveth. To daughter Elizabeth Moss 150 acres of Land which I bought of Patrick Norton and is adjoining to the above mentioned 600 acres of Land I have given to my son William. Also to daughter Elizabeth 200 acres of Land where Thomas Newman now lives together with the Plantacon and all things belonging to it she to enjoy the same as soon as the lease is out. To each of my daughters aforesaid two feather beds and furniture belonging to them and each of them one paire of Curtains and Vallence one of their beds to be new and the other ordinary and I give to my daughter Elizabeth one great blew Rugg and a pair of cotton blankets to be for the furniture of her new bed. To daughter ffrances one Cubbard that standeth in the Parlour and to my daughter Elizabeth one small Iron Bound Cabinett. And to each of my daughters two chests and a little trunk and a great one apiece and to my daughter ffrances one hoop gold Ring that is now in the house and to my daughter Elizabeth three small silver spoons and one small Dram Cup but not the smallest of all. And to my daughter ffrances one silver sack Cup and to my two daughters aforesaid one piece of fine seirge containing twenty seven yards to be equally divided between them. To daughter ffrances one black silk gowne that was made for her mother and not worn. To my brother Robert Moss one new suit of cloaths to be delivered to him at my decease that will fitt him. To Edward Westbury as much of the best cloth in the house as will make him a suit of Cloaths wth buttons to make it up and that the making be paid for. To Thomas New one silver seale that I had given me by my sister Crask. To my two said daughters one half of my Pewter both new and old to be equally divided between them and half of all the Cattle I am possessed of at my decease except the six draught oxen given to my son William both male and female to be equally divided between them share and share alike to be delivered to them at the day of marriage or when they come of age which shall first happen. To my two aforesaid daughters the two or three Remnants of fine Linen to make up for them. To daughter Elizabeth one negro boy called Docee to be delivered to her at the day of Marriage and to my daughter ffrances one man servant to serve the Custom of the Country to be delivered to her at the day of Marriage. It is my will and desire that my two aforesaid daughters do Continue wth my son William until they come of age or day of Marriage. All other goods merchandise household stuff and implements of household stuff cattle chatells and other Estate to my son W^m (except what is hereby given and bequeathed away). Only out of my stock of horses I do give and bequeath unto my two above said Daughters ffrances and Elizabeth each of them one horse and one mare to be delivered to them at the days of their respective marriages. To daughter ffrances three ewes and one ram to be delivered to her at the day of Marriage. To daughter Elizabeth one heifer and four sheepe wch heifer and sheepe do go by the name of her stock the said heifer and sheepe to runn on her Brothers Plantacon until her Marriage day and then to be delivered to her together wth the female increase that shall happen to come of them. If either of my sons or daughters die without lawful issue then their real estate to be equally divided among the survivors. Executor my son William.

Wit. ELIAS X WILSON, JOHN X MILLS, ROBT. MOSS, THOS. NEW.

Page 53.

5 October, 1684;
1 September, 1685.

COGHILL, JAMES, of Sittingburne Parish in Rappahannock County, Plant^r.

To wife Mary the Plantacon whereon I live during her life with all my household goods hogs and cattle one mare and one horse and if she dies a widow then to be divided among all our children. To my eldest son 225 acres of land one mare with all my coopers and carpenters tools to be equally divided between William and James. To son James 225 acres of land one mare my own gun and sword. To son David 200 acres of land and one mare and one gun. To son ffrederick 200 acres of land. To a child unborn if a boy 200 acres of land if not to return to within four sons above mentioned And to my son ffrederick I bequeath one mare. All wch land given of one dividend to be equally divided according to quantity and quality every one taking their portion as they are capable to manage it every one according to age to take their choice. To daughters Margrett and Mary 600 acres of land lying in another Divident 200 acres of this land to a child unborn if a girle if not to Remain to the above Margrett and Mary and of the increase of David and ffrederick Maryes to Returne to Margrett and Mary each of them a mare of one year old apiece. I do appoint David and ffrederick to be at age at eighteen and to enjoy their estate if their mother Marryeth. Executor my son [not named] and my wife Mary.

Wit. CHRISTOPHER X MAN, THOMAS X HENLEY.   Page 59.

SAMPSON, JOHN,
7 September, 1680;
25 November, 1685.

In the Name of God Amen. I John Sampson at the psent in the County of Rappa. in Virginia Merch. being of sound mind and memory praised be God, do make and declare my last Will & Testam^t: as followeth: first & principally I do hereby recomend my Soul into the hands of the Almighty who gave it me & my Body I Commit to the Earth to be decently buried as herein Expressed trusting it shall partake of that glorious Resurrection purchased by the blessed Redeemer of the World Christ Jesus but my desire is no sermon be preached at my funeral my Body to be put into a decent Coffin & Carryed to the grave by six Merchants if they may be had otherwise by six of the Commission of this County And desire that there be no more than Three gallons of Strong Liquor (without Victualls) be therefore Expended And as for that Worldly estate God of his goodness hath blessed me with I dispose thereof as is herein Exprest.

My mourning Ring I give and bequeath unto my Loveing Sister Rebecca Sampson.

I give & bequeath unto Mrs Sarah Suggett my little Ring my little Bible wth Silver Clasps my Silver Spoon my Silver Punch Cup my Book in ffolio written by Herne and two other books: one Heaven Opened by R. A. ye other the Life & Death of Mr John Janeway. To my brothers Jacob and Isaac Sampson 30 sh. to buy each of them Mourning Rings wch said Rings & Mony or Tobo the value of the said Mony to be sent by some trusty friend to the use aforesaid Vizt My Mourning Ring to my sister & the thirty shillings to my brothers my silver seale I give to my brother Jacob. To my loving friend Mr John Taverner my Book entitled Religio Medici & the french Acedemy. My Tobacco to my honoured father Mr Ptolomeus Sampson of Tattons. My wearing apparel and all other things not disposed of to be sold at an outcry and when my debts are paid the overplus to go to my father but in case he dies before such consignment is made then to go to my brother Isaac in London for the use of himself my brother Jacob and my sister Rebekah viz. one half to my brothers Jacob and

Isaac and the other half to my sister Rebekah. My mind and further
will is that all my books of account remain in the hands of Mr John
Suggett and when the business of my Estate is performed to consign
the said books of account to my honoured father but if he be deceased
to either of my Brothers. I desier My Body may Be Buryed At M^r
John Suggetts the First house I Lived at in these Parts.

No witnesses.

Page 61.

29 September, 1684;
4 November, 1685.

REYNOLDS, CORNELIUS, in the ffreshes of Rappahannock.

Wife Margery to be whole and sole Executrix of all and every
parcel of my Estate and all moveables only the seat of land where I
now live to be divided equally either of them a Plantation my son
William to have the Choice and my son John the other halfe with one
Plantacon. To grandson Goss the first mare foal with her increase.

Wit. Thos X Hope, Mary X Hope, Matt X Lafry.   Page 60.

9 November, 1685;
21 December, 1685.

JONES, HONORIA, Widdow & Relict of M^r: George Jones.

To daughter Margaret Blagg that Seat & Tract of Land wch I
purchased of Coln^ll: John Vassall Lying & being on the south Side
of Rappa River contayning Eleven hundred seventy and five acres the
sd Land to be at her absolute and sole disposall forever. To daughter
Elizabeth Gardiner my Wedding Ring w^ch: Joyned me and my husband Maj^r: John Weire in Matrimonie. To son-in-law M^r: Abraham
Blagg and my son M^r: Richard Gardner each twenty shillings to buy
them Mourning Rings. To my grandchildren Richard Watts Edward
Blagg Abraham Blagg Luke Gardner and Jno: Gardner each one Silver
Spoone and one Silver Trencher Salt. I Constitute and Ordaine my
Well beloved Daughter Margrett Blagg wife of M^r: Abraham Blagg
my sole Executrix.

Wit. James Harrison, Arth: X Oneby, Michall X Bassey.

Page 63.

8 January, 1685/6;
3 February, 1685/6.

BOYCSS, (BOYCE, BOYESS), GEORGE,

To Mr. John Daingerfield 250 acres of Land of that Tract of
Land called the Range Land the said 250 acres of Land to be on that
side the said Tract next to the Land that Bryan Ward now liveth on.
To Jeremiah Parker 250 acres of Land of the same Tract Called y^e.

Range and Joyning to the above said 250 bequeathed to Mr. John Daingerfield. The residue of the above Tract of Land called y^e : Range all whole and singular with the appurtenances (saving and Excepting what is above bequeathed) to my Loving sister Dorothy Boycss als Browne. To my God daughter Sarah Shipley daughter of Daniel Shipley 250 acres of Land that I hold by Patent and Conveyance Lying in this County of Rapp^a on the south side of the River in the Parish of South ffarnham and Joyning to the Land of Mr. Joseph Goodrich and the Land of Thomas Wood. To ffrances Daingerfield daughter of Mr. John Daingerfield one gold ring with three barrs and a stone in it being the least of three rings that I have. I will that my horses and mares and what Debts are due unto me go to pay my Debts with all and the residue of my personall Estate after my Debts are paid I give and bequeath to my beloved sister Dorothy Boycss als Browne. Executrix my sister Dorothy Boycss als Browne and Mr. John Daingerfield to join with her as overseer and assistant. What Tobb. of mine in the hands of Mr. John Daingerfield be by him expended and disburst in the Paying of my sisters passage into the country. I will that my man Grace be and remain wth Mr John Daingerfield until my sister comes into this country unless he can dispose of him on a good Acc^t : towards the defraying of charges either of my sisters Passage or other charges that he may be at in the Managing my Estate in whose hands (to wit) Mr John Daingerfield I will that my Estate may remaine until my sister may arrive in Virginia. Requests that Mr John Daingerfield see that his funeral be solemnized at the house where he dies and that a funeral sermon be Preached for him at the Lower Church of Sittingburne Parish at the first opportunity of a Minister. If my sister should not come into the Country Then my will is that my Land that is not already above bequeathed (to wit) the Residue of that Tract of Land called the Range be disposed of and I do dispose of it thus Viz. : I give unto Mr John Daingerfields children 800 acres of the said Land Residue to be equally divided between them and to Thomas Parkers children 800 acres of the said Land to be equally divided between them and to Daniel Shipleys children 900 acres of the said Land to be equally divided between them being 3000 acres in the whole.

Wit. Tho: Parker, Danl. X Shipley, Alice X Shipley.

Page 65.

9 January, 1685;
YEATS, JAMES,   3 March, 1685/6.

Executor William Clapham to whom he bequeaths all his estate both personall and reall horses and hogs and all my goods that is to me belonging.

Wit. Thomas Paice, Rowland Thornton, John X Jackson.

Page 68.

27 January, 1685/6;
GODSON, FRANCES,   7 April, 1686.

In the Name of God Amen.

I ffrances Godson being Sick & Weake in Body but in perfect memory do make this my last Will and Testam^t. in manner & forme as followeth—

1. I bequeath my Soul to the hands of Almighty God my Creator & maker in full and assured hopes of Salvation in & through the meritorious death & Passion of my deare & blessed Saviour Jesus Christ.

2. I bequeath my Body to the Earth from whence it Came to be Christian-like buried by the discretion of ffriends—

3. I give & bequeath all my worldly Goods & Estate both reall & Personall in manner & forme as followeth—

4. I give & bequeath all the money that is due to me by Rappa: County Court Records to be Equally divided between Toby Smith & Hen: Smyth and their heires for ever—

5. I give & bequeath unto Hen: Smyth all my Estate of Land that is Joyning to Bridgetts Land it being to the sd Henry Smyth & his heires for ever—

6. I give & bequeath unto M^{rs}: Elizabeth Smyth all other things of my Estate and what may Come out of England from my Unkle to her own proper use and behalf In Witness whereof I have sett my hand & fixed my Seale this 27th day of January 1685/6—

signum
Sign^{e}d Sealed and   FFRANCES O GODSON   Seale
delivrd in the p^{r}sence of

    GERARD X FFITZGERRALD
    his marke

    EDW: ADCOCK

Wee the Subscribers do depose & say that wee saw the within Testat^x: signe & Publish the above Will as her last Will & Testam^t & that at the Signing & Publishing the Same she was of perfect Sence & Memory to the best of our knowledge and further Saith not

EDWARD ADCOCK
Garrett X FFITZGERALD

Probat^r P Sacramenteorum in Cur Com Rappa: 7°. die Aprilis An^o 1686 Et Record^r: 22° die Ejud Men Anoq Supradit Tes^{te} Wm Colston Cl Cur   Page 71.

22 October, 1676;
GUNSTOCKER, EDWARD,   No date of probate.

Whereas I Edward Gunstocker being now designed upon an Expedition with the English against my Countrymen the Indians do make Ordaine Constitute and appoint this my last Will & Testament. I Constitute and appoint my beloved Wife Mary Gunstocker my sole Executrix and to her alone give and bequeath my Plantacon & all housing thereunto belonging or appertaining my above sd Plantacon Containing one hundred and fifty acres of Land Scituate lying and being upon the ffreshes of Rapp^a River wth all my stock of Cattle & hoggs Yonge and old with all my household goods and bedding and every moveable belonging and appertaining to me my above sd wife paying all my due Debts.

Wit. JAMES KAY, DAVID JONES, CHARLES HICKS.   Page 75.

1 April, 1686;
Proved 5 May, 1686 & recorded 17 May, 1686.
BOWEN, JOHN,

Sick of Body yett thanks be unto God of perfect memory.
To my two sons Mathew and John Bowen Two hundred & fifty Acres of Land where I now live to be Equally divided between them when please God they shall live to the age of Twenty one years. To my other two sons Stephen & Alexander Bowen my part of a parcell of Land lying in the forke bought by Alexander Doniphan & myself of George Jones Containing five hundred Acres to be Equally divided between them when they shall Live to the Age of Twenty one years and if either of my sons die that then my Daughter Martha to have his part of Land and if any issue of my sons should die or all the Remainder of my sons die that then my daughters Martha and the Child my Wife goeth with all to have the above remaining part of my Land. To my son Matthew my horse Jack. To my Daughter Martha a young mare now Running in the woods a grey Colour she and her increase forever. To my Loving Wife a gray horse Hector. I give also a mare and Two horses to my sons Stephen John and Alexander and the Child my Wife goeth with all wth. the encrease of the Mare forever. To my Loving Wife and John Stephen and Alexander Martha and the Child my Wife goeth withall my female Cattle to be equally divided between them and for the male Cattle I bequeath unto my Loving Wife and also to her all the Hoggs and what household goods I have.

Wife Executrix and son Matthew Executor.

Wit. MOSES HUBBERT, ALEX^R. DONIPHAN, FFRAN : X WILLIAMS.

Page 75.

28th day of 9ber, 1685;
WILLOUGHBY, HENRY, Gent.,   21 December, 1686.

All my lands in Virginia to my daughter Rebecca Hull during her life and after her decease to my two grandaughters Sarah and Mary Hull. The rest of my estate I give to my daughter Rebecca Hull whom I make executrix of this my will.

No witnesses.   Decemr: 21st. 1686

Mr Charles Harris & Edward Nelbett did in Court upon Oath declare that Mr: Henry Willoughby did in their hearing owne that this was his Will & Testamt. & died before he could signe the same.

Vera Copia Test Tho: Hobson Jun Cl Cur North
            Test WM Colston Cl. Cur.   Page 76.

7 September, 1685;
GIBSON, MAGDALEN,   4 August, 1686.

To son Tobias Ingram and his first child lawfully begotten my whole estate to be equally had and enjoyed between them saving such legacies exceptions and cautions here underneath set downe alwaies provided in Case of the Death of the sd. Child that then the second Child of my son or the third wch shall be the eldest survivor shall enjoy my Estate Joyntly with my son as above sd but what stock of hoggs I have I will to my son Tobias Ingram have hold and enjoy them to his own proper use & behoof saving six sows and four barrows wch I will that he pay sd Child in Copartnership with him at the time that it shall attain the age of eighteen years. To John Gray one gray gelding horse branded with JB about three years old. To Arabella White one heifer of a year old. Executor Tobias Ingram Joyning with him John Gray to be his oversere & assistant.

Wit. Tho: Parker, Nathll: Allen.   Page 78.

16 September, 1686;
PALMER, JOHN,*   6 8bris, 1686.

Executor William Barber who is to pay his debts and funeral charges and send what is left to his wife in England except his wearing cloaths which he gives to John Peterson.

Wit. Ralph Graydon, John X Welch, John Peterson.
                                           Page 82.

22 July, 1686;
PAGE, JONAS,   6 8bris, 1686.

My executor Henry Clarke living in Totaskey Creek to take into his hands all that pertaines and belongs to me for such use as followeth— My two mares and two colts I do give to Henry Clarke son

*Signed John *Pallmer* to original will.

unto the said Henry Clarke with all the increase thereafter also to sd Henry Clarke the younger seven breeding cattle and two male cattle the same being desired to remaine in the hands of his father Henry Clarke until his son is capable to make use of them himselfe all this I desire may be performed.

Wit. RICH^D DUDLEY, HENRY X TILLERY, THO: X DUDLEY.

Page 82.

11 January, 1685/6;

FULLER, THOMAS,   3 9^{bris}, 1686.

To daughter Susanna all my land and one Red pied heifer known by the name of Primrose. To Wm Witt one brindled heifer of three years old. To daughter Susanna the first mare foal that my mare brings and the rest of my moveable Estate I give to my loving wife.

Wit. JOHN HANSFORD, ZACHA X HEFFORD.   Page 83.

8 February, 1684/5;
3 November, 1686.

RICE, ANN, widow and relict of Dominick Rice, decd.

Appoints her son Tho: Dew* to be her sole Executor and leaves all her children to him during their minority desiring him only to be careful of them. In case of mortality of my son Tho: Dew the children to be kept by my son Andrew Dew and if he dies before the children come to age then my son William Toone to take them in his custody until they come of age. To daughter Ann Toone all my wearing Cloaths. I appoint my said Executor to act and do in all things belonging to me in my husband Dom. Rice's last Will & Test^{mt}.

Wit. WILLIAM BARBER, JOSEPH JEFFERSON, SAM^{LL} WHITEHEAD.

Page 83.

20 November, 1686;

GUBB, NATHANIEL,   5 January, 1686/7.

To sister Michah all what came in the Exiter Merchant this year and all what is at Mr Thornburys And to Mr Swan for his Mare fifteen hundred pounds of Tobb and to Coln^{ll} Loyd fifty sh. which he lent me of wch some part is in my Chest and I allow for my funeral Charges Two Thousand Pounds of Tobb and all debts being paid I

*My mother's desire in her last sickness to me was to be acted to her will as followeth to Give and Record to her son Stephen Rice Two Cows with their Female increase to be marked a Crop in the Right Ear and an under Keele in the left a feather bed Bolster Rugg and Blanketts and a pair of Sheets Two Puter dishes Puter Candle stick one Iron Pott which I do here present under my hand to this Court to be Recorded.

Acknowledged before me
This Sixth day of Jan. 1686/7.

SAM^{LL} TRAVERS   THO^S. DEW

Deed Book 7, page 354.

do make my mother whole and sole Executrix of this my last Will & Testam^t: and after her decease all to my Couzens equally divided and this to be delivered Mr Joseph Harniger & Mr Robinson attorney at Law for the due discharge of this I do allow to them foure hundred and fifty pounds of Tobb.

Wit. JAMES STANFORD, (or SANDFORD), HEN: TAYLOR.   Page 84.

Virginia X^ber 18th 1686;
LINCOLNE, JOHN,   5 January, 1686/7.

In the name of God Amen I John Lincolne of Rapp^a County of ffarnham Parish being very sicke & weake of body but of perfect memory thanks be to God for it doth make this my last Will & Testam^t Revoking all other wills before made in forme following Imprs I bequeath my soul to Christ my Redeemer & my body to Christian buriall according to the discretion of my Execu^trs hereafter mentioned.

I do give to my deare wife Elizabeth all what Land I now am possessed of During her natural Life not to be destroyed by her & likewise a Childs part of all my stock & moveables.

I do give all my lands to my son John after his mothers decease to be quietly possessed by him and like wise one younge horse named Nabb branded with J L on the further buttock and two Cowes & Calves marked with two Crops & Two Slitts of the neare Eare one slitt of the Right Eare & under Keeled on the same with their encrease not to be removed of my now dwelling Plantacon.

I do give to my Daughter Eliz: one mare big with foal named betty wth her encrease not to be removed as aforemenconed & two Cowes & Calves marked as aforemencined wth their encrease not to be removed of my now Dwelling Plantacon.

I give to my Daughter Margaret one young horse named Ball of Two Years old & Two Cowes & Calves of the former marke with the encrease to Remaine upon the now dwelling Plantacon I do give to my Daughter Catherine one Mare Called Figg with her encrease with Two Cowes & Calves with encrease not to be Removed of my now Plantacon.

I do give to my foure Children aforemenconed and to each of them one Sow & Two Barrows of one yeare age.

We the subscribers are able to attest that this is the Reall dictate of John Lincolne sensible to the last word writing and likewise that he did urge to have Charles Dodson to be his Execut^r severall times when his wife was named.

JOHN X MILLS
HENRY X HARTLEY
GILBERT X CROSWELL
W^M BRASSEY

Henry Hartley John Mills & Gilbert Croswell made Oath to all & every the above sd Will & attestation by them signed the Hoggs only Excepted.

Test W^M COLSTON Cl.   Page 85.

2 April, 1686;
WITHERS, JOHN,　　　　　　　　　5 January, 1686/7.

What goods or Estate I am seized of after my decease as soon as Can be Conveniently to be Equally divided into three parts one part to be reserved and Kept for my daughter Margaret Withers to be possessed by her when she shall Come to the age of sixteen years or day of Marriage wch shall first happen. The other two parts I give unto my well beloved wife Sarah Withers for her own use as also for the Child with which she now goeth whether it be male or female to be equally divided. I also desire that my wife shall have the Keeping of my Daughter Margaret Withers in her own Custody whome I Ordaine the sole Executrix of this my last Will & Testam^t: as well in Paying as Receiving & in all other Cases.

Wit. THO: KENDALL, JOHN X CROW, W^M HEATHER.　　　Page 86.

25 January, 1686;
BILLINGTON, LUKE,　　　　　　　2 March, 1686/7.

The Last Will of Luke Billington decd the 25th of January 1686 first bequeathing his soule to God Almighty and his Body to the Ground &c.

Impris I bequeath to Teige McDonnogh my sword & Belt with all my wearing Cloaths.

It. I bequeath to my Couzens ye Remainder of my Estate (after my sister Barbara & Sam^ll Bayly are Paid) Equally to be divided between them

It. my Brass Pistolls to little Daniell

It. My Turkey Barrell Gun to Wm Robinson but after a little better recollection of his Sences bequeathed the same to his Brother Carty saying y^t he thought he would have nothing else

It. To Ann Robinson I would leave something but what I cannot tell, but upon some small Recollection bequeathed her the first foal y^t any of his Mares brought.

his
TEIGE ——— MACKDONNOUGH
mark
LAWRENCE X HUNNINGS
his mark
March 2^d 1686/7
Sworne to in Rapp^a Court
Test W^M: COLSTON Cl. Cur.

But after two or three hours were past & his brother Carty was gott out of his bed and asked him how he did he Replyed he was indifferent well, M^r: Carty said, Brother I understand you made a Will, & he Replyed yes then Mª Carty Demanded whether he remembered his will, and Desired y^t he may hear him Repeat it, he replyed yes, and so began as followeth I give my Cloaths, sword, &

Belt to ye Irishman, and ye first mare foal y^t any of my mares bring to Ann Robinson, & after my Debts are Paid, the Remainder of my Estate to be Equally Divided between my five Couzens, Then m^r: Carty demanded what five Couzens and he replyed I mean my foure Cozens wch be them sd M^aCarty, he made answer your three Children & Robert Baylys Child, and I think I owe Sam^ll Bayly two thousand weight of Tobacco or thereabouts. Then Mr Carty demanded whom do you appoint to performe your Will and he replyed whom should I but you, for I think you have most right to it, and after your Death Sam^ll: Bayly if he survives you is to see it performed, & oversee it till ye Children comes to age, and my horse Turk I Leave him also Then Mr Carty Demanded do you give him ye horse over & above his Debt & he replyed Yes.   Page 86.

                                                22 January, 1686;
TAYLOR, THOMAS,   2 March, 1686/7.
                        Jan^r 22 1686

    In ye Name of God Amen
    I Thomas Taylor being sick and weak of Body: but of perfitt Memory: doe here make my last will & Testament
    Imprs. I Bequeath my Soul to Almighty God that gave itt and my Body to have such Decent Buriall in ye Earth as my Exer^es: shall think fitt
    It. I give to Each of my Godsons John Taverner Junr: & Samford Jones one thousand pounds of tobb.
    It. I give to Isaac Webb son to John Webb one thousand pounds of tobb.
    It. I give to friend Rees Evans one thousand pounds of tobb.
    It. I give to Thomas White foure hundred pounds of tobb.
    It. I give to Eliz: Pond foure hundred pounds of tobb.
    It. I clearly discharge & set free my Boy Thomas Huitt giving him My woolin & linen Cloaths
    It. I give six pounds Sterling to my friends Mr Edward Jones Mr. Elisha Jones Mr. Thomas Baylis Mr^s Catherine Baylis Mr. John Webb & Mr Isaac Webb Each of them twenty shillings of ye fore sd money and desire each of them to buy a Ring of ye value
    I will and order Mr James Samford & Mr William Colston to be Exer^s: to this my last will and testament
                                        THOMAS TAYLOR   Seal
Signed & sealed in
    p:rsents of us
            ISA: WEBB
            JOHN BLAKE
                Signum
            JOSEPH X DAVIS

Wee the subscribers do make Oath that the within Testat[r]: did signe Seal & Publish the within Will as his last Will & Testam[t]: & that he was of perfect sence & memory at the signing & sealing of the same and further say not

ISAAC WEBB

JOHN BLAKE

Proved by the oaths of Isaac Webb and John Blake in Rappahannock County Court 2 March, 1686/7 & recorded 11 March, 1686/7.   Test W[M]: COLSTON Cl. Cur.   Page 87.

	14 February, 1686/7;
TRAVERS, WILLIAM, Gent.,	2 March, 1686/7;

Weak & sick of Body but of Perfect mind & memory.

To my Deere mother Rebecca Rice five thousand Pounds of Tobb during her Naturall Life to be left in the hands of my brother Samuell Travers to be at her disposall when she shall be Pleased to Call for it & after her death to Return to my sd brother Sam[ll] Travers & Rawleigh Travers their heires Execut[rs] & Admst: &c.

It. I bequeath to my father in Law John Rice my Riding horse with furniture.

It. I give to Katherine Reyley five hundred pounds of Tobb in Caske.

It. I give & bequeath unto Sam[ll]: Robinson son of Elias Robinson one Heifer w[ch]: is at the house of John Battin with all her encrease & if the sd Sam[ll]: shall die before he arrives to the age of one & Twenty years that then it shall Returne to the sd Elias Robinson.

It. All the Rest of my Estate to my Two Loving Brothers Sam[ll]: & Rawleigh Travers their heirs Exect[s]: Admst: forever Equally to be divided between them. My Will is that if my father in Law M[r]: John Rice Pay fifteen Thousand Pounds of Tobb as part of my Estate unto my sd Loving Brothers their heirs or Order on the 10th day of March which will be in the year of our Lord 1687/88, that then he shall have the Liberty to Pay the Remayning Part at any time from thence untill the Tenth day of October w[ch]: will be in the yeare of our Lord God 1689.

It. I do Constutute & appoint my Two Loving Brothers Sam[ll] & Rawleigh Travers my Lawfull Execut: of this my last Will & Testam[t].

Wit. W[M]: SLAUGHTER, GEO. X BAKER, JOANNA GRAYDON.

Page 88.

18 March, 1679/80;
Proved by comparison of hands 2 March, 1686/7.

CAWTHORNE, RICHARD,

In the Name of God Amen I Richard Cauthorne of the Parish of Sittingbourne in the County of Rappa in Virginia Plant[r]: being in health Praise be given to God for the same and knowing the uncertaintie of this Life on Earth and being desirous to settle things in

Order do make this my last Will & Testam^t. in manner and forme following That is to say first and Principally I Commend my Soule unto Almighty God my Creator assuredly believing that I shall Receive full Pardon and free Remission of all my sins and be saved by the Pretious deth and meritts of my blessed saviour and Redeemer Christ Jesus and my Body to the Earth from whence it was taken to be buried in such decent and Christian manner as my Execut^x: hereafter named shall be thought meet and Convenient And as touching such Worldly Estate as the Lord in mercy hath lent me, my Will and meaning is the same shall be Imployed and bestowed as hereafter by this my Will is Expressed my just Detts first paid

Imprs I give and bequeath unto my eldest son Richard Cauthorne and his heires forever the one halfe of five hundred Acres of Land w^ch: was Acknowledged by Capt: Tho: Goldman being part of a dividend of Two and Twentie hundred acres lying upon the head of Hodgkins Pocoson.

It. I give and bequeath unto my son Thomas Cawthorne and his heires forever the other halfe of my above said Land;

It. I will and desire that the Rest of my Estate be equally divided between my children;

It. I do Ordaine and appoint my deare and Loving Wife Ann Cawthorne to be Execut^x: of this my last Will & Testam^t: Revoking and annulling by these psents all and every Testam^t: or Testam^ts: Will or Wills heretofore by mee made or declared either by word or writing and this to be taken only for my last Will & Testam^t: and no other in witness whereof I have hereunto sett my hand and affixed my seal this 18th of March 1679/80.

RICH CAWTHORNE   seal

signed and sealed in
the psence of us
    EDMUND CRASKE
      his mark
    ROBERT RR GULLOCK

Proved by comparison of hands the 2d day of March, 1686/7 in Rappa County Court and recorded the 11th

Test W^M COLSTON Cl. Cur.   Page 89.

Richard Cawthorne, citizen and Merchant Taylor of London and Anne, his wife, Admrs. of the goods, &c., of her late husband, Thomas Abrahall, late citizen and Skinner of London, deceased, makes their son, Richard Cawthorne, of Rappa County now resident in London, their attorney to collect anything due to Robert Abrahall of New Kent County, Gent.

Dated, September 15, 1680.

RICHARD CAWTHORNE
ANNE CAWTHORNE

Deeds, &c., No. 2, page 21, Middlesex County, Virginia.

15 January, 1686/7;
2 March, 1686/7.

PARKER, ROBERT, of the Parish of Sittenburne, in the
County of Rappa plant[r]

My wife to enjoy the home Plantation during her life but all my
Land being Eight hundred Acres by Computation I give & bequeath
unto my foure Children to each Two hundred Acres still Reserving
to my wife the Plantation for her life then my son John to have his
first Choice of Two hundred Acres which I give unto him & his heires
forever so alsoe unto the other three Children save only if any of my
three Daughters dye before Marriage or the Age of twenty their Parts
of Land I give unto My Son & his heirs forever but if my sd son shall
dye before he be of Age I give my Land to be Equally divided between
my surviving Children to them and their heirs forever My Cattl[e] I
give to be Equally divided between my wife & my sd foure Children
the Tobb I have I give to buy a Younge Negro my goods household
stuff Mill & the Rest of my Estate I give unto my Loving wife Save
only a Negroe to each of my Children after their Mothers decease.
Wife Executrix.
Wit. ED: KEELING, HENRY KEEYS, CALEB X LYON.

Sarah Lyon makes Oath upon the Holy Evangelist that she stood
by & saw the within Testator sign seale & Publish the within will as
his last Will & Testam[t]. and that he was of perfect sense & memory
at the signing & sealing the same and further sayeth not

her mark
SARAH X LYON

Note: Proved by the oath of Sarah Lyon all the witnesses being dead.

Page 90.

29 January, 1686/7;
Sworn to 27 February, 1686/7
& 2 March, 1686/7.

JOHNSON, EDWARD, of the County of Rappa & Parish
of ffarnham.

Very Sick of Body but of perfect mind & memory.

I leave unto W[m] Macanrico three Cowes & one heyfer & one yearling being upon the Plantacon of Ennis Macanrico & one Mare bigg
with foale & one bed & what belongeth to it, and all other things that
doth belong to me the above sd Cattle to be delivered in kinde when
he Cometh to the Age of sixteen & the Mares to Run with encrease
from the Day of the Date hereof and do make Charles Dodson my
full Execut[r]: to see this my Will fulfilled when my Debts is Satisfied
& what is left to Returne to Ennis Macanrico.
Wit. DAN[LL] EVERARD, ALEXANDER X DUKE, PETER X ELMORE.

Page 89.

Original Wills Between 1682 and 1692, In Metal Box 101.

Not in any Record Book in the
Clerk's Office, Tappahannock, Va.

MALLE, DANIEL, (Nuncupative Will),

Rich: Bennett Aged 24 or thereabouts being Sworne Saith That being with Daniel Malle when he was sick on his death Bedd heard the [said] Malle Give and dispose to Rich. Pains Children one Cow & a hayffer, and another Cow to Jn° paine, Junior, and a hayffer to George payne, as allso two hoggd of tobb to W^m paine, and one hhd tobb to Jn° paine junior and a fflock bed and ffurniture to W^m paine: 1 paire of woosted Stocking 1 paire of French falles to John Sanders: 1 piece of dimity 1 piece of sarge to be equally divided between W^m paine and Rich. paine 1 steer Aged 2 years to be left to them that take most pains about his burall

his marke
RICHARD RB BENNETT

Sworn to in Rappahannock County Court the 19th day of May 1686 & Recorded the 29th Ejus Men.

Tes^te: W^M: COLSTON Cl. Cur.

John King Aged 20 (or 28) or thereabouts being Sworne Saith being with Daniel Malle when he was sick on his death bed heard the [said] Daniel Malle give and dispose to Rich. pains Children one Cow and a hayfer: and another cow to John paine Junior & one hayfer to george paine as allso two hoggd of tobacco to W^m paine and one hoggd of tobacco to John paine junior and A flock bed and furniture to W^m paine: 1 paire of wosted stocking 1 paire of French falls to John Sanders: 1 piece of dimity 1 piece of sarge to be equally divided between W^m paine and Rich. paine 1 stere Aged 2 years ould to be left to them that take most pains about his buriall

his marke
JOHN O KING

Sworn to in Rappahannock County Court the 19th day of May an° 1686 and Recorded the 29th Ejusd Mens

Tes^te: W^M COLSTON Cl. Cur.

KEELING, EDWARD, Gent.,

IN THE NAME OF GOD AMEN I Edward Keeling of the County of Rappa. in Virga Gent. Being Sicke and weake and In a low condition But of Sound and perfect Sence & Memory Blessed be God And Calling to minde the frailety of man Doe therefore make and ordaine this to be my last Will & Testament in Maner and forme foll. (VIZ)

Imprs. I give and Bequeath my Soule to God that gave it hoping by the merrits of Jesus Christ to Inherrit Everlasting Life And my Body I Commit to the Earth from whence it came to be Decently burried in Such Christian Like Burriall as Shall be thought fitt and Convenient by my Execut. hereafter named.

first and principally I Desire that all Just debts wch. I owe be paid forthwith after my decease wch. are here Inserted To Capt. George Tayler by Bill 840 lbs Toba: To Robert Wells Boatwright on Account 540 lbs. Toba.: To Richard Bray by change of Toba. 398 lbs. Toba: To Jno. Moodee if he lives till ye last of Xber 1000 lbs Toba: To Mr. William Colston 200 lbs Toba: To Mr. Joshuah Davis 200 lbs Toba.

Next I Order that five pounds worth of Childrens Books be sent for from England by ye first opportunity to be given to Children of this Parrish of Sittingborn and Farnham Pish on ye South Side at ye discretion of my execrx.

Item I give unto ye boy Wm. Jordan half a years time & the charge of schooling him some time before he is free.

Item I give to ye two Children of Elizabeth Brutnell 500 lbs. Toba. to be paid for their Schooling when she will sett them to school.

Item I give to my Sister Lidia Goodall of Churchells near Leengwood in ye Isle of Wight one thousand pounds Toba. of my own Crop that Shall be made this year or five pounds Sterl. to be Sent to Mr. Tho: Cresser at ye Brasen Serpent in ye old Bayley, London Apothecary Alsoe to ye said Mr. Tho: Cresser five hundred pounds Toba. or fifty Shill. Sterl.

Item I give unto my Godson Edward Gouldman one Cow Called Pretty to be disposed of by my execrx. toward the good of his schooling & all the future increase.

Item All & Singular ye Remaining part of my Estate I give and Bequeath to my Beloved Wife Mary whome I appoint to be my whole & Sole Execut^rx of this my last Will and Testament Revoaking by these prests. all other Wills by me heretofore made eyther by word or writing.

Item I Except my own Rideing horse which I give to him that my Wife Shall Chuse Or appointe to be her Assistant.

lastly I desire Mr. Joshua Davis to assist my Sd. Executrix.

signed Sealed & acknowledged   EDW. KELING.
to be my last will & testament
in presence of the witnesses on the other side

Test

WILLIAM BRUDNELL

LAWRENCE X YOUNG
      his marke

post Script I give unto William Brutnell one yeare residence in my wife house & halfe the Corne Ground next adjoyning

I give unto Tho New halfe a Crowne for writing my will on the other Side Edw: Keling

I the subscriber do depose & say that I saw the within Testator Signe Seale & Publish the within Will & Testament as his Last Will & that he was of perfect Sence & memory at the time of signing & Sealing the same & further say not.

                                                    marke
            June 16th   LAWRENCE X YOUNGE
      Sworne in Rapp. Court April the *6th 1687*
                        Test. WM. COLSTON Cl. Cur.

I ye subscriber do depose and say that I saw ye within Testator Signe Seale and Publish ye within Will and Testament as his Last will and yt. he was of perfect memory at ye Signing and Sealeing ye Same and further Say not.   WILLIAM BRUDNELL

      Jurat est Brudnell in Cur. Com. Rapp.
      1 die Junis Ano: 1687 T.W.C.
      Probat per Sac: Young et Brudnell in Cur. Com. Ejusd. &
      Record: 8 die Junis Ano: 1687 Test Wm. Colston Cl. Cur.

                                          27 February, 1686/7;
BURK, DAVID,   6 April, 1687.

In the name of God Amen I David Burk of the County of Rapp\ :sup . being weake and sick of body but in my perfect sens and memory make this my Last will and testament:

Impris: I Recommend my Soule unto my saviour Jesus Christ when hee is pleased to Call upon on mee and my body to the ground to be buried by my friends and Neighbours In a Decent manner. I Doe Give and Bequeath unto my Countryman Walter Wallace one hundred acres of Land Next Joyning unto that Land I formerly sould to William Cambell to him and his heirs forever.

Item I doe Give and bequeath unto William Grymes a black heffer of two years owld.

It^m I Doe Give and bequeath unto Christopher Jones a bull yearling and farther I doe order and appoint that the said Jones doe Live and Abide and plant upon the said plantation where he now Is for and During the full terme and time of Six Yeares.

It^m I Doe Give and Bequeath unto my Countryman Michael Scurlocke one hundred Ackres of Land being the uppermost part of my Devident wth. the Cleared ground the howses and fences therein Contained.

It^m I Doe give and Bequeath unto the said Michaell Scurlocke all my moveable Estate as household goods Cowes hoggs horses and all other things that belongeth unto mee and to receive all Debts that is Due or owing unto me from any psone or psones whatsoever: and to pay all Debts that I Doe owe or am Indebted.

It^m I Doe ord^r & appoint that the said Michaell Scurlocke bee my Execut^r to see this my will pformed. In wittness whereof and for the true acknowledgement of this my Act I have hereunto put my hand and seale this twenty seventh Day of February 1686/7.

his mark

Signed and sealed   DAVID X BURK   seal
in presence of us

 WILLIAM GRYMES aged 38 years or thereabouts
  signum
 JNO. X McCOMICO
  signum
 CHRIST. X JONES
  signum
 BRIAN X HARKINS aged 40 years or thereabouts

And further your deponents Declareth that David Burk did Give y^e. said hundred Acers of Land that is in this will mentioned to Michaell Scurlock and his heirs for ever & further Saith not

WILLIAM GRYMES
the marke of
BRIANT X Hargin

MASON, JOSIAH,

In ye name of God Amen

I Josiah Mason of ye County of Rappahannock being very sicke & weake but of perfect sence & memory blessed be God doe make this my last will & testam^nt: in man^e:r & forme following viz.: first I bequeath my Soule into ye hands of Almighty God my Creato^r in sure & Certaine hope of ye pardon of all my sines & everlasting life through ye merits of Jesus Christ my redeemer & my body I Commit to ye earth from whence it was taken decently to be interred at ye discretion of my Execut^r hereafter named as to ye worldly estate y^t God hath given me I do bestow as followeth

Imp^r: I give & bequeath to my loving daughter Ann Mason ye plantation whereon I now live wth ye land thereunto belonging & to her heirs forever

It^m I give & bequeath to Saynty Gay her & her heires of two of my Cows wth their Calves & one mare named Tibb wth the increase as alsoe two hog^{sds}. of tobacco for her present necessity together wth one flock bed bolster & rug

It^m it is my desire that all my debts be fully pd & y^t y^n ye legasie be pd to Saynty & ye undermentioned of my personal estate I give to my aforesaid daughter Ann & to her heirs to be returned in kind after all my lawful charges & funerall rites be defrayed

It^m: it is my des^{re} my loving friend Wm Und^{er}wood of this County take my daughter Ann Mason whome I solely commit to his care & tuition till she shall come to ye age of eighteene years or till she is married together wth her estate & y^n her estate to return to her for her proper use & behoofe & if my sd daughter should dye before she be married or arrive to ye age aforesaid y^t y^n I bequeath my plantation & land belonging to ye aforesaid Saynty Gay & to her heires whom I desire y^t she continue thereon as long as she continue a single woman & my personal estate to my daughter before given & freely give & bequeath to my before mentioned friend Wm Und^{er}wood & to his heires whom I desire should educate my daughter aforesaid at ye charge of my estate according to ye discretion of him ye sd Und^{er}wood

It^m it is my will & desire my aforesaid f^{rnd} Wm Und^{er}wood be my whole & sole executor of this my last will & testam^{ent} as witness my hand this 28th of March 1687

                                        JOSIAH MASON   Seal

Signed sealed & delivered as
my last will & testam^{nt}
in ye presence of us
        JOHN H PARSONS
            his marke
        MOSES HUBBERT
        JOHN X WILLIS
            his marke

Proved in Rappahannock County Court by the witnesses 4 May, 1687 and recorded 23 May, 1687 by William Colston Clerk of the Court.

                                        25 January, 1686/7;
DUNBAR, WILLIAM,   4 May, 1687.

                    In the name of God Amen

Be it known that I William Dunbar of the parish of farnham in the County of Rappahannock doe here in the presant of God and thes witnesses acknowledge this to be my last will and testament first I bequeath my [soul] to God that gave it and my body to Christian

buriall and my worldly Estate as followeth I gife unto my true and
well beloved wife Mary fifty ackers of land which was my one fourth
part with all my moveable estate only one gelding colt excepted which
I give and bequeath unto Joseph White the Sone of Richard White
which said colte is towe years olde being baye branded on the near
buttock with W.

Item I doe impower my only true and well beloved wife Mary to
be my only true and lawful executor and to pay this one legacy and
all such debts that I do owe and to receive all debts that is due to me.
In witness whereof I set my hand and seal this 25 day of January,
1686/7.

WILLIAM X DUNBAR   Seal

sind & sealed in the
    presence of
RICHARD X WHITE
THOMAS X MORSORE
WILLIAM SMOOT

24 February, 1686/7 ;

SIMONS, JAMES,   4 May, 1687.
                         Soli Dei Gloria

The last will and Testament of James Simons

I being very weak of body but of perfect mind and memory first
of all commit my soul to God Almighty mi body to the ground in
decent and Christian order to be interred.

Imprimis I do make Gerard Grienwood the German Doctor his
heirs assignes or order mi only executor of this my last will to order
my corps decently to be buried, to pay my Debts, to have and to hold
and possess that medium Estate which God has given me and plantation till the eldest girl come to age.

Item I do give unto my youngest daughter in law Two female
yearlings with male & female increase.

Item if my mare live to bring too female Colts the said youngest
daughter to have one.

Item I do give unto Abraham Cock my great coat.

Item I do give unto my servant William Wilitt all my wearing
Cloath.

Memoranda. If the youngest daughter should die her sister to
have her legacie with all the increase.

JAMES SIMONS   Seal

Test
RICHARD BENGEE
JOHN X CRUTCHETT

HUDSON, ISAAC,

The Will of Isaac Hudson to witt four cayne [kine?] and a Meer [mare] and some hogs wich he leaveth to his wiff only the read hifer wich is caled bay the name of doe and one each ear tow [two] crops and tow holls and tow under kells and the first mear coult wich ye mear brings and tow sows of a year old and a pott and pane wich he leaveth to his sone* and when he comes to seventeen years of age he my be free and he Desireth Master alexander Newman to see the same recorded in court and when fourtune cometh to be sixteen years of age to be free and to have tow suits of new apparel and in case that death should take away his wiff that Master alexander Newman should tak the child and kep him and putt him to shool until such tyme as he be free and as for the corn and to—

ISAC HUDSON Janu'y 3 1686/7

bacco I leave it to my wif and any debts that I owe or is owe to me that she pay and be payd

Witness
> CORNELIUS C HAWKINS
> his mark
> JOHN D HANCOCK
> his mark

Aprill ye 6th 1687 The deposition of Cornelius Hawkins & John Hancock aged twenty two years or thereabouts declareth that your deponents was present when Izack Hudson made this within written Will and that Izack Hudson did acknowledge it to be his last Will & Testament and that the said Izack Hudson was in perfect sence when he acknowledged this to your Deponents and further saith not

Probated and recorded 6 April, Ano Dom 1687

W^M. COLSTON Cl Cur

	7 September, 1688;
NORTON, PATRICK,	7 November, 1688.

In the name of God Amen I Patrick Northen being very sick and weak of body but of sound and Pfect memory thanks be to Almighty God for it doe make and ordaine this my last will and testament in manner and form as followeth, first I bequeath and give my soule to God Almighty in sure and certain hope of a Joyfull resurrection in and through Jesus Christ my beloved Saviour and Redeemer and my body to be decently buried at the discretion of my Ex^r. hereafter named. It. I give and bequeath all my Estate reall and personall to my Sonn Thomas Northen and his heirs for Ever excepting a Cow calfe y^t I give to Nelly Kelly and her heirs wth her increase and my

---

*Note. Court Orders 2, page 28. 4 May, 1687, Isaac Hudson, orphan of Isaac Hudson in care and charge of Alexander Newman until he come of age.

Original Will of Isaac Hudson,
Written January 3, 1686/7, Rappahannock County Records, Metal Box 101.

desire is y^t this plantation be kept in as good occupation as possible can be and that my Ex^r Keepe the Same stock on the plantation and use his endeavour for the keeping it for the good of my Child untill he shall attaine to his full age. It. It is my will and desier y^t if my Sonn Thomas Dies wthout Issue of his body lawfully begotten that then I give and bequeath my land to Daniel ^{ma} Carty and his heirs for ever. I give to my late wife Margrett Northen, one shilling in bar of any Claime or right in or to any part of my Estate reall and personall. It: I make and ordaine my trusty and well beloved friend Dennis ^{ma} Carty my whole and sole Executor in testimony and Confirmation of which I have hereunto sett my hand and seale this Seaventh day of September in the year of our Lord God 1688 the name Margrett interlined before the signing and sealing hereof.

signed sealed and pub-
lished in the p^{r}sents of us
    EDWARD X GEFFERYS
      his marke
    WILLIAM X BELL
      his marke
    ELIZABETH X CAMELL
      her marke

           his
PATRICK X NORTHEN   Seal
   mark and seal
after the signing hereof
the testator did give unto
Elizabeth Camell a Cow
calfe to be delivered to
her the next Calfing time
if she stays on the plan-
tation.

Court held 7 November, 1688.

A Writing in forme of a Will under the hand & seale of Patrick Norton of this County decd bearing date the 19th day of Septem: 1688 being p^{r}sented to this Court for proofe is by this Court disallowed having no Execut^r. therein expressly named and for that it was alledged that the sd Patrick Norton consented to this sd Writing through Importunities in his sickness whereas a Will under the hand and seale of Patrick Norton bearing date the seventh day of Septem^r: was p^{r}sented to this Court for proofe by Den: Ma Carty Execut^r: therein named w^{ch}: sd Will being duly proved by the sd witnesses thereunto due Probat was granted to the sd Exect: of the sd Last Will

Orders, 1686-1692, page 122

24 January, 1687;
4 July, 1688.

WILLIAMS, GEORGE, of Sittingbourne Parish

    In ye name of God Amen ye 24th day of January 1687

    Imprimis I Give and bequeath unto Elizabeth Robins one Cow After ye decease of my wife.

    Item after ye decease of my wife I Give and bequeath unto Alexander Robins one Cow.

    Item I Give unto Anne Robins after my wifes decease one Cow.

Item I give and bequeath unto my Wife & her heirs ye Land I now live upon.

Item I give and bequeath unto my wife Ann Williams my personall Estate moveable & immoveables wth all bills bonds dues & accounts that is due to me from any person or persons w^tsoever & doe make my Wife Ann Williams sole Executrix of this my last will & Testament.

Signed in ye presence of   GEORGE X WILLIAMS   Seal
        GEORGE PLEY   his mark
     RICHARD LEIGHTON

                                        14 March, 1686;
                                        10 March, 1688.

WILLSON, HENRY, of Farnham Parish

I give and bequeath unto my son Thomas Willson this devident of Land whereon I now live being seven hundred akers more or less Binding on ffarnham Creek & ye Branches thereof to be holden by him and his heirs forever.

Item. I give and bequeath unto my two grandsons Will & [Thomas] Jeffery ye sons of Edward Jeffery & Elizabeth his wife that devident of Land Called Willsons quarter being a tract of four hundred & fifteen acres Joyning on the Land of Coll: griffin to be held by them & their Heirs for ever w^th: this pvision that they nor their heirs shall never hinder nor molest my son Thomas nor his heirs to Cutt & Carry of all such Timber as he or they shall att any time have accation for.

Item. I give and bequeath unto my four grandchildren Will: Thomas prudence & Elizabeth Jeffery ye sons and daughters of Edward Jeffery & his wife Elizabeth ffour two year old heifers to be payed to them when they Come of age, that is one heifer p Child.

Item. I give unto my son in Law Edward Jeffery one shilling to be payd one twelve months after my decease.

Item. I give and bequeath unto my daughter Elizabeth Jeffery one shilling to be payd one twelve months after my decease.

Item. I give & bequeath unto my nephew Henry Willson the son of my Brother Charles Willson one Cow & Calf to be payd one twelve months after my decease.

Item. I give & bequeath unto my son Thomas all other my Lands goods Chattles stocks & servants & whatsoever else I am now possessed of & do like wise Constitute make & ordaine he ye sayd Thomas Willson my Executor to Execute this my Last will & testament.

Item. I give & bequeath unto Will Brasier all Chirurgion my weights and scales & w^t other Instruments belonging to a Chirurgion to be delivered to him on demand after my decease.

Lastly it is my Request & desier that my two loving ffriends & naybours Capt. Samuel Travers and M^r. Gregorie glascoke be my

over seers of this my Last Will & testament & to be an aid unto my
son and assist him in managing of his affairs w^{t}soever & that he doth
nothing wthout their consent untill he Comes of ye age of twenty one,
& more especilie to keep him from ye Companie of Edward Jeffery
not Removing him nor anything from ye plantation & that ye sayd
Capt. Travers & Mr gregorie glascoke wth Two men more when they
please do Inventorie my Estate (but not apprays it) for which Care
& trouble they may be att to be payd out of ye Estate as ye Estate
shall prove it & Likewise twentie shillings Each man to bye him a
Caster hatt.

HENRY WILSON   Seal

Wit. BENJAMIN MASON, SARAH BOYCE, J. BRASIER.

WILCOCKS, RICHARD,

The Deposition of Thomas Colly aged 53 years or thereabouts
being Examined and Sworn Saith that about ye Beginning of 9^{ber}
Last past in Company with Richard Wilcocks and Luke Williams
at ye house of Henry Williams he this deponent heard ye s^d Willcocks
say that if it pleased God y^t. he should dye he would give all y^t he
had to ye a bove s^d Henry Williams and his wife & further said there
stands my chest and I give y^t. and all y^t. I have to him and his wife
and further sayth not

his
THOMAS   COLLY
mark

Sworn to 2 January, 1688 and recorded the same day.

The Deposition of Luke Williams aged 23 years or thereabouts
Examined and Sworne Saith That about ye Beginning of 9^{ber} Last
past being in Company wth Richard Wilcocks & Tho: Colly at y^e
house of Henry Williams he this deponent heard ye s^d Wilcocks say y^t
if it pleased God y^t he should dye he would give all y^t he had to y^e
a bove s^d Henry Williams & his wife & further said there stands my
chest & I give y^t all y^t I have to him & his wife & further Sayeth not.

his
LUKE X WILLIAMS
mark

Sworn to 2 January, 1688 and recorded the same day.

8 August, 1685;

MOSS, ROBERT, 3 April, 1689.

In the name of God Amen I Robert Moss of the County of Rap-
pah^k., being of perfect sence & memory, & knowing the fragility uncertainty & the brevity of mans Life, & being willing to get my affairs
in order before I die, doe make this my Last will & Testament In
manner & forme as followeth;

Imprimis I bequeath my soule to God that gave it, and my body to y^e
dust from whence it was taken, In sure & Certaine hope of Resur-

rection to Life at ye Last day, through my Lord & Saviour Jesus Christ, & dispose of my Estate as followeth I^tm I give & bequeath unto my Son Robert Moss all & singular my Lands & Lands in this Colony of Virginia & Else where to have hold & Enjoy to him & his heires for Ever. Item. I give & bequeath unto my beloved Wife Rebeckah Moss the one halfe parte of my Plantation with the Moiety of the housing fencing gardens and orchards thereupon, to her to have hold and Enjoy for & during her Life. Item. I give & bequeath all & sole my personall Estate to wit, my goods & Chattles Unto my beloved Wife Rebeckah, & my son Robert, to be Equally devided between them saveing & Excepting some Legacies hereafter mentioned. Item. I give unto Laomedon Tucker or his two Children already borne (to wit) Daniell & Mary one mare fold of one yeare old to them & their heires for Ever, & also two Earling [yearling] heifers to the said Daniell & Mary I give to be them & their Increase in Common between them ye said Daniell & Mary for Ever. Item. I give unto Daniell Tucker the Use & benefitt of housing & ground to plant his Cropp on and his Diett from time to time & at all times as Long as the said Daniell shall Live. Item. I give & bequeath unto my brother Thomas Mosses two daughters, (Elizabeth & Frances) two Gold Rings, of ten shillings price apiece Each of them one. Item I give & bequeath unto William Mosses Son & daughters (to wit) William Moss, ffrances Moss & Elizabeth Moss, three Gold Rings of ten shillings price apiece; to Each of them one. Item. I give & bequeath Unto my two grand-daughters (the daughters of Abraham Stapp by my daughter Dorothy) (to wit Rebeckah & Martha Stapp) two mare folds of the age of two yeares Each, to have & to hold the said mare folds & their Increase in Common to them & their heires for Ever, always be it provided that when Either of ye said daughters shall attain ye age of Eighteene yeares that then she may make an Equall division of this said Legacie & Enjoy her Due part. Item. I give & bequeath unto my daughter Dorothy, the wife of Abraham Stapp, one gold Ring of Eighteen shillings price. Item I give Unto Jeremiah Parker the son of Thomas Parker one heifer of a yeare old. Item. I Will, ordaine, & appoynt my beloved Wife Rebeckah, & my Son Robert Moss, to be Joynt Executrix & Executor of this my last will, & doe Revoke annull all former Will or Wills by me had and made appoynting this and no other to be my Last Will & testament. In witness hereof I hereunto publish my name, & affixe my Seale, & make publication hereof In the p^rsence of honest & Lawfull witnesses; this Eighth day of August in the yeare of our Lord & Saviour Jesus Christ, one Thousand sixe hundred & five.

Signed sealed & Published   Robert Moss   Seal
in the presence of us
    Abraham Stapp
    John M Mills his mark
    Tho: Parker

12 April, 1688;
PARSONS, JOHN,   6 November, 1689.

In ye name of God amen

I John Parsons Thanks be to God being in good and perfect health
but bound out of the country and knowing that all flesh is Mortal
Doe ordain this as my Last Will in manner and form following first
I Bequeath my soul into ye hands of Almighty God hoping by ye
meritts of Jesus Christ to have full pardon and remission of all my
sins and my Body to ye dust from whence it Came.

Imprimis I give that point of Land where my son Walter liveth
& ye next point to it to my son Walter to he and his heirs for Ever.

Item I give to my son John Parsons my plantation where I now
Dwell and all yᵗ Belongeth to it both wᵗhin and without and a Mallatoe
Girle.

Item I give him all my Stock only tow Cow Calves to be allowed
to my grand Children and This I Doe ordaine as my Last Will Revoking all other Wills In Witness I sett my hand and Seale the 12
of Aprill 1688.

Test   JOHN H PARSONS   Seal
    JOSEPH HEMINGE   his mark
    THOMAS T SPILLMAN
    his mark

7 May, 1689;
WELCH, WALTER,   6 November, 1689.

In the name of God Amen the Seventh day of May Anno Domini
1689 According to the Computation of the Church of England I
Walter Welch in the County of Rappʰ: being in perfect memory and
Remembrance praised be God do make and ordain this my last will
and Testament in Manner and form following Viz—First I bequeath
my Soul into the hands of Almighty God my maker hoping that
through the Meritorious death & passion of Jesus Christ my only
Saviour and Redeemer to receive free pardon and forgiveness of all
my Sins and as for my body to be buried in Christian burial at the
discretion of my Executrix hereafter nominated Item—I give & bequeath to my two Sonns Richard & Thomas all my land in Generall
& them both equal and if it please God that either of them should
die without issue then to returne to the other. Item it is my desire
that Charles Falem should be as an overseer to look after my two
Sonns till they come of age. Item I do make my two Sonns above
nominated at age when they bee Eighteen years old Item I do give
to my Sones each of them when they come to be of age one horse or
mare apiece. Item I doe give to my two Sones when they come to the
Same age Three Cowes & Calves apiece that is to say each of them:
Item I give to my two Sones that is to say each of them apiece five
Sowes & a Boar Item I give to my two Sones above mentioned each

of them a flock bedd with two Rugs and blankets any werable & a Couple of pillows: & each of them a pott made of Iron. Item it is my will that my two Sones when they come to age shall not Sell nor dispose of any of the above mentioned Land except it be to each other: Item I give each of my Sones two pewter dishes Item I do make my wife Jane Welch my whole & Sole Executrix upon condition She shall pay all my debts and Legacies Item I give to my son Richard Welch my little gunn: Item I give to my son Thomas Welch my musquet Item it is my will that neither of my sons shall have nothing of the above said estate in their tuition till they bee one & twenty years of age as witness hereof I have hereunto set my hand & Sealed with my seal this day above mentioned

Signed Sealed & Declared In the Presence
off

JOSEPH OKAINE   WALTER WELCH   Seal
   his mark

BARTHOLEMEW B WOOD
   his mark

JOHN X MORTONN

Proved in Rappahannock County Court 6 die 9^{bs}. An^o Dom 1689.

                                       6 January, 1687/8;
RILEY, EDMOND,   4° die 7^{brs}. 1689.

Bee it knowne that I Edmond Riley of the parish of ffarnham in the county of Rappahannock do hear in the present of god and thes witnesses acknowledg this to be my last will and testament finding my selfe of boady weake and sickly but of memory sond and parfit first I bequeath my soul to god that gave it and my boady to be lade in the earth and my worldly estate as folloeth Item I give and bequeath one year old heifer to be paide unto my god son Edmond Corlobe the son of Michael Corlobe to be paide at my death with her increase for ever Item I give to Briant Larbell one of my waring coats as also one pare of briches and one hatt to be paid at my death Item I give and bequeath unto my dafter Elizabeth Grade my plantation and fifty ackers of land belonging to it with all my moveable estate to my dafter in law Elizabeth and to her heirs for ever paying such legacys as I have willed making my dafter in law Elizabeth Grade to be my full and only executrix to pay all my debts that I do owe and to recover such debts as is due to me and pay these legacys as I have given and it is my will that my loving friend William Smoot is to looke after this my dafter in lawe Elizabeth Grade and that my said dafter in law shall not make Salle nor make any bargain with any person nor persons whatsoever for any of this my Worldly estate nor the increase of the said hoggs nor catell nor the increase of the mare wich of the said Edmond Riley do leave her without the advise of William Smoot and his free consent untill the day of her marriage as witness my hand and seal this 6th day of January 1687/8.

Signed sealed in the presence of   EDMUND X RILEY
    WILLIAM SMOOT   his signum
    RICHARD X WHITE his marke
    the marke of
    RICHARD X DRAPER

                                        24 September, 1689;
SUGGITT, JOHN,   2 April, 1690.

In the name of God Amen the four and twentieth day of September Anno Domini 1689 I John Suggitt of ye County of Rapp^a Planter being sicke & weake in body butt of sound mind and Memory Praysed be God Doe make & Declare my Last Will & Testament in Manner following Viz My soul I commend into ye hands of ye Almighty my Creator and my body I commit to ye Earth to be decently buryed att ye Discretion of my Executor hereafter named Trusting & assuredly believing itt shall partake of that gloryous Resurrection by ye pretious meritts Death & passion of our deare Lord & Saviour Jesus Christ and as for y^t little worldly Estate God of his goodness hath blessed me with I give and dispose thereof as followeth not Desiring itt should come to an appraisement after my decease but to be paid in kind as I dispose of it, that is to say, I give unto my son James Suggitt and confirme two young Cows with Calves by side of y^m————————with calfe and a thousand pound of good sweet scented Tobacco to be paid when hee arrives at ye age of one and twenty as also two sows with pig ye Cowe and sows to be paid ye next Spring after my decease. Item. I give and confirme to my son Edgcome Suggitt three young Cows with calf by their sides and two sows with pig and a feather bed with boulster pillows blanketts & rug & my little gun to be delivered when he comes to twenty years of age and my black horse to bee delivered immediately after my decease. Item. I give unto my son Thomas Suggitt two young Cows with calves by their sides———— with calfe and two sows with pig and a bed with boulster pillows blanketts & rug ye bed to be a good feather bed to be confirmed by being delivered to him when he comes to bee twenty years of age also I give unto my son Thomas Suggitt my black mare only ye first mare colt she brings after my Decease I give unto my son James with its increase ye aforesaid mare to be confirmed with the rest of her increase and Delivered immediately after my decease to my said son Thomas Suggitt. Item. I give unto my wife twenty shillings to buy her a ring. Item. I give unto Elizabeth Thomas a Cow with calfe to be delivered to her when she is free.

Item. I give & devise unto my son John Suggitt & to his heirs forever all that pcell of land wch was found to bee ye surplusage of what was found to bee ye contants of y^t Tract of Land which I now˙

live on and Lately surveyed by Mr Willm Moseley And all ye Rest of my Estate both personnall & reall not before hereby given after my Debts pd and funerall expences discharged ———————— servants horses Mares Cattell & Chattels whatsoever I give & bequeath unto my sd son John and do make him full & sole Executor of this my Will and further that here given unto my son Edgcombe Suggitt a years schooling finding him Clothes & Diet besides paying ye school-master in case he stays with him but if he goes from him then only to pay for his schooling and to my son Thomas Suggitt two years upon ye same terms before expressed and further in case it appears upon sufficient proof y^t my Executor Doe embezell this my Estate before he hath paid the Legacies y^t then hee be forst to give security for ye performance of this my will if not my will is y^t ye rest of ym choose them guardians and y^t their estates be taken out of my Executors hands. Revoking and making void all other former wills or testaments and Doe make this my last will & testament. In witness whereof and affixed my seal & subscribed my name ye day & year above written.

Signed sealed & published by ye testa-   JOHN SUGGITT   Seal
tor as his last will & testament in
presence of
    JOHN DUVALL SAM^{LL} PEACHEY

I the subscriber do depose & say that I saw the within Testator Signe Seale & publish the within will as his last will & Testam^t. & that he was of perfect sence & memory at the time of signing & sealing the same & further sayeth not.

    J^{NO}. X DUVALL

Probat^d P sacram Duvall in Cur. Com. Rapp. 2° die Apr^{ls} An^o 1690 et Record^d. 25° die ejus Anoq supradid.

    Teste
    W^M. COLSTON Cl Cur

Memord the 28th of this Instant September The sd Testat^r caused the several Interlynings in the Will wthin menconed to bee made (vizt) The word (Devize) & these words (aft^r my Debts pd & my funerall expences discharged) & the words (I give & bequeath unto my sd Sonn John) And Did then Likewise declare by these psent^s that he Constituted & appointed his wife Sarah Joynt Executrix of this his last Will wth their sd Sonn John As witness his hand & Seale ye day & year above written

And published as his Last   JOHN SUGGITT   Seal
Will & also Sealed in p^{r}sence of
    SAM^L PEACHEY
    JO: TAVERNER

24 April, 1687;
5 November, 1690.

LOYD, LEWIS, of Rappahannock Co., Planter.

Weak and sick in body but of perfect mind and memory. He bequeaths his soul to God and his body to be decently buried at the discretion of his Executrix.

To his Grandchild Ann Phillips a Cow calfe.

To Henry Thornton son of Roger Thornton a Cow calfe.

To Elizabeth Phillips a Cow calfe to be paid them at the discretion of his Executrix hereafter named.

To Ruth Williams my daughter-in-law the first mare colte as either of my mares bring.

To my loving wife Joane Loyd my whole heire and sole Executrix of all my lands goods Chattels & Cattle moveables and immoveables.

Teste: LEWIS LOYD   Seal

WILLIAM X SMITH, aged 39 years or thereabouts.

WILLIAM DAVIS, aged 48 years or thereabouts.

10 November, 1690;

BROWN, FRANCIS,   3 February, 1691.

In the name of God Amen

I ffrancis Brown senior in the parish of South ffarnham in the County of Rapp^a being very sick and weake of body butt of perffect sence and memory doe make this my Last Will and Testament in manner and forme ffolowing I give and bequeath my soule unto Almighty God that gave it me with a sure and certayne hope of a joyfull Resurrection through the merits of my Blessed Lord and Saviour Jesus Christ and my body unto my mother the earth to be decently interred and for my worldly Estate in manner and form following after my just and Lawfull debts are satisfied.

I give and bequeath unto my son ffrancis Brown after mine and my Loving wife Elizabeth decease all that necke of Land Lying on the north side of my devident of Land I now live on bounded as followeth that is to say strayt away through and ould field from the Run of the deviding branch the mill road which goes to my son Daniel goes over & for a small branch neare my ould dwelling house called by the name of the spring branch which sayd Land I give and bequeath unto my said son ffrancis to him and his heirs forever.

I also give and bequeath unto my son Daniel Brown after my and my Loving wife Elizabeth decease all that Rest of my land I am now possessed with all my plantation and housing to him and his heires to have and to hould in fee simple for ever also itt is my will and desier that my household goods be equally divided between my two sons ffrancis and Daniel both in quality and goodness to them and their heirs to have and to hould in fee simple for ever also it is my will and desier there be a row of orchard trees planted along ye sayd ould field to devide the above sayd Land. I also give and bequeath unto my sons ffrancis and Daniel my parcell of Land Lying on the south side of pescataway Creeke called by the name of ye wading place poynt equally between them and their heirs forever I alsoe give and bequeath unto my fower daughters Elizabeth, Sarah, Mary and Rebecca one shilling apeace to be payd them by my lawful executor or executrix I also give and bequeath unto Daniel Brown the son of my son Francis Brown one feather bed with the furniture belonging unto itt to him and his heirs forever after my and my wifes decease.

I give and bequeath unto my Loving wife Elizabeth all the Rest of my moveable Estate that I am now possessed with to have and to hould without any Lett or molestation to her and her heirs forever I also give and bequeath unto my ffower Godsons that is Joseph and John Edmondson and ffras Brown the son of Daniell Brown senior my neighbour and ffra^s Graves the son of ffra^s Graves deceased to every one of them one pocket bible of fiue or six shillings price to be truly payd them after my decease by my Lawfull executor or executrix I alsoe apoynt my Loving wife Elizabeth my sole and whole executrix of this my Last will and testament and this my Last will to cut off and disannull all fformer wills whatsoever as witness my hand and seal this 10th day of nov^{ber} 1690

signed sealed and delivered   FRANCIS BROWN   Seal
in the presence of us JOHN FERGUSON, THO WHEALER

Probat est sacrum in Cur. Com. Rappa. 3° die ffeby ano 1691
                                      Test W^M COLSTON Cl.
Recorded 26 Feb. 1691.

                                      14 September, 1688;
                                      1 July, 1691.

OVERTON, JOHN, of Rappa County in the
          parish of Farnham planter.

My will & desier is that if the Child my wife now goes wth is a Boye that then my divident of Land be Equelee divided into three p^{ts} that is to say one p^t to my Eldest son Edmond and that to be the now dwelling plantation where I now Live & unto my son John one other third and that the middle p^t & to the child unborne if a Boye one other third But if the Child that my wife now goes wth: proves to be a girle that then my Land Be Equalie devided between my sons Edmond & John & that Either of them or all then that is if the Child my wife now goes wth is a Boye shall admite one another to cutt & fall w^t timber they may have accation for the use of the plantation of their Respect. dwelling & that if Either chance to dye before he comes of age then his p^t: to be Equalie divided between the other two: & if two dies then to the survivor & never to be embezeled or sould butt to return from heir to heir forever & if all dye then w^thout issue then to return & be Equalie divided among all the girles then surviving.

Item. I give & bequeath unto my Daughter Ann the Bedd & furniture wch stand in the hall that is to say Bed Boulster & pillows Blankets sheets Rugs Curtains & Valians to be delivered at the day of her marriage.

Item. I give & bequeath unto my Daughter Elizabeth my feather bed that I had out of England wth Ruge sheets & Blankitts Bolsters & pillows wth w^t Curtains & Valians is thereunto belonging.

Item. I give & bequeath unto my Deare & well beloved wife penelope the remaining p^t of my Estate & likewise make her my whole & sole Executrix of this my last will & testament & that she shall pay my debts & Legacies & defray my funerall Charges in witness whereof I have hereunto sett my hand & seale this fourteenth day of September 1688.

	his marke	
Signed sealed and delivered in the	JOHN X OVERTON	Seal
presence of		

RICHD. X WHITE
CHARLES X DICKSON
W^M BRASIER

STERNE, DAVID,	8 September, 1691; 2 March, 1691/2.

In the name of God Amen I David Sterne of the parish of Sitting-borne in the County of Rapahannock Planter Being sick and weak in body but of pfect mind & memory (thanks be to Almighty God) doe make this my last Will & Testament in manner & forme following. First I comend my Soul into the hands of Almighty God hoping through the meritts and mediation of Jesus Christ my Redeemer to have and receive eternall life And my body to the Earth from whence It came decently to be interred according to the discretion of my Executors hereafter named hoping for a glorious resurrection & re-union with my soul at the last day according to that Article of my Faith X^t Item I give & devise unto my Loving Brother Francis Sterne all my Trooping Furniture that is to say Bridle Saddle Pistolls and holsters. Item I give and bequeath unto my Loving Wife Agitha Sterne and my Daughter Frances Sterne by my former Wife And my daughter Ann by my now wife Agitha all those Lands goods Cattels & chattels unto them & their heyres forever to be equally devided amongst them which now I have or shall dye possessed of. Item I give and bequeath unto Sarah Wilden daughter of Jane Wilden one two year old heyfer to be delivered unto her when she shall attaine to the age of sixteen years And lastly I doe by this my last will & testament desire M^r: Arthur Spicer & M^r: James Scott to be overseers of this my last Will & Testament hereby revoking annulling and making void all and every former will and wills heretofore by me made to all intents constructions and purposes whatsoever And my desire is that my Overseers herein above named see that my debts be first paid before my Lands and personall Estate be proportioned and divided as above I have willed and ordered In testimony whereof and that this is my last will and Testament I have hereunto set my hand and affixed my Seale this Eight day of September 1691

the mark of
[Signed] Sealed & delivered   DAVID D S STERNE
   in the presence of
      JOHN DAVIES Clk.
      NATHANIEL X HALL

16 August, 1690;
Proved in Northumberland Co., 16 Xᵇᵉʳ 1691,
Recorded in Rappahannock Co., 27 February, 1691.

WELSH, RICHARD,

   In the name of God Amen the sixteenth day of August 1690 Viz according to the computation of the Church of England I Richard Welsh of the County of Rappahannock being in perfect memory and remembrance praised be God doe make and ordaine my last will and testament in manner and form Following Viz first I will & bequeath my soull unto the hands of Almighty God my maker hoping that through the meritorious death and passion of Jesus Christ my only Saviour and Redeemer to receive ffull pardon and forgiveness of all my sins and as for my body to be buried in Christian lyke sort att the discretion of my Executor hereafter named. Item. I will and bequeath to my son Thomas Welsh in Ireland five hundred and twenty five acres of land and one Cow and one pot and one bed bolster and blanketts that is to say if he Comes from Ireland to Virginia within ten years after the date hereof and if the said Thomas Welsh doe not come within the said ten years then what is left to him ————— to Walter Welsh my grand child and ——————— Margaret Welsh ——————— three Cows and whatever else there is belongs to me in her hand and for her use so long as she lives and after her death to be Equally divided amongst my three Grand Children that is Richard Welsh and Thomas Welsh and Walter Welsh the bed that is to be left to my son Thomas Welsh is to be a feather bed & the one halfe of the household furniture and one halfe of the horses doe belong to me I will and bequeath to John Hoster one Heifer——— things above said being done as I would have it I sett my hand & seale the day and year above said—Charles Hallin to be my Executor.

his
Test   RICHARD X WELSH   Seal
      JAMES MONTGOMERIE   mark
      JOHN X MORTONN

5 September, 1682;
WOODBRIDGE, PAUL,   2 7ber 1691.

In the name of God Amen I Paull Woodbridge of the County of Rappahannock and in Farnham Parish in Virginia being weake of body but perfect of mind and memory knowing nothing more unsartaine than the time and where I die for whilst I am in perfect memory shall make my Last Will & Testyment as followeth. In the Name of God I bequeath my Soule to the Lord Jesus Christ and hope to be saved through the meretts of his only Son our Lord and my body to the ground Next I doe give to my wife [Bridget] the plantatyon where I doe now live during her life. Next to my two sonnes: I give to Will: Woodbridge the Eldest the plantatyon after his mothers decease with what land belongeth to it to be jointly betweene his brother George and himself and to them and to their heirs for Ever to have and to hould. My plantatyon where Tho: Clonton now lives my Will is Elizabeth Woodbridge with one hundred and fifty akers of land to have and to hould. Also to my daughter Anne I give one hundred and fifty adjoining her sister to have and to hould. And for the remaining three hundred akers to be jointly betweene my two sones Will: and George Woodbridge and their heirs. The rest of my personall estate when my debts are paide to be equally divided between my wife and Children; and my loving and kind wife and my son Will: to be my hole and sole executors with my brother Mr. Will: Fitzherberts care; and *god* alone and you mentioned I leave this trust. Look to *god* and to your trust farewell
Sept. 5, 1682

PAULL WOODBRIDGE

Witnesses: ROGER HABERS, ANN X PHILLIPS, ANN X MORGAN,
   WILL: FITZHERBERT.

William Fitzherbert aged 60 years or thereabouts, Anne Phillips aged 32 or thereabouts Sworne say that they these deponents did see the within Testator Signe Seale publish & declare the within written as his last Will & Testament & that he the said Testator at the time was in perfect sence & memory & further sayth not.

Sworne in Rappa County Court by Wm. Fitzherbert & Anne Phillips the 2nd day of 7ber 1691 and recorded the 16th day of the month Ano.

Test   WM. COLSTON   Clk.

Wills in the Record Book entitled Order Book, 1683-1686.

WHITNALL, WILLIAM,* (Nuncupative Will),

Whereas it manifestly appeared to this Court by the oaths of Edward and Philip Parry that William Whitnall upon his death bed did verbally give & bequeath his Whole Estate both Reall & Personall unto Sam^{ll}: Parry Junr: Whereupon this Court granted Probat of the Nuncupative Will of the sd W^m. Whitnall decd unto the sd Sam^{ll}: Parry Junr: And Ordered that he take into his Possession all & singular the Goods Rights and Credits of the sd Decd giving in securitie to this Court to be accountable for the same whensoever thereunto Lawfully Required.

Court held 7 April, 1686.   Page 218.

---

*Not in Torrence's "Virginia Wills and Administrations."

Wills in the Record Book entitled Book of Land Trials, 1711-1716.

REEVES, HENRY, Sr.*

In Y^e name of God Amen I Henry Reeves Senr of the County of Rappa. in Virginia being sick and weak & in a low Condition but of Sound & perfect memory blessed be God do therefore make ordain Constitute & appoint this to be my last Will & Testam^t. in manner & forme following First and principally I give & bequeath my Soule to God that gave it me in Shure & Certaine hope of a blessed Resurrection at ye Last day and my body I commit to y^e. ground from whence it came to receive shuch decent Christian like burial as by my Ex^{rs} shall be thought fitt & Convenient Imprimis I give & bequeath unto my well beloved wife Eliz^a. Reeves one third part of all my psonall Estate of what nature kind or quallity soever it bee Item I give unto my s^d. wife the plantation where I now live wth two hundred Acres of Land adjoining to it for & During her naturall life; and then my will is that Aft: her decease y^e. s^d. Land descend to my son Henry Reeves & to his heirs forever Item I give and bequeath unto my s^d. son Henry Reeves all the remaining part of my Land on this side the Beeverdam that runneth up by the plantation that Thomas Streshley liveth on and bounding on the River adjoining to the Land given to my s^d. wife to my son Henry and his heirs forever Item I give & bequeath unto Son Joseph Reeves & James Reeves all the Land belonging to the Aforesaid dividert given to my son Henry and my loving wife that lyeth on the Oth^r.side the s^d Beeverdam Including Thomas Streshley's plantation aft^r. his time by lease is Expired Equally to be divided between them both to them and their heirs forever Item I give and bequeath unto my s^d. son Henry Reeves my plantation at James River now in the possession & Occupation of Bridgett Ascough beginning at a marked Pine standing neere a wolf pitt in the fork of the Indian Bog branch so running So: to a marked gum Standing at the lower end of a thickett by the side of a great meadow so down the meadow branch Containing the breadth of 450 acres of Land wch I purchased of Godfrey Hunt running from thence to the head of a Spring branch So soe running down the s^d branch so far as that Deed extends to him & his heirs forever. Item I give & bequeath unto my s^d. Son Joseph all the Remaining part of the Western side of the above s^d. Deed together with three hundred & fifty acres of Land which I took up bearing date the 18th March 1672 lying by the side of the Beverdam Swamp to him & his heirs forever. It. I give and bequeath unto my son James all the remaining part of the Above Mentoned pcell of Land wch I purchased of Godfrey Hunt on the East side of a branch called the Spring

*Original will in metal box 101.

branch to him & his heirs forever. It. I give & bequeath unto my three youngest Daughters Martha, Mary & Anne two Cows a piece to run for their use aft^r. my Decease and they to be delivered to them as they shall respectively attaine to ye Age of Sixteen years; or day of Marriage together wth their female increase my will is also that my sons Joseph and James be at full age to Receive their Estate when they Attaine to Eighteen years. It. I give & bequeath unto my eight Children Henry, Joseph, James, Elizabeth, Rebecca, Martha, Mary, and Ann, All the remaining part of my personal Estate that is not here above given away to be Equally Divided between all Shear & Shear alike. It. I do hereby appoint my Loveing wife Elizabeth & Son Henry to be my whole Exect^{rx} & Ex^r of this my last will and Testament revoaking and disannulling all former wills heretofore by me made either by word or writing it is also my will that my two sons Joseph and James have one years schooling a piece out of the s^d Estate given them speedily after my decease. In Witness whereof I have hereunto set my hand and fixed my Seale this ninth day of January Anno Domi 1686 ————————
Interlined before signed these words (viz) & son Henry Ex^r.)

Signed Sealed in the   the mark of
presence of us   HENRY X REEVES   seal
     THO: NEW
       mark
     THO X JONES
     AND^w STRELLEY

The within named Tho: New Andrew Strelley do hereby testify & declare upon their Oaths that they did see the within named Testat^r signe seal & publish this within written to be his last Will & Testament and that he was then in prfect Sence & memory to the best of their Knowledge and further say not.   THO: NEW
                                        AND^w. STRELLEY

Probated 6° die April Anno Dom^i 1687 and Recorded 20th day.
                                         Pages 124-127.
A true copy.

TOMLIN, ROBERT,*

To son Robert Tomlin all my land and plantation at Arraricke with all the household goods & stock upon it to him & his heirs forever & likewise one negroe due to me from Mr Malachiah Peale with one feather bed boulster & Rugg which lyeth in my wife's Chamber And my Great Iron Gray Mare with all her Increase to him & his heirs for ever. Item I give unto my Cozen George Tomlin one young Mare about two years old, one feather bed which Lyeth in the hall with

————————
*Original will in metal box 101.

the furniture to itt belonging, one Iron pott about four or five Gallons & nineteen hundred pounds of Tobo. which John ffenner oweth me to build him a house upon his owne Land And Likewise a man servant which I am Indebted to him, And likewise itt is my will that he shall have his own Cattell which was brought over to my plantation. Item. I give & bequeath unto my son William Tomlin all the Land & plantation which I formerly bought of M^r. Thomas Gordon all the household goods & stocke of Cattell which are upon itt with the negroes & feather bed with the furniture to itt belonging which Lyeth in my wifes Chamber, & one feath^r. bed more with the furniture thereto belonging about eight or nine pounds price which I will my Execut^r. hereafter named to buy for him & all the horses & mares which he always Claimed as his owne, to him & his heires forever, and Likewise I give more to my son William halfe a dozen pewter dishes one Table, four paire of sheets & two suits of Table Linen. Item. I give unto my Loving wife one third p^{ts}. of the plantation & Land whereon I now live & leaving noe more Land but towards the poynt of woods next the River & to Keep everything in repaire as now itt is, And likewise one third part of the plantation & Land I formerly bought of Thomas Rawson during her life, five and twenty head of Cattell & one third part of my horses & mares not before bequeathed & Likewise this psent Cropp she paying my debts out of itt & maintaininge my son William and 3 daughters with necessaries for this psent year & afterwards with the pfitts of my negroes & stocke to maintain my 3 daughters & give them convenient Learnynge during the time they live with her which my desire is till they marry or come to age.

Item. My will is that if my said wife Rebeccah Tomlin doe not assent of this my will then she shall have no more than an equall childs part of my personall Estate. I will & bequeath unto my daughter Rebecca Tomlin all the plantation & Land whereon I now live after her mothers decease unto her & her heirs forever. Item. I will & bequeath unto my daughter Hannah Tomlin the Land I formerly bought of Thomas Rawson aft^r: her moth^{rs}: decease to her & her heirs forever. Item. I will & bequeath unto my daughter Martha Tomlin my mill with all the priviledges to me belonging or in any wise appertaining to her & her heirs forever also my will is that my Execut^r. shall keep my Mill in repaire with the pfitts that shall come of the Mill and the remaind^r. of the profitts shall be & remaine for the use and benefitt of my aforesaid daught^r. to be returned to her at the age of one & twenty years or marriage which shall first happen according to the discretion of my Execut^r: Item itt is my will & desire that if all or any of my said daughters shall attain to ye age of one & twenty years or marry before my s^d wife shall depart this life, then my will is that my Execut^r. shall equally divide the negroes Cattel & horses which are upon my plantation as they come of age or marry respectively except my wifes thirds during her life of her personal estate & after her death to be equally divided between my three daughters but if itt should happen that any of my daughters should die before the age of 21 years or marry then the Lands Negroes & stocks to goe to the survivor equally. Item my will is & I freely bequeath unto my brother Capt. George Taylor one of my saddle horses which are upon my plantation which he shall please to accept of after my decease. Item I give unto my Cozen Martha Taylor my mare about two years old with her increase to her & her heirs forever. Item I give unto my sister Mrs Martha Taylor one Gold ring about 12 shillings price. Item I give unto Robt Brooke two pieces of eight two New England shillings & six pence which is [in] my Lett^r. Case in my Truncke. Item I give & bequeath six hundred pounds of Tobacco to be Laide out in Mourning Ribbon to be given to my friends at my funerall according as my executor shall think fitt. Item my will is that the two dwelling houses upon my son William's plantation shall be both new covered & the Tobacco house in the bottom new posted & mended out of the produce of the Tobacco of this p^rsent Cropp Also my will is that if my Execut^r shall thinke fitt that my son William Tomlin be not capable of managing the plantation to him bequeathed that then my will is that my Executor shall keep the plantation in his owne hands till my son comes of age only the profits in the meantime to return to the boy.

Also that whereas I have already consigned seaventy five bushells of wheat to new England as by bills of Laidinge will appear, my will is that the produce of itt att the returne may be equally divided between my wife son William & her three daughters And likewise my will is that the wheat which I have att home in my Barne & my mill, which I suppose may be about 200 bushells may be shipt & consigned to New England accordingly as I formerly took Care pposd by my Letters writt to M^r: Saffin & the pduce of that at the return to be equally divided between my wife son William & my three daughters. Exr. my loving Brother Capt. George Taylor my Loving wife Rebecca my full & sole Execut^r. & Likewise if they see fitt for the good of my wife & children to dispose of any horses & mares according to their discretion. If my brother dies before this will be fulfilled I desire my son Robert Tomlin to join with my wife & to assist her according to his endeavour.

Witnesses: ROBERT TOMLIN   seal
      HEN AWBREY
      WILL MOSELEY
      RO: BROOKE.
                        7 March, 1683; 3 October, 1688.

                                        Pages 28-32.
A true copy.

Wills in the Record Book entitled Orders, 1692-1694.

23 September, 1663;

PETTIT, THOMAS,*   7 June, 1665.

September y^e. 23th in ye year of our Lord 1663

I Thomas Pettit of ye County of Rapp^a. and in ye parish of ffarnham being in a Weak Estate of body but in perfect mind & Memory make this my last Will & Testament, first I bequeath my soul unto Almighty God & my body unto ye ground to be buried with assured belief of the Resurection and that after this life my Soul & body shall be united in one & enjoy that Eternall bliss where my Redemer liveth, First I give and bequeath unto my Daughter Dorothy† three ffemale Cattle, one Cow named Cherry, and two heifers Comonly called by ye name of Goodluck, & Slow them & their female Increase, I give unto my afores^d. Daughter & her heirs for Ever but ye Male to remaine to those that look after them until she come of age I do also give and bequeath all my Land y^t is Really mine y^t is to say a pattent of one hundred acres adjoining to ye Land I now live on ye which Land encludes two hundred & Eighty acres by conveyance specified this Land heretofore mentioned my aforesaid Daughter Dorothy is to have when she cometh to age for her & her heirs for Ever, and in case of ye death of my afores^d. Daughter Dorothy before she cometh to Enjoy this Land according to ye term of my will then the s^d Land here given unto my Daughter to my Wife Katherine for her & her heirs for Ever & in ye meantime untill my Daughter be of age as afores^d. my wife Katherine to inherit & enjoy for her use in every kind whatsoever not destroying any timber nor to make sale nor diminish any more than what shall go for ye use of her own housing and Cropps & likewise I doe also include that in case my wife Katherine afores^d. keep her self a Widow that she shall freely and wholly enjoy the Land with the proffits thereof according to ye tenor afores^d. during her life I do also give & bequeath unto my Wife after my Death my debts Satisfyed all ye rest of my personal Estate both within doors & with-

---

*Not in Torrence's "Virginia Wills and Administrations."

†Married 1st., 1675, James Fugett; 2nd. Godfrey Stanton.

Thomas Pettit married Katherine, daughter of Major George & Eleanor Morris. Besides his daughter Dorothy he had a son Capt. Thomas Pettit "born in the Spring after the death of his father Vizt. April or May." *Land Trials* 1711-1716, page 19.

3 June, 1665, Katherine Pettit makes a deed of gift to her son Thomas Pettit. Deeds &c. 1656-1664, page 418.

out unto her & her h^rs for Ever I doe also here ordaine and appoint my friend Nicholas White and my friend Thomas Cooper overseers of this my last will & Testament ye day & year above written

THOMAS PETTIT   Seal

Witnesses

RICHARD GLOVER, aged 37 years or thereabouts.

his

RICHARD RN NIGHTINGALE, aged 27 years of thereabouts.

mark

ROBERT DAVIS Cl. Cur.

A true copy THOS. NEW Dep. Cl.

Truly recorded according to an order of Essex Court dated y^e. 11th : March, 1694.

Test FRANCIS MERIWETHER Cl. Cur.

Page 33.

Wills in the Record Book entitled Deeds, &c., 1695-1699.

COX, JOHN,

9 November, 1669;
Recorded 10 February, 1695.

Virginia this 9th day of Novemb: in ye year of our Lord *1669*. In the name of God amen I John Cox of the County of Rappahannock being at psent very Sick & weake of Body but in perfect Sence and memory blessed be ye Almighty for ye Same do hereby make & declare this to be my last Will & Testament.

It: my Soul I give into the hands of Almighty God and my blessed Saviour ———— Jesus Christ in & through whose meritts only I hope for Salvation & my body to ———— earth from whence it was taken decently to be buryed in Sure & certaine hopes of resurrection at the last day.

It: for my worldly Estate my debts & ffunerall Charges being paid I do dispose of as ffolloweth

It: It is my Will that what ffraight I have taken this year by my freind m^r Henry Mees may by my Executor hereafter named be performed as neare as possible————

It: I give unto Henry White Son of Nicholas White———————— with all the Lands & buildings thereon or thereunto belonging, to be delivered ———————— hands of his said ffather two years after my decease and during the said Tearme my executor hereafter named for the profitt of the same to give ye sd Henry his Education but if my Executor shall refuse————————————forthwith upon his refusall the premises be surrendered into the hands of Nicholas White ffather to y^e ———————— and he out of ye said profitts give him education by being————————————

It: I give unto John White Sonne of Nicholas White———————— years old and to his sister Elizabeth White four Cowes or Heifers to be———————— the next Spring after my decease.

It: I give unto Eme Johnson two Cowes & one ffeather bed whereon she now lieth And I farther desire she be paid other two Cowes it being in leiu of her Wages.

It: I give unto James ffackett (?) Sonne of the said Eme one Cow or heifer to be delivered with his mothers Legacie in april one thousand six hundred Seventy & one but hir Wages to be delivered in Januarie next after the date hereof.

It: I give unto my Godsonne John Moseley three Ewe Lambs to be delivered in april next after my decease.

It: I do hereby constitute & ordaine my well beloved Kinsman Henry Cox ye Sonne of my brother William Cox & now present in

Virginia my sole ———————— this my last Will & Testament
to whom I doe hereby give all my esta———————————reall &
personall both Lan—————————————————else doth or of
right may belon——————————————————————— or any
other place whatsoever——————————————————— and
Legacies hereby given and ————————————————————
Lawfully begotten for ever but if so it——————————————
his part hereby given I doe heer————————————————
brother William Cox and the Child———————————————
of them as shall be then livei—————————————————
Henry Cox my Kinsmen I do ——————————————————
Capt: John Hull, m^r William Moseley, m^r John Mott, m^r George
Mott ————— or the survivor or survivors of them to be overseers
of ye same in ye behalfe of my said Neeces & Nephewes, and I do
desire my said ffreinds or ye survivor or survivors of them that the
same may be by them or him sold at an outcry both Lands Goods &
Chattles as before specified & that they make return home of ye produce made to my forementioned Nephewes & Neeces.

It: It is my Will if Henry White before menconed in ye fourth
Article of this my Will do dye without heires of his body Lawfully
begotten that then ye Lands & plantation there to him given do fall
to his two sisters Elizabeth & Sarah.

It: I do hereby revoake, null & make voide all or any Will or
Wills Testament or Testaments heretofore made & have & do confirme
this to be my last Will for confirmation whereof I have hereunto set
my hand & Seale ye day & yeare before mentioned.

Signed Sealed in presence of us   JOHN COX   seale

    Signum
    JOHN B BIBBEY   DAVID FFOX Junr
    Signum   Signum
    RICHARD X BECKLEY   RICHARD R: HALES

        Vera Copia Test EDMUND CRASKE Cl: Cur:

Truely Recorded according to an order of Essex County Court
bearing date ye 10th: day of ffeb^ry: Ano Dom 1695

        Test FRANCIS MERIWETHER Cl Cur

            Page 12.

Wills in the Record Book entitled Will Book No. 2, Richmond County.

WALKER, JOHN,* Col.,

22 February, 1665;
3 February, 1668.

In the name of God Amen. I, John Walker of the county of Rapp[ck]: being in good health and sound and perfect memory yet considering the uncertainty of human life do make and ordaine this my last Will and Testament in Manner and forme following, vizt:

Imp[rs]:—I commend my soule unto Almighty God my Creator trusting & verily believing in the merritts of my blessed Saviour Jesus Christ to receive full pardon and remission of all my sins my body I give to the earth to be decently buryed my worldly goods which God hath pleased to bestow I give & bequeath as followeth

It:—to my daughter Anne Walker I give six cowes and in lieu of two cowes given her by Francis Baylie, also I give her one feather bed bolster &c.

It:—I give to my daughter Frances Walker one Cow and one feather bed & boulster &c.

It: I give unto my daughter Jane Walker one cow and one feather bed & boulster, &c.

It: I give unto my Daughter Elizabeth Walker one cow and one feather bed, boulster, &c.

It:—I give unto my said Daughters Anne Frances Jane & Elizabeth all my lands lying and being in the County of Gloster to be Equally divided and delivered to each of them when she shall attaine to the age of sixteen years or day of marriage which shall first happen to enjoy to her & her heirs forever.

It: my will is that if either my daughters decease before sixteen years of age or day of marriage then the land given to her I give to the surviv[rs]: to be equally divided among them if two of my said daughters decease as aforesaid then theire land to descend to my two surviving

*The Deposition of Mr John Deane aged 58 yeares or thereabouts, 6 February, 1706.

"That he Intermarryed with one of the Daughters of Coll John Walker and that by Virtue of a copy of a will which was the will of said Coll John Walker attested by Robert Davis als Payne then Clk of Rapp'ac County Court he recovered a some [a Legacy] left by the said Walker to his the said depo'ts wife."

Recorded in Richmond County x[th] Feb[ry]: Ano Dom *1706*

Test.

J. SHERLOCK Cl. Cur.

Richmond County, Virginia, Will Book 2, page 108.

daughters to be equally divided and if three of my said daughters decease before the time aforesaid then the surviving daughter to enjoy all the said land to her and her heirs forever.

It: I give unto my two daughters Sarah Walker and Hester Walker all my land in the county of Rapp^ck : one thousand acres equally upon my decease and the Residue att their mothers decease &c.

It: my will is that either my sd. two daughters Sarah and Hester decease before she attaine the age of sixteen yeares or day of marriage then my other daughter to enjoy all the said land and her heirs and assigns forever, and in case both of said daughters decease before they attaine the age aforesaid then my will is that my four aforesaid Daughters enjoy all the said land lying in Rapp^ck : County to them and their heirs according to the tenure aforesaid.

It: I give unto my daughters Sarah and Hester Walker four cowes and two feather Beds Ruggs & boulsters &c.

It: I give unto my loving wife Sarah Walker all my land in Rapp^ck : (not before given to my two daughters viz:) four hundred acres from the beginning of the land bounden upon the land of Lt: Coll: Fleete Extending northwest and six hundred acres beginning att the end of the Land bounding upon Gibsons which said land I give unto my said Loving wife during her natural life in lieu of her thirds of my land belonging to her according to law.

It: my debts legacies and funerall Expenses first satisfied I give the remainder of my sole Estate unto my said loving wife Sarah Walker making and ordaining my said loving wife sole Executrix of this my last will and Testament revoking and nulling all former wills and Testaments before made as Witness my hand seale the 22nd of Febry. 1665

JOHN WALKER   seale

signed sealed and
delivered in the presence
of   RICH^D : Fox
ABRAHAM WARREN

Whereas, I have two parcels of land due unto me since the writing above said the one being 1030 acres the survey and right being entered in the Secretary's Office the other parcell being 900 acres by patent both lying on the Eastw^d. side of Rapp^ck : Creeke I give unto my loving wife Sarah Walker and her heirs prov'd she relinquishes her right of her thirds of the land of Gloster County which my will is should be sold and the produce to be given to my four daughters vizt: Anne Payne, Frances Walker, Jane Walker and Eliz^b : Walker equally and in case of the death of any of them before sixteene yeares of age or day of marriage to the survivo^rs : equally.

It: the Legacy Given by this my will of Cattle and beds to my Daughter Anne her husband John Payne hath Received therefore void.

The postcript or addition I have thought fitt to add knowing the uncertainty of life as Witness my hand and seale this 6th day of July *1668*

JOHN WALKER   seale

Signed sealed and
declared
according to the tenure
thereof in presence of
sign
JOSEPH X CHISSELL

    The Deposition of Richard Fox aged thirty nine yeares or thereabouts sworne and Examined saith that he both heard and saw the within mentioned Coll: John Walker, Esqr: signe seale and publish the within mentioned will and Coddicell as his last will and testament and that he was then in perfect mind & memory and further saith not

RICHARD FOX

Jurat^r. in Cur Com. Rappa. 3°.
die Feb^{ry}. 1668

Test ROBT. PAYNE C. C. Cur.

    The deposition of Joseph Chissell age 27 years or thereabouts sworne and Examined saith that he hath heard and saw the within named Coll: John Walker Esqr: sign seale and publish the Codicill annexed to the within mentioned writing as his last will and Testament and further saith not

sign
J°. X CHISELL   seale

Jurat^r. in Cur Com Rapp^{ck}. 3° die Feb^{ry}. 1668

Test.

ROBT. PAYNE Cl Cur

Record^{tr}. X° die Feb^{ry}. 1668

Test ROBT. PAYNE Cl. Cur.

Vera copia

    Test Edm^d. Craske Cl. Cur.

Recordat^r. in Cur Com

Richmond xth die Feb^{ry}. Ano Dom *1706*

Test.

J. SHERLOCK Cl. Cur.

Page 108.

INDEX

www.ingramcontent.com/pod-product-compliance
Lightning Source LLC
Chambersburg PA
CBHW070425270326
41926CB00014B/2941